SLAVERY, PHILOSOPHY, AND AMERICAN LITERATURE, 1830–1860

Examining the literature of slavery and race before the Civil War, Maurice Lee demonstrates for the first time exactly how the slavery crisis became a crisis of philosophy that exposed the breakdown of national consensus and the limits of rational authority. Poe, Stowe, Douglass, Melville, and Emerson were among the antebellum authors who tried – and failed – to find rational solutions to the slavery conflict. Unable to mediate the slavery controversy as the nation moved toward war, their writings form an uneasy transition between the confident rationalism of the American Enlightenment and the more skeptical thought of the pragmatists. Lee draws on antebellum moral philosophy, political theory, and metaphysics, bringing a fresh perspective to the literature of slavery – one that synthesizes cultural studies and intellectual history to argue that romantic, sentimental, and black Atlantic writers all struggled with modernity when facing the slavery crisis.

MAURICE LEE is an Assistant Professor of English at the University of Missouri. His work has appeared in *American Literature*, *PMLA*, *ESQ*, and *African American Review*.

SLAVERY, PHILOSOPHY, AND AMERICAN LITERATURE, 1830–1860

MAURICE S. LEE

CAMBRIDGE
UNIVERSITY PRESS

CAMBRIDGE UNIVERSITY PRESS

Cambridge, New York, Melbourne, Madrid, Cape Town, Singapore, São Paulo

Cambridge University Press
The Edinburgh Building, Cambridge CB2 2RU, UK

Published in the United States of America by Cambridge University Press, New York

www.cambridge.org
Information on this title: www.cambridge.org/9780521846530

© Maurice S. Lee 2005

First published 2005
Reprinted 2006

Printed in the United Kingdom at the University Press, Cambridge

A catalogue record for this book is available from the British Library

Library of Congress Cataloguing in Publication data

ISBN-13 978-0-521-846530 - hardback
ISBN-10 0-521-846536 - hardback

To Marisa and Nico

Contents

Acknowledgments

At the end of one of his standup routines, Steve Martin says, "I want to thank each and every one of you for coming by. Thank you, thank you, thank you, thank you, thank you, thank you . . ." I feel a similarly overwhelming and more serious sense of gratitude for the skill, generosity, and good cheer so many have contributed to this book. Martha Banta, Barbara Packer, Eric Sundquist, and Richard Yarborough helped shape my understanding of nineteenth-century American literature. Luke Bresky, Joanna Brooks, Kris Fresonke, Bill Handley, Greg Jackson, Karen Keely, Meredith Newman, and Mark Quigley shared classes, suggestions, and support. Frances Dickey, Mark Gallagher, Noah Heringman, Andrew Hoberek, Patricia Okker, Tom Quirk, Kristin Schwain, Paul Stasi, and Jeff Williams provided comments on various chapters and are most excellent colleagues. John Evelev and Samuel Otter went beyond the call of duty in sharpening my thinking and prose. Fellowships from the University of California, Los Angeles and the University of Missouri helped me along the way. So, too, did an NEH summer institute, led by Russell Goodman and graced by an array of enthusiastic Emersonians. Responses from readers at the Cambridge University Press greatly improved what follows. Many thanks to Ray Ryan and Ross Posnock for their editorial support, as well as to *American Literature*, which published two sections from this book. With undiminished pleasure, my gratitude goes out to Michael Colacurcio, whose wisdom, irony, and faith first inspired this project and helped to bring it to light. Thank you, Mom, for reading to me as a child. Thank you, Andrew, for setting a good example. Thank you, Grandma, for keeping things in perspective. Thanks to friends who have indulged my interests and idiosyncrasies. Finally, thank you Marisa; "Forever – is composed of Nows –."

Introduction

Moby-Dick (1851) begins with a provocative question and some advice on how to approach it. When Ishmael wonders, "Who aint a slave?" he asks his readers to ponder the subject "either in a physical or metaphysical point of view," thereby announcing a dialectic that governs much of the book.[1] The *Pequod* is an American ship-of-state run by a tyrant who masters his multiracial crew. It is also a stage for speculative rhapsodies about freedom, fate, and the tragedy of being enslaved by the quest for truth. Just as the white whale can represent chattel bondage and the boundaries of human understanding, *Moby-Dick* treats slavery as a political and a philosophical crisis as Melville, like many of his peers, struggles to reconcile the two points of view. What were the social consequences of antebellum metaphysics? By what criteria and method should slavery be judged? Could philosophy settle the slavery controversy, or was it part of the problem? Such questions loomed over United States literature between 1830 and 1860 as the slavery crisis exposed the limits of national consensus and rational authority.

Among the antebellum thinkers who strained against such limits were Edgar Allan Poe, Harriet Beecher Stowe, Frederick Douglass, Herman Melville, and Ralph Waldo Emerson. Although these authors are rightly regarded as literary figures, all brought sophisticated philosophical arguments to the slavery debate. Poe derives a theory of slavery and racism from German and British romanticism. Stowe invokes sentimental philosophy in support of abolition, while Douglass agitates for similar ends in the logic of Scottish commonsense. The slavery crisis turned Melville toward the political philosophies of Machiavelli and Hobbes, and for Emerson the conflict both vexed and inspired his particular brand of transcendentalism. What all these authors have in common is that the slavery crisis forced them to face interrelated philosophical

---

1 Herman Melville, *Moby-Dick, or The Whale* (New York: Library of America, 1983), 798.

problems – skepticism, representation, subject/object dualism, the foundations of moral and political law. The slavery crisis thus brought new impetus to abiding intellectual quandaries, instantiating in tragic social experience the failure of rational authority. This breakdown would culminate with the Civil War, which proved to be unavoidable. But before it came, antebellum authors tried to mediate the slavery conflict not as disengaged minds or as prophets of postmodernism so much as writers participating in a history of ideas and their use.

Reconstructing their work requires attention to an array of overlapping contexts – the slavery debate in its manifold forms, antebellum philosophy (including metaphysics, moral philosophy, and political theory), the careers, sources, and writings of authors whose thinking shaped and was shaped by events leading toward the Civil War. To study these topics is to move among disciplines and ground textual interpretation in history. It is also to synthesize what seems to be a divided critical legacy. American romanticism, particularly transcendentalism, has long been linked with philosophy, while slavery and race are clearly important to a variety of antebellum literary works. There have been, however, no extended attempts to examine the period's literature of slavery within philosophical contexts, to see how authors adapted and applied philosophy to the most demanding civic issue of their age. Some found that their speculative projects could not escape the vortex of the slavery debate. Others discovered that their inability to settle the conflict practically forced them to engage theoretical problems at the core of their liberal beliefs. That none of them reached a peaceful solution to the slavery crisis marks the shortcomings of their era's philosophy and the scope of their ambitions.

To say that literature uses philosophy to intervene in politics is to invite a host of definitional questions, though the general tendency of this book is to complicate, not make, such distinctions. Richard Rorty pointed out decades ago that "philosophy does not have an essence, any more than do literature or politics," a claim borne out in the antebellum period where disciplinary formations were often inchoate, where the slavery debate cut across multiple fields, and where enlightened thinkers attempted to bring all learning into coherence.[2] It is true that antebellum novels, stories, poems, orations, and autobiographies are usually too anecdotal and improvisational for the logical rigor of analytic philosophy. Literature also

---

2 Richard Rorty, *Consequences of Pragmatism: Essays, 1972–1980* (Minneapolis: University of Minnesota Press, 1982), 62.

differs from political discourse if only in terms of genre and rhetorical occasion. However, the writers treated here are not bound by narrow traditions, for their productions are not so much shaped by abstract disciplinary forms as they are driven by cultural forces such as the slavery conflict. Indeed, one reason why their texts are so committed to philosophical and political questions is that the antebellum era could not agree upon frameworks for the rational discussion of slavery.

Alexis de Tocqueville was both right and wrong when he wrote in 1835, "Less attention . . . is paid to philosophy in the United States than in any other country of the civilized world."[3] Today, most philosophers pay little heed to antebellum America, and even some sympathetic intellectual historians find the period too derivative of the Scottish Enlightenment and too embroiled in provincial theological debates. Between Jonathan Edwards and the pragmatists, Emerson is the most likely figure of philosophical repute, and yet he remains too whimsical for more systematic thinkers. Who in the wide world of great ideas reads an antebellum book? Apologists point to constraining piety and scant institutional resources. As transatlantic observers, subsequent scholars, and antebellum writers themselves remarked, the dearth of an educated leisure class and a wealth of economic opportunity made the new nation a material culture governed by what Margaret Fuller deplored as a "love of *utility*."[4]

In this respect, however, philosophy mattered before the Civil War – even if its importance is best asserted not in the name of great ideas but under the aegis of cultural work, even if to do so is to accept what Adorno and Horkheimer (and more cheerfully, William James) call the "instrumental" ends of philosophy.[5] Some antebellum commentators certainly objected to speculative hairsplitting, logic chopping, and skylarking. But in a country that prided itself on putting abstract ideals into practice, philosophy was vital to public life – from lyceums and moral philosophy courses, to sermons and religious pamphlet exchanges, to legal and political discussions that were closely allied with philosophy. What Emerson called

3 Alexis de Tocqueville, *Democracy in America, Vol. I,* ed. J. P. Meyer and Max Lerner (1835; New York: Harper and Row, 1966), 1: 393.
4 These sentiments are generally expressed by Bruce Kuklick in *A History of Philosophy in America, 1720–2000* (Oxford: Clarendon Press, 2001), 1–94. For transatlantic commentary, see for instance Gustave de Beaumont, *Marie, or Slavery in the United States* (1835; Stanford: Stanford University Press, 1958), 107–10. Margaret Fuller, *Summer on the Lakes* (1844), in *The Portable Margaret Fuller,* ed. Mary Kelley (New York: Penguin, 1994), 72.
5 Max Horkheimer and Theodor W. Adorno, *Dialectic of Enlightenment,* trans. John Cumming (1944; New York: Continuum, 2001), 39; William James, *Pragmatism* (1907), in *William James: Writings, 1902–1910* (New York: Library of America, 1987), 571.

"the philosophy of the street" was supposed to have practical value; and while philosophy was not equally available to all, neither was it restricted to privileged academics and romantics running through Concord. Though Thoreau wrote in *Walden* (1854), "[T]here never was and is not likely soon to be a nation of philosophers," Richard Hildreth argued in a treatise on the political theory of abolitionism, "[I]n the present age, we are all growing to be philosophers."[6] From the perspective of a social history of ideas, the issue is not if philosophy mattered in antebellum United States culture but rather how it moved and was moved by the course of civic events.[7]

William E. Channing suggested as much when he wrote in 1835, "[S]lavery, regarded only in a philosophical light, . . . involves the gravest questions about human nature and society."[8] Whether whites could know the experience of slaves became a problem of intersubjectivity. Discussions of reform entailed debates over the will and the mystery of iniquity. Attempts to determine the rectitude of slavery could not logically prove first principles and led to struggles over contract theory, natural law, and definitions of humanity. Such conundrums were not new except that the antebellum era could not effectively defer them, especially after the Compromise of 1850 served chiefly to exacerbate tensions. The years before the Civil War witnessed the devastating irony that as the slavery conflict came to dominate intellectual life, America's supposed empire of reason lacked philosophical clarity.

Poe, Stowe, Douglass, Melville, and Emerson had motive and opportunity to jump into the fray, though this does not explain why figures we

6 Ralph Waldo Emerson, "The American Scholar" (1837), in *Ralph Waldo Emerson: Essays and Lectures* (New York: Library of America, 1983), 68. Henry David Thoreau, *Walden*, in *Walden and Other Writings*, ed. William Howarth (New York: The Modern Library, 1981), 50; Richard Hildreth, *Despotism in America: An Inquiry into the Nature, Results, and Legal Basis of the Slave-Holding System in the United States* (1840; Boston: John P. Jewett, 1854), 302.

7 Some of the many sources providing a background for the broad cultural work of philosophy in the antebellum era include: Gilman Ostrander, *Republic of Letters: The American Intellectual Community, 1776–1865* (Madison: Madison House, 1999); Daniel Walker Howe, *The Unitarian Conscience: Harvard Moral Philosophy, 1805–1861* (1970; Cambridge: Harvard University Press, 1988) and *Making the American Self: Jonathan Edwards to Abraham Lincoln* (Cambridge: Harvard University Press, 1997); and Rush Welter, *The Mind of America: 1820–1860* (New York: Columbia University Press, 1975). Though Kuklick holds that "for the most part politics has not shaped American philosophy," he does provide helpful cultural and institutional contexts (*A History of Philosophy in America*, xiii). Though limited to transcendentalism, Ronald Zboray and Mary Zboray indicate the variety of American audiences who experienced philosophy in diverse ways ("Transcendentalism in Print," in *Transient and Permanent: The Transcendentalist Movement and Its Contexts*, ed. Charles Capper and Conrad Edick Wright [Boston: Massachusetts Historical Society, 1999], 310–81).

8 William E. Channing, "Slavery" (Boston: James Munroe, 1835), 8.

have learned to call literary theorize slavery as provocatively as they do. Perhaps, as Sacvan Bercovitch and Wai Chee Dimock suggest, literature is the "very domain of the incommensurate," a type of writing that refuses to abide by totalized systems of thought.[9] More specifically, romanticism, sentimentality, and the black Atlantic play a role, for often their transatlantic transmission occurred along literary lines and their resistance to rationalism is powerfully evident in the American literature of slavery. Another reason why antebellum authors so creatively take up philosophy is that the slavery crisis eroded faith in the enlightened public sphere. The controversy was a wildly allusive, highly intertextual dialogue, but such discursive density only revealed the futility of deliberation. When Douglass marveled in 1852, "What point in the antislavery creed would you have me argue?" he played upon the widespread fear that there was little left to say.[10]

Paradoxically, such anxieties actually led to literary achievements. Obfuscation, banality, and feckless aggression do mar much of the slavery dialogue; and as in current discussions over, say, the death penalty and abortion, ideological claims were attacked and defended with almost ritualistic repetition. Nonetheless, some authors kept writing of slavery in desperate and compelling ways, striving to overcome or at least ascertain the limitations of the national debate. Their texts suggest that dramatic power rises when discursive strategies fail and that the elusive meanings of some works come not from the facile desire to obscure with willful ambiguities but rather from the frustrated drive to understand and be understood. When defending his inflammatory rhetoric, and using a figure that *Moby-Dick* would employ, the abolitionist William Lloyd Garrison described chattel bondage as (in part) a literary problem, "The whole scope of the English language is inadequate to describe the horrors and impieties of slavery . . . Canst thou draw out the leviathan, slavery, with a hook?"[11] For some antebellum authors, the slavery crisis required, among other things, extraordinary words. That their writings speak in various registers demands no less from readers.

9 Sacvan Bercovitch, "Games of Chess: A Model of Literary and Cultural Studies," in *Centuries' Ends, Narrative Means*, ed. Robert Newman (Stanford: Stanford University Press, 1996), 15–57; Wai Chee Dimock, *Residues of Justice: Literature, Law, Philosophy* (Berkeley: University of California Press, 1996), 10. Martha Nussbaum also sees a special role for literature, particularly regarding questions of moral philosophy (*Love's Knowledge: Essays on Philosophy and Literature* [New York: Oxford University Press, 1990]).
10 Frederick Douglass, "What to the Slave is the Fourth of July?" (1852), in *My Bondage and My Freedom*, in *Frederick Douglass: Autobiographies* (New York: Library of America, 1994), 432.
11 William Lloyd Garrison, "Harsh Language – Retarding the Cause," in *Selections from the Writings and Speeches of William Lloyd Garrison* (1852; New York: Negro University Press, 1968), 122.

In the field of American intellectual history, the antebellum literature of slavery forms an uneasy transition between David Brion Davis's *The Problem of Slavery in the Age of Revolution:* 1770–1823 and Louis Menand's *The Metaphysical Club*, which traces pragmatism to the Civil War.[12] Poe, Stowe, Douglass, Melville, and Emerson show how slavery factored in the turbulent shift from the American Enlightenment's rational confidence to the more self-conscious, skeptical modernity that the pragmatists helped to shape. In political theory and political philosophy, Paul Gilroy, Charles Mills, and Ivan Hannaford examine slavery, enlightenment, and race, depicting racism and chattel bondage as fundamental ideologies of modern Western thought.[13] A purpose here is to argue that antebellum writers actively and often insightfully interrogate the relationship of slavery and philosophy, even if their thinking does not always accord with current sensibilities. A less explicitly political perspective comes from the philosopher Stanley Cavell, who has shown that the best antebellum metaphysics appear in literary forms. Along with Cornel West, Cavell reveals the philosophical acuity of American transcendentalism by placing it between European romanticism and subsequent anti-foundational thought.[14] What follows shares an appreciation for the proleptic power of antebellum literature while including a broader selection of writers and more attention to social milieus.

Yet for all the welcome work in adjacent scholarly fields, the primary locus of reference for this book is the study of antebellum literature. Literary critics committed to philosophy seldom examine the slavery crisis, while those investigating chattel bondage and race tend more toward political contexts. As a result, the field has suffered from a problem of "double consciousness" – not exactly W. E. B. Du Bois's Hegelian concept of "two warring ideals" but rather Emerson's struggle with the

12 David Brion Davis, *The Problem of Slavery in the Age of Revolution: 1770–1823* (Ithaca: Cornell University Press, 1975); Louis Menand, *The Metaphysical Club* (New York: Farrar, Straus, and Giroux, 2001). Though focused on the Civil War years, George M. Frederickson offers a largely compatible account of intellectual changes in the mid-nineteenth century (*The Inner Civil War: Northern Intellectuals and the Crisis of the Union with a New Preface* [1965; Chicago: University of Illinois Press, 1993]).

13 Paul Gilroy, *The Black Atlantic: Modernity and Double Consciousness* (Cambridge: Harvard University Press, 1993); Charles Mills, *The Racial Contract* (Ithaca: Cornell University Press, 1997); Ivan Hannaford, *Race: The History of an Idea in the West* (Washington, DC: The Woodrow Wilson Center Press, 1997).

14 For Cavell, see *The Senses of Walden* (San Francisco: North Point Press, 1981) and later essays on Emerson in *Emerson's Transcendental Etudes*, ed. David Justin Hodge (Stanford: Stanford University Press, 2003); Cornel West, *The American Evasion of Philosophy: A Genealogy of Pragmatism* (Madison: University of Wisconsin Press, 1989).

disjunction between "Materialist" and "Idealist" ways of being in the world.[15] Emerson's loose usage of these terms is, to quote Lawrence Buell, "cavalier"; and his notion of double consciousness is capacious enough to encompass a number of dualisms.[16] Most immediately, he points to a tension between Lockean empiricism and Kantian idealism, between a passive perception of the physical world and an active, constructivist view. Emerson also sets at odds the inductive methods of natural science and the *a priori* methods of metaphysics. But keeping in mind Bruce Kuklick's point that nineteenth-century American philosophy is dominated by "idealism" (insofar as it tends to hold that "existence is essentially mental"), Emerson's double consciousness additionally indicates a more general distinction between the material practices of politics and the abstract theories of philosophical idealism, between what Ishmael roughly calls the "physical" and "metaphysical."[17] In Emerson's words, these two outlooks "diverge at every moment, and stand in wild contrast," even as they offer in a diction that is simultaneously national and transcendental the promise of a coming and yet unrealized "fuller union."[18] Whether or not such a synthesis is possible is a main concern for Emerson and his contemporaries; and just as they struggled with double consciousness, generations of critics have been split not only over questions of canon but on methodological lines.

In 1867, Emerson remembered antebellum life and letters as a field of "divides," "dissociation," "severance," and "detachment." In the early twentieth century, George Santayana, Van Wyck Brooks, and D. H. Lawrence agreed, finding in American literature and culture an irreconcilable "double allegiance" to theoretical speculation and practical power.[19]

15 W. E. B. Du Bois, *The Souls of Black Folk* (1903), in *W. E. B Du Bois: Writings* (New York: Library of America, 1986), 364; Ralph Waldo Emerson, "The Transcendentalist" (1842), in *Essays and Reviews*, 205, 193.

16 Lawrence Buell, *Emerson* (Cambridge: Belknap Press of Harvard University Press, 2003), 206.

17 Kuklick, *A History of American Philosophy*, xii. See also William James, "Even the professional critics of idealism are for the most part idealists – after a fashion" (*A Pluralistic Universe* [1909] in *William James: Writings, 1902–1910*, 653).

18 Emerson, "The Transcendentalist," 205, 209.

19 Ralph Waldo Emerson, "Historical Notes of Life and Letters in New England" (1867), in *Emerson's Prose and Poetry*, ed. Joel Porte and Saundra Morris (New York: Norton, 2001), 415; George Santayana, "The Genteel Tradition in American Philosophy" (1911), in *The Genteel Tradition: Nine Essays by George Santayana*, ed. Douglas Wilson (Cambridge: Harvard University Press, 1967), 62; Van Wyck Brooks, *America's Coming-of-Age* (New York: B. W. Huebsch, 1915); D. H. Lawrence, *Studies in Classic American Literature* (New York: Viking Press, 1923). Recent critics who trace a similarly divided story in the early-twentieth century include Peter Carafiol, *The American Ideal: Literary History as a Worldly Activity* (New York: Oxford University Press, 1991), and Paul Jay, *Contingency Blues: The Search for Foundations in American Criticism* (Madison: The University of Wisconsin Press, 1997), especially 57–80.

F. O. Matthiessen's definitive *American Renaissance* (1941) moved toward a fuller union by claiming a synthesis of romanticism and "the possibilities of democracy." Yet in doing so Matthiessen built what Jay Grossman calls a literary–historical "fortress" that so narrowly conceives of political questions as to neglect such issues as slavery and race.[20] Cold War scholars continued to emphasize the metaphysical strain of Matthiessen's canon, setting the ecstatic transcendentalism of Emerson, Thoreau, and Whitman against the speculative caveats of Hawthorne, Melville, and, less frequently, Dickinson and Poe. The possibilities of democracy did not go unnoticed, but most critics downplayed socio-logical factors, defining the genius of the American Renaissance over and against material discourses. Despite the rise of American studies and critics like C. L. R. James, writings about slavery, even from major figures, were considered minor works, while the shadow of blackness that cast itself over more canonical texts seemed less about chattel bondage and race and more about the psychology and theology of sin.[21]

Then the Culture Wars came, bringing with them a kind of wild contrast. Famously, the American Renaissance became a flashpoint in the 1980s and beyond as feminist, multicultural, and New Americanist critics, often bolstered by theories of historical materialism, objected to the field's exclusive canon and purportedly disengaged scholarship.[22] To dwell on philosophy seemed to miss more pressing political points as Stowe, Douglass, Fuller, Harriet Jacobs, and others formed a new canon, while slavery and race came to the fore in a host of scholarly books. Older methodologies endured in the age of political criticism, but one reason and measure for the success of cultural studies in antebellum literature is that it discovered and continues to discover exciting synergies between the old canon and the new.

20 F. O. Matthiessen, *American Renaissance: Art and Expression in the Age of Emerson and Whitman* (New York: Oxford University Press, 1941), ix. Jay Grossman, *Reconstituting the American Renaissance: Emerson, Whitman, and the Politics of Representation* (Durham: Duke University Press, 2003), 19.
21 See, for example, Harry Levin, *The Power of Blackness: Hawthorne, Poe, and Melville* (New York: Knopf, 1958); and R. W. B. Lewis's *The American Adam: Innocence, Tragedy, and Tradition in the Nineteenth Century* (Chicago: University of Chicago Press, 1955), which defines its interest in the "history of ideas" against "sociology," "economic geography," and "political history" (1). Teresa Goddu argues a similar point in *Gothic America: Narrative, History, and Nation* (New York: Columbia University Press, 1997), 7–8.
22 For general accounts of this moment in literary history, see *The American Renaissance Reconsidered*, ed. Walter Benn Michaels and Donald Pease (Baltimore: Johns Hopkins University Press, 1985); Russell J. Reising, *The Unusable Past: Theory and the Study of American Literature* (New York: Methuen, 1986); and Frederick Crews, "Whose American Renaissance?" *New York Review of Books* 27 (Oct. 1988): 68–77.

At the start of the twenty-first century, it is clear that a range of antebellum writers treat political topics, including slavery. It turns out that much conversation is possible – that, for instance, Hawthorne and Thoreau talk about slavery with Fuller and Stowe; that Emerson, Douglass, Dickinson, and Jacobs converge on issues of freedom and self; that Poe, Melville, Whitman, and Martin Delany explore the dynamics of democracy and race. With race and slavery seeming to enter into every sphere of antebellum life, with diverse authors engaging in dramas of resistance and mutual influence, and with the sense that race, class, gender, and citizenship all variously inflect each other, sociological models that once seemed reductive have become more nuanced and expansive without ceding their original conceptual terms. The Culture Wars are not over in the study of antebellum literature but a kind of détente has been reached. During the middle third of the nineteenth century, a generous grouping of texts interact in a decidedly material idiom – one occasionally still lamented as the politicization of literature, one that continues in accusations of American Renaissance "monoculturalism," and one often celebrated in the name of diversity and cultural work.[23]

That said, some slow growing signs suggest that criticism committed to idealism is rising, and not simply in the manner of a scholarly pendulum tracking a well-worn arc. Just as the American Renaissance proved amenable to political interpretation, more recently canonized traditions appear increasingly open to philosophical inquiry. Such inquiry need not entail deconstruction, neo-Marxism, or psycholinguistics, which have for decades been projected back on nineteenth-century texts. The more historically minded can turn to ideas available at the time to invoke, for instance, Hobbes before Foucault, and Schelling instead of Lacan, and to view language not through Derrida but through someone like Thomas Reid. In this way, the literature of slavery can be read within philosophical history not to attenuate theory or cultural studies but rather to advance them through an effort of synthesis that does not exclude philosophy from the domain of politics and culture.

Already such work is underway within subfields that are often treated as discrete. Len Gougeon and Albert von Frank have shown how slavery was a fundamental concern of transcendentalism. Other scholars demonstrate how sentimental literature before the Civil War broadly calls on eighteenth-century moral philosophy when advocating social reforms.

23 Timothy Powell, *Ruthless Democracy: A Multicultural Interpretation of the American Renaissance* (Princeton: Princeton University Press, 2000), 4.

Gilroy, Helen Thomas, and Henry Louis Gates, Jr. show how black Atlantic writers test the limits of enlightenment when resisting slavery and racism, while Dimock, Brook Thomas, and Eric Sundquist explore the relation of antebellum literature and law. Perhaps closest to the work at hand is Gregg Crane's recent (and excellent) book that reads nineteenth-century American literature in terms of race and higher law.[24] Sharing Crane's sense that the slavery crisis demanded new and often proto-pragmatist ways of establishing moral and rational consensus, this book explores how romantic, sentimental, and black Atlantic literatures all work with varying degrees of doubt within and against philosophical traditions.

In the crucible of the slavery crisis some standard distinctions do not easily hold, though the blurring of such boundaries need not be an act of deconstruction nor (as Russ Castronovo warns) a "liberal methodology" erasing all differences.[25] Rather, by focusing on the slavery debate as a widely experienced cultural problem, antebellum authors of various affiliations mix and match on both materialist and idealist ground as canonical diversity comes to entail a synthesis of methodologies. The problem of double consciousness thus leads toward what Emerson called "Idealism as it appears in 1842," a formulation that embeds philosophical abstractions in specific historical conditions and suggests that the practical work of politics cannot be divorced from theoretical frameworks.[26] In the middle third of the nineteenth century, an inclusive gathering of seriously considered, richly written texts desperately tries to realize ideals in the material world. The literature of slavery is a site for this prospective fuller union, even if disparate methods and canons cannot be smoothly or symmetrically integrated.

24 Len Gougeon, *Virtue's Hero: Emerson, Antislavery, and Reform* (Athens: The University of Georgia Press, 1990); Albert von Frank, *The Trials of Anthony Burns: Freedom and Slavery in Emerson's Boston* (Cambridge: Harvard University Press, 1998). Gilroy, *The Black Atlantic*; Helen Thomas, *Romanticism and Slave Narratives: Transatlantic Testimonies* (Cambridge: Cambridge University Press, 2000); Henry Louis Gates, Jr., *Figures in Black: Words, Signs, and the "Racial Self"* (New York: Oxford University Press, 1987); Brook Thomas, *Cross-Examinations of Law and Literature: Cooper, Hawthorne, Stowe, and Melville* (Cambridge: Cambridge University Press, 1987); Eric Sundquist, *To Wake the Nations: Race in the Making of American Literature* (Cambridge: Belknap Press of Harvard University Press, 1993); Gregg Crane, *Race, Citizenship, and Law in American Literature* (New York: Cambridge University Press, 2002).
25 Russ Castronovo, *Necro Citizenship: Death, Eroticism, and the Public Sphere in the Nineteenth-Century United States* (Durham: Duke University Press, 2001), 21.
26 Emerson, "The Transcendentalist," 193.

The writers treated in the following chapters do not form an exclusive or exhaustive group, but they cover something of a range demographically, ideologically, philosophically, and aesthetically. Chapter 1 looks at Poe, the first American writer to talk about slavery in transcendentalist terms. Poe commences his prose career as the slavery conflict and transcendentalism come to the national fore, a telling coincidence that sets the stage for his peculiar double consciousness. From his first published story, "Metzengerstein" (1832), to more recognized fictions including "Ligeia" (1838) and *The Narrative of Arthur Gordon Pym* (1838), to later prose works such as *Eureka* (1848) and "Mellonta Tauta" (1849), Poe seeks what he calls an "absolute oneness," a synthesis of the material and ideal, even as he maintains prejudicial distinctions between black and white, slave and master, brutish other and rational self. Borrowing concepts from Schelling and Coleridge, Poe cannot square transcendental unity with his racist anti-abolitionism. What he does is turn his contradictions into affective narratives that theorize a metaphysic of slavery that operates in the unconscious. In this way, three aspects of Poe's thought uneasily coincide – his ambivalence toward transcendentalism, his foreshadowing of modern psychology, and his surprising investment in the national conflict over chattel bondage.

Chapter 2 explores Stowe's sentimentality as a metaphysical system drawn from various affective traditions – sentimental philosophy, educational theory, and New England theology. In *Uncle Tom's Cabin* (1852), *Dred* (1856), and *The Minister's Wooing* (1859), Stowe refines a theory of abolitionism. The irony is that her antebellum novels retreat from the slavery crisis at the very moment the United States verge on civil war. The arc of Stowe's antebellum career reflects her struggle with philosophy; for as social experience belies her faith in sympathy as a means of reform, she revises her sentimental theory and faces troubling issues indulged by Poe – skepticism, uncontrollable affect, and the gap between subject and object. Such questions ultimately lead Stowe's novels away from secular perfectionism toward a more partisan, more Puritan sense of a failing American mission.

Just as Stowe encountered opposition as a female philosopher, Douglass in chapter 3 must assert his capacity, and by extension the capacities of blacks, for philosophy. Douglass has yet to be historically situated as a metaphysician, though his most ambitious autobiography, *My Bondage and My Freedom* (1855), makes a sophisticated abolitionist case based in Scottish commonsense. With the help of the African-American abolitionist James McCune Smith, Douglass uses the example of his mind to prove that blacks possess common faculties at a time when scientific racism extended into the field of mental philosophy. In his *Narrative* (1845), during his British tour, and in his subsequent work in America, Douglass deploys his era's dominant metaphysic even as he learns too well its practical limitations.

In chapter 4, Melville has a different reaction. Whereas Douglass adopts a popular philosophy, Melville invokes Machiavelli and Hobbes, whose political theories subvert enlightenment in general and American republicanism in particular. For Melville, the failure of rational discussion threatens not only democracy in America but the very basis of civil society. In "Benito Cereno" (1855) and beyond, Melville doubts the accuracy of linguistic and political representation, suggesting that in his suppressive time and from his peculiar authorial position, no one could truthfully talk about slavery or for that matter anything else. Melville offers a damning description of the United States in conflict, indicating how hard it could be to believe in America's empire of reason.

Finally, there is Emerson, who as seriously as any antebellum thinker faces up to the slavery crisis as a crisis of double consciousness. Chapter 5 traces Emerson's thinking on slavery from his lectures in the early 1840s, to "Experience" (1844), to his later antislavery speeches, and ultimately to "Thoreau" (1862). Emerson initially holds that the transcendental poet will come to settle the national conflict, not through politics as such but by prophesizing ideals. This is the Emerson who has been castigated for liberal irresponsibility, but when encountering the slavery crisis he ruefully adjusts his convictions about the calling of the poet-hero and the powers of transcendent speech. Slavery, then, is not simply a topic that Emerson tactically addresses; it is a problem that constitutes his transcendentalism in its subtly shifting forms. As the slavery conflict became increasingly dire, Emerson called the abolitionist cause a "terrible metaphysician," by which he meant exacting, daunting, and hard to bring to fruition.[27] In Emerson's experience, slavery demanded and escaped philosophical resolution, a crisis that Poe, Stowe, Douglass, and Melville also witnessed as America headed for war.

How useful their responses were and are is a complicated question. Antebellum authors (and this book itself) may risk using philosophy, in Toni Morrison's words, as a "strateg[y] of escape" that sublimates horrific

27 Emerson, "Woman" (1855), in *The Complete Works of Ralph Waldo Emerson, Vol. 11*, ed. Edward W. Emerson (Boston: Houghton Mifflin, 1883), 416.

physical facts that demand more direct interventions.[28] If so, the literature of slavery offers less a blueprint for progressive reform and more a cautionary lesson about intellectual evasion, particularly when authors scrutinize an atrocity that today is so obviously wrong. However, in the decades before the Civil War precious little was obvious about slavery, and this problem is precisely what drove some writers to seek philosophical answers.[29] Rational deliberation, for all its limitations, remains the most powerful way of ordering a peaceful and democratic world, and the literature of slavery kept faith with this hope during its most strenuous trial in America. For William James, "In our cognitive as well as in our active life we are creative."[30] Such humanism seems an appropriate posture of inquiry for this book – not only because James saw himself as a mediator of the material and ideal, and not only because pragmatism refuses to separate ideas from social consequences, but also because pragmatism and its frustration with philosophical legacies form a kind of horizon that antebellum authors move toward but never quite reach. The literature of slavery before the Civil War is both shortsighted and forward looking, for despite the potential abuses of philosophy, there remains a need to assert broadly shared, ameliorative truth-claims in the face of skepticism and political brutality. In this sense, the struggles of the antebellum period are by no means finished.

28 Toni Morrison, "Unspeakable Things Unspoken: The Afro-American Presence in American Literature," *Michigan Quarterly Review* (winter 1989), 11.
29 John Perry notes that even today "the philosophical issues involved with slavery are by no means fully understood, much less resolved" (introduction to *Subjugation and Bondage: Critical Essays on Slavery and Social Philosophy*, ed. Tommy L. Lott [New York: Rowman and Littlefield, 1998], x).
30 James, *Pragmatism*, 599.

CHAPTER I

Absolute Poe

Dim memories, dead lovers, old sins, former selves – almost nothing passes utterly away in Poe. Nor does faith in rational systems finally expire in his writings, for although Poe is preternaturally sensitive to the limits of enlightenment philosophy, and although he appears to anticipate post-modernism as uncannily as anyone in the nineteenth century, he remains like so many of his desperate characters driven by the crises of his moment. Melville, Emerson, Douglass, and Stowe have for decades been associated with political questions. Now somewhat belatedly but with sudden intensity a historically grounded and culturally embedded Poe is being unearthed. Whereas deconstruction and psycholinguistics used Poe in a decidedly ahistorical manner, recent scholarship sets his work within social, economic, and mass cultural contexts of the antebellum period.[1] The problem is that Poe is becoming something of a divided figure bound by his era's political discourse but divorced from the philosophy of his day. It may be possible, however, to synthesize this instance of double consciousness by finding a more stubbornly historical Poe who not only participates in his era's broader cultural milieus but who uses historically available ideas to theorize his American world. Like Emerson, Melville, Douglass, and Stowe, Poe tries to bring philosophical order to the slavery conflict. Unlike them, the order he comes to announce is pro-slavery and virulently racist, indicating one possible use of transcendentalism in the antebellum United States.

---

1 For deconstruction and psycholinguistics, see *The Purloined Poe: Lacan, Derrida, and Psychoanalytic Reading*, ed. John P. Muller and William J. Richardson (Baltimore: Johns Hopkins University Press, 1988). Historical works include *A Historical Guide to Edgar Allan Poe*, ed. J. Gerald Kennedy (New York: Oxford University Press, 2001); Terence Whalen, *Edgar Allan Poe and the Masses: The Political Economy of Literature in Antebellum America* (Princeton: Princeton University Press, 1999); Jonathan Elmer, *Reading at the Social Limit: Affect, Mass Culture and Edgar Allan Poe* (Stanford: Stanford University Press, 1995); and *The American Face of Edgar Allan Poe*, ed. Shawn Rosenheim and Stephen Rachman (Baltimore: Johns Hopkins University Press, 1995).

Taking its impetus from a Toni Morrison chapter, the recent collection, *Romancing the Shadow* (2001), puts slavery and race at the center of Poe studies and, despite the diversity of its essays, offers up a kind of consensus from some of Poe's most distinguished readers.[2] With varying degrees of interpretive will, race and slavery become powerfully explanatory not only in *The Narrative of Arthur Gordon Pym* (1838) but in an array of Poe's poems, stories, essays, and reviews. Such claims are justified by the intensity and frequency of blackness and bondage in Poe's writings, but what is striking is how often Poe's treatment of slavery seems to be beyond his control as ideology and unconscious desire determine textual meanings. Poe thus presents the crucial irony that while his work bears sophisticated readings of antebellum politics and culture, Poe remains for many a figure who fails to look critically at chattel bondage and race.

This chapter takes the unlikely stand that Poe thinks seriously about the slavery crisis, which became for him a political, metaphysical, aesthetic, and psychological problem. This is not to say that Poe achieves a coherent theory of slavery and race. Far from it. The terror, disruption, and violence that mark his accounts of the national sin originate from his failure to reconcile his philosophy and racism. On the one hand, Poe insists on enlightenment dualisms – black versus white, slave versus master, brutish object versus reasoning subject. On the other hand, he indulges what he calls "the appetite for Unity," the transcendental urge to synthesize dualities in an "absolute oneness."[3] This tension appears in various forms – from the radically subjective racial fears described in *Pym* and "Ligeia" (1838), to satires of transcendental amalgamation such as "How to Write a Blackwood Article" (1838), to Poe's metaphysical opus *Eureka* (1848), which fails to disentangle absolutism and race, to the psychological theories of racism implicit in his aesthetic theory and practical criticism. Of particular interest here is "Metzengerstein" (1832), an instructive story that renders a relatively cogent position on the slavery debate, and one that understands blackness and bondage through the transcendentalism of Schelling and Coleridge. In "Metzengerstein" and throughout Poe's career, dualistic order threatens to collapse into terrifying absolutism as race and slavery are figured as dangers lurking in the unwitting white mind. The slavery crisis turns out to be a crisis of the unconscious that

2 Toni Morrison, *Playing in the Dark: Whiteness and the Literary Imagination* (New York: Vintage, 1992), 31–59; *Romancing the Shadow: Poe and Race*, ed. J. Gerald Kennedy and Liliane Weissberg (New York: Oxford University Press, 2001).
3 Edgar Allan Poe, *Eureka* (1848), in *Edgar Allan Poe: Poetry and Tales* (New York: Library of America, 1984), 1280. Hereafter cited in the text as "PT."

Poe dramatizes with a repetition more compelling than compulsive. Poe, that is, may be less an author bedeviled by buried racial fears and more a writer who prejudicially enacts a strategic philosophy of slavery and race.

UNGOVERNABLE FIRE

The "facts" of Poe's politics are open to argument but can look something like this. Poe himself never owned a slave and was ambivalent about southern plantation culture. Later in his career, he was loosely affiliated with the literary wing of the Democratic Party, even as he resisted the increasing conscription by the nationalists of "Young America." But while Poe learned to resent the aristocratic mores he enjoyed as a youth in Virginia and Britain, he also expressed reactionary ire against egalitarian causes in general and abolitionism in particular. Poe lambasted the anti-slavery movement in critiques of Lowell and Longfellow, and his correspondence with pro-slavery thinkers can imply his concurring beliefs. Less surely, he may have condoned as writer or editor the disputed Paulding-Drayton review, a text that celebrates chattel bondage as a positive good. For the most part, Poe's literary criticism and practice tend to conform to the demeaning black stereotypes of plantation fiction. At the same time, Terence Whalen offers an intriguing caveat. Aspiring to a national litera-ture and attuned to market forces, Whalen's Poe for the most part manages to avoid the slavery controversy, displaying instead an "average racism" that a range of readers could support. One might doubt Poe's willingness and ability to consistently pander to popular tastes, especially given his lifelong penchant for self-destructive behavior. More crucially, as Whalen knows, a larger question looms; for even if Poe eschews explicit discussion of the slavery conflict, to what extent might the crisis shape his literary work?[4]

Poe commenced his writing career with *Tamerlane and Other Poems* (1827), and from 1827 to 1831 he poured his energies into verse, little of which suggests an interest in specific political controversies. Poe's first work of literary theory, the prefatory letter to *Poems: Second Edition* (1831),

4 David Leverenz, "Poe and Gentry Virginia," in *The American Face of Edgar Allan Poe*, 210–36 ("plantation culture"). Meredith McGill, "Poe, Literary Nationalism, and Authorial Identity," in *The American Face of Edgar Allan Poe*, 271–304 ("Young America"). For Poe and slavery, see Whalen, *Edgar Allan Poe and the Masses*, 111–46. Whalen's chapter provides an excellent critical history of Poe's relation to slavery and race. Here and elsewhere, biographical information comes from Kenneth Silverman, *Edgar A. Poe: Mournful and Never-ending Remembrance* (New York: Harpers, 1991).

denies the didactic role of poetry, claiming instead indefinite pleasure as the poet's main estate. Poe associates proper poetry with "all that is airy and fairy-like" (PT 16), and much of his dreamy, introspective verse seems set, not within American contexts, but in places not of the world. This does not mean that scholars have not found ideology in Poe's poems. For John Carlos Rowe, Poe's escapist aesthetics attempt a retreat from history that ultimately does not exempt him from political critique or social responsibility. Betsy Erkkila applies a similar logic, arguing that "Tamerlane" (1827) and "Al Aaraaf" (1829) engage in a "poetics of whiteness" that re-enacts antebellum ideologies of Indian removal and racism.[5]

To a limited degree, Poe's later poems speak less elliptically to slavery and race. "The Haunted Palace" (1839), especially when placed within "The Fall of the House of Usher" (1839), potentially invokes dark others to hint at the horrors of a slave revolt, while "The Raven" (1845), particularly if alluding to the color-changed raven of Ovid's *Metamorphoses*, can be seen to play on antebellum fears of whites becoming black.[6] Yet taken as a whole, Poe's poetry seldom and only indirectly treats slavery and race, if only because the bulk of his verse appeared prior to the rising conflict over slavery. Genre is also a likely reason, for even if Poe finally fails to escape from history into art, his poetic theory and practice emphasize rarified, self-contained beauty, whereas he more clearly associates prose with temporal referents.[7] Critics are correct to find in Poe's prose his most sustained engagements of slavery and race, though the focus on *Pym* and subsequent stories obscures an importantly formative tale.

Poe's first published story, "Metzengerstein," describes the horrifying death of a Baron who becomes obsessed with a mystical horse that, in familiar gothic fashion, materializes out of a tapestry. The tale does not seem particularly political, nor is its setting overtly American. In his preface to *Tales of the Grotesque and Arabesque* (1840), Poe probably had

---

5 John Carlos Rowe, *At Emerson's Tomb: The Politics of Classic American Literature* (New York: Columbia University Press, 1997), 42–62; Betsy Erkkila, "The Poetics of Whiteness: Poe and the Racial Imaginary," in *Romancing the Shadow*, 41–74.

6 For racial readings of "The Haunted Palace," see David Leverenz, "Spanking the Master: Mind-Body Crossings in Poe's Sensationalism," in *A Historical Guide to Edgar Allan Poe*, 112–14. For "The Raven," see Erkkila, "The Poetics of Whiteness," 60–67. Joan Dayan has also politicized Poe's early love poetry in "Amorous Bondage: Poe, Ladies, and Slaves," in *The American Face of Edgar Allan Poe*, 179–87. To my knowledge, no one has noted the connection between "The Raven" and Ovid's story of a white bird that the gods punish by turning black.

7 Poe's literary criticism generally bears this out. See especially his 1847 review of Hawthorne, which distinguishes poetry and prose (*Edgar Allan Poe: Essays and Reviews* [New York: Library of America, 1984], 573; hereafter referred to in the text as "ER").

"Metzengerstein" in mind when he wrote that one story in the collection favored that "species of pseudo-horror which we are taught to call Germanic" (PT 129). Poe in this way associates "Metzengerstein" with E. T. A. Hoffmann's *phantasystück* tradition, a comparison that scholars tend to accept if only to watch Poe burlesque such supernaturalism.[8] Yet by this token Poe's prefatory claim itself may be ironic, for despite the Hungarian setting of "Metzengerstein" and its tongue-tying Teutonic names, its fantastical terror is not solely Germanic but also profoundly American. Published in January of 1832, five months after Nat Turner's Revolt,[9] "Metzengerstein" stands as Poe's first literary handling of slavery and race, a treatment he offers in the form of a cautious – and cautionary – political commentary.

Even at this late critical date when politics seem everywhere in Poe, it is wise to be wary when reading Poe's work for political analogues. As early as 1839 but most famously in his 1847 review of Hawthorne's tales, Poe charged, "In defence of allegory (however, or for whatever object, employed) there is scarcely one respectable word to be said" (ER 582).[10] Poe dislikes the didacticism, popular appeal, and overly delineated meanings of allegory, though "Metzengerstein" may simply pre-date an opinion that Poe would significantly qualify. In an 1845 review of the poet Henry B. Hirst, Poe wrote, "*[A]ll* allegories are contemptible: – at least the only two which are not contemptible (The Pilgrim's Progress and The Fairy Queen) are admired in despite of themselves (as allegories) and in the direct ratio of the possibility of keeping the allegorical meaning out of sight" (ER 600). Poe is thus willing to countenance allegory when it is somehow hidden, a conviction pointing less to his love of formal unity and more toward his infatuation with hoaxes and cryptology. "Metzengerstein" indulges this subversive impulse in a subtle political

8 Edward H. Davidson, *Poe: A Critical Study* (Cambridge: Belknap Press of Harvard University Press, 1957), 138; G. R. Thompson, *Poe's Fiction: Romantic Irony in the Gothic Tales* (Madison: The University of Wisconsin Press, 1973), 39–44.

9 As "Metzengerstein" came soon after Nat Turner's Rebellion, specific dates matter. Turner's Rebellion occurred August 23, 1831 with coverage in the popular press appearing quickly thereafter. Poe had been writing short fiction in Baltimore from as early as April of 1831. On May 28, *The Saturday Courier* announced a short story contest, though details were not announced until July 9. We do not know when Poe submitted "Metzengerstein," but the deadline for the contest was December 1 and Poe has a history – and, in "The Imp of the Perverse" (1845), a theory – of procrastination. It is thus likely that Poe did not finish his "Metzengerstein" manuscript until after he heard of Turner's Rebellion through various sources. See *The Poe Log: A Documentary Life of Edgar Allan Poe, 1809–1849*, ed. Dwight Thomas, David K. Jackson (Boston: G. K. Hall, 1987), 120–24.

10 Earlier attacks on allegory appear in Poe's 1839 review of Baron de la Motte Fouqué's *Undine* (ER 257) and in his 1841 review of Edward Lytton Bulwer's *Night and Morning* (ER 159).

story that presents what Poe described in Hawthorne as a "not unpleasant *appositeness*" (ER 583).

Poe begins by unsettling the setting of his tale, "Horror and fatality have been stalking abroad in all ages. Why then give a date to the story I have to tell?"[11] He then adds geographic uncertainty to chronological doubt by introducing metempsychosis and, in a footnote probably added in 1849, naming "Ethan Allen, the 'Green Mountain Boy'" as a "serious metempsychosist." No hard evidence exists to suggest that Ethan Allen believed in the transmigration of souls; and though the Allen allusion may come from Poe's tendency to encode his own name in his texts, it makes the most sense as a strategic indication of American themes, particularly themes suggested by Allen's role in political rebellions and border disputes.[12]

In Poe's story, the families of Berlifitzing and Metzengerstein represent two "contiguous" and "mutually embittered" estates that had "long exercised a rival influence in the affairs of a busy government." This tense situation is analogous to political conditions in the United States, for tensions between the North and South spiked in 1831 when South Carolina threatened to nullify Andrew Jackson's tariff on the dangerous ground that States' rights superseded federal authority. Commentators of the time recognized that the nullification crisis had serious bearing on the slavery conflict, which was entering a new and more militant phase.[13] In the two years preceding "Metzengerstein," David Walker's "Appeal" (1829) and Garrison's *Liberator* outraged the pro-slavery sentiments of the South; and in 1831, John Calhoun renounced his ambitions for national office, pursuing instead a sectional course increasingly marked by secessionist rhetoric and aggressive defenses of slavery. Most dramatically, Nat Turner's Revolt stoked the slavery debate, unifying pro-slavery forces and engendering harsher slave codes even while convincing many observers that slavery needed to end. In 1831, the peculiar institution was seen as a threat to the Union by Americans in both the North and South, including the twenty-two-year old Poe, who that year crossed the Mason-Dixon line twice before settling near Frederick Douglass in Baltimore to begin a career in prose.

11 "Metzengerstein" quotes are from Edgar Allan Poe, *Collected Works of Edgar Allan Poe, Vol. 2: Tales and Sketches, 1831–1842*, 3 vols., ed. Thomas Mabbott (Cambridge: Belknap Press of Harvard University Press, 1978), 2: 5–31.

12 In a footnote, Thompson hints but does not pursue the possibility that the Allen allusion may have a "political or historical implication" as a result of Allen's involvement in a border dispute between Vermont and New York (*Poe's Fiction*, 54).

13 Richard E. Ellis, *The Union at Risk: Jacksonian Democracy, States' Rights, and the Nullification Crisis* (New York: Oxford University Press, 1987), 187–94.

Poe's first production was "Metzengerstein," a story that speaks to sectional tensions. The Berlifitzing house is headed by a count who possesses "so passionate a love of horses, and of hunting, that neither bodily infirmity, great age, nor mental incapacity, prevented his daily participation." In the antebellum era, hunting and horsemanship were standard features of the southern cavalier; and by 1831 the South was depicted as a passionate, feudal, failing place. In such writings as *Pym*, "The Man That Was Used Up" (1839), "The Fall of the House of Usher," and "The Gold-Bug" (1843), Poe exploits this regional stereotype, showing both fealty and resentment toward a South (and an adopted father) that was for him an occasional home in which he never felt welcome. "Metzengerstein" expresses these turbulent feelings in the "loftily descended" but "infirm" Count Berlifitzing, whose "honorable" but "weaker" estate falls to its neighboring rival.

This rival, the Metzengerstein house, is headed by the young, Byronic Baron Frederick who, among other immoral acts, purportedly sets fire to the Berlifitzing stables. Poe could be indulging a fantasy of vengeance against his father John Allan and authority in general, but also slavery and race at this point irrupt into the tale. As the Baron listens to the crackling stables, he fixates on an ancient tapestry featuring an "unnaturally colored horse" that once belonged to a "Saracen ancestor" of the neighboring Count. Against the backdrop of a Metzengerstein stabbing a fallen Berlifitzing, the horse's eyes glare with a "human expression" and its teeth show through "distended lips." Spiritualist gambits and horrifying teeth are, of course, favorite Poe tropes; but racial connotations of the "Horse-Shade" increase when it takes physical form, seemingly emerging from the tapestry under the Baron's monomaniacal gaze. The origins of the fiery beast are unclear, except that it is branded with Berlifitzing's initials, indicating to one servant that the animal belonged to the "old Count's stud of foreign horses." The antebellum era linked horses and slaves as branded, bred, and brutish chattel – a fact decried on the masthead of *The Liberator*, which conflated slave and horse auctions; and one stretching back in southern thought to Thomas Jefferson and William Byrd, who warned as early as 1736 that African slaves require "tort rein, or they will be apt to throw their rider."[14] If the horse of

---

14 Thomas Jefferson, *Notes on the State of Virginia* (1785; New York: Harper, 1964), 133; William Byrd II to John Perceval, 12 July, 1736, in *The Correspondence of the Three William Byrds of Westover, Virginia, 1684–1776, Vol. II*, ed. Marion Tinling (Charlottesville: the University Press of Virginia, 1977), 488.

"Metzengerstein" represents a slave, then the Baron becomes an abolitionist figure; for just as Turner's Southampton Revolt was blamed on "incendiary" abolitionists, the Baron is called an "incendiary" villain implicated in the disastrous end of his neighbor's chattel institution.[15]

Poe's basic position seems anti-abolitionist. Count Berlifitzing, decrepit though he is, dies when attempting to rescue his horses. Like the loving masters of plantation fiction, he is too fond of his chattel, a weakness that was a cause for concern in the fearful post-Turner South. Poe also broaches what was for many the most troubling prospect of abolition: What happens with masterless blacks? The question arises time and again in discussions of American slavery, particularly after Turner's Revolt when the fear of free blacks made colonization a popular (albeit unworkable) scheme and states passed laws more severely restricting the rights of free persons of color. In 1832, Thomas Dew, an architect of proslavery thought, saw "[e]mancipation without deportation" as the single greatest danger to the South; and Poe himself was well situated to note such anxieties as Baltimore's thriving free-black population came under increasingly hostile scrutiny in the wake of Turner's Revolt.[16]

"Metzengerstein" shares such fears about the control and ownership of chattel. When the Baron first meets the mysterious steed, he immediately asks, "Whose horse?" To which a servant replies, "He is your own property, . . . at least he is claimed by no other owner." Despite the "suspicious and untractable character" attributed to the masterless brute, the Baron muses, "[P]erhaps a rider like Frederick of Metzengerstein, may tame even the devil from the stables of Berlifitzing." This line echoes a frequent complaint brought against abolitionists. Northern reformers foolishly think that they can handle intractable blacks, an optimism born of perfectionist ignorance and one that leads to Metzengerstein's death. Obsessed with his horse to the scandalous point that he "disdained the company of his equals," Baron Metzengerstein's "perverse attachment" grows into an "unnatural fervor" exacerbated by the horse's "peculiar intelligence" and "human-looking eye." William Gilmore Simms wrote in 1853, "The moral of the steed is in the spur of his rider; of the slave, in

---

15 "Incendiary Publications," *National Intelligencer*, Sept. 15, 1831, in *Nat Turner*, ed. Eric Foner (Englewood Cliffs, NJ: Prentice-Hall, 1971), 87–89.

16 Thomas Roderick Dew, "Abolition of Negro Slavery" (1832), in *The Ideology of Slavery*, ed. Drew Gilpin Faust (Baton Rouge: Louisiana State University Press, 1981), 50; Barbara Jeanne Fields, *Slavery and Freedom on the Middle Ground: Maryland during the Nineteenth Century* (New Haven: Yale University Press, 1985), 40–62.

the eye of his master."[17] Such is not, however, the case in "Metzenger-stein," for in a lurid conclusion in which Poe brings his fledgling literary powers to bear, the Baron is mastered by his semi-human chattel and borne into his own burning palace. As the "ungovernable fire" dies to a "white flame," Poe ends "Metzengerstein," "[A] cloud of smoke settled heavily over the battlements in the distinct colossal figure of – *a horse.*"

This scene does not exactly enact the "white spirits and black spirits" that Nat Turner reportedly saw fighting in the sky. It is not precisely William Blake's "The Little Black Boy" (1789), where colored clouds form a tenuous line between African and white. Nor does Poe's cloud quite cast the shadow of "the Negro" that darkens the conclusion of "Benito Cereno" (1855).[18] However, like Melville's subversive story, "Metzengerstein" covertly imagines the potential of American slave revolt by ostensibly setting itself outside of immediate antebellum contexts.[19] The South, as Berlifitzing, is a dying culture, but the Count remains something of a romanticized martyr. The abolitionist Baron Metzenger-stein is the one who comes under relentless abuse as Poe takes up what was becoming a national anti-abolitionist stand.[20] The Baron relishes the destruction of his neighbor and then slyly possesses his chattel, suggest-ing – as did some pro-slavery radicals – that the North practiced its own form of bondage and coveted the labor of freeman. Deadly to himself and his neighbors alike, Metzengerstein prefers the company of a brute, a fact Poe describes in sexualized language thus voicing an anti-abolitionist

17 William Gilmore Simms, *Egeria: Or, Voices of Thought and Counsel for the Woods and Wayside* (Philadelphia: E. H. Butler, 1853), 15.
18 Thomas R. Gray, "The Confessions of Nat Turner" (1831), in *The Confessions of Nat Turner and Related Documents*, ed. Kenneth S. Greenberg (Boston: Bedford Books, 1996), 47. Herman Melville, "Benito Cereno," in *The Piazza Tales and Other Prose Pieces, 1839–1860*, ed. Harrison Hayford, Alma A. MacDougall, G. Thomas Tanselle, and others, *The Writings of Herman Melville, Vol. 9*, 116.
19 One can also read "Metzengerstein" as a more local political tale about abolitionism versus anti-abolitionism in 1831 Virginia. Some of the North/South tensions emphasized here are analogous to those of the slavery debate that raged between eastern and western Virginians before and after Turner's Rebellion. Perhaps Wilhelm (originally "William") von Berlifitzing represents the pro-slavery Prince William County, which disagreed with the antislavery voters of nearby Frederick County. Some of Poe's revisions (the change of "William" to "Wilhelm"; the addition of the Ethan Allen reference) suggest that Poe may have made his story more national as opinion in the South became more unified. The best historical support for this local reading is Alison Goodyear Freehling, *Drift Toward Dissolution: The Virginian Slavery Debates of 1831–32* (Baton Rouge: Louisiana State University Press, 1982).
20 Larry Tise, *Pro-Slavery: A History of the Defense of Slavery in America, 1701–1840* (Athens: University of Georgia Press, 1987).

jibe he repeats in subsequent works.[21] Most importantly, the Baron tragically discounts the savagery of the chattel he frees. Just as accounts of the Southampton Revolt dwelled on Turner's "spirit of prophecy," Poe's story begins with an "ancient prophecy" predicting the fall of both houses.[22] Like an incendiary abolitionist fanatic, the Baron ignores such warnings. He fails to tame the devilish brute that survives the fire of Berlifitzing's stables, bringing to pass the darkest fears of anti-abolitionists – that the emancipation of chattel slaves would destroy both North and South, that blacks would come to rule over whites, and that America would go up in flames in the shadow of slaves without masters.

Such a reading of "Metzengerstein" may too aggressively posit slavery and race, except that the whole of Poe's career suggests a pattern of interest. Slave rebellion potentially lurks in a number of Poe texts – from vague intimations in "Silence – A Fable" (1835), "The Fall of the House of Usher," and "The Black Cat" (1843) to *Pym*, "The Murders in the Rouge Morgue" (1841), "The System of Doctor Tarr and Professor Fether" (1844), and "Hop-Frog" (1849). Like these later works, "Metzengerstein" takes a racist, anti-abolitionist stand at least insofar as Poe dwells on black savagery and the dangers of masterless chattel. Reflecting the fears of post-Turner America, "Metzengerstein" fits a familiar Poe profile, even as the story remains distinctive in at least two critical ways. First, "Metzengerstein" shows that Poe's prose addresses slavery from the beginning. Poe did not discover the national sin as a literary topic during the writing of *Pym*, nor is his early political commentary limited to lesser satirical pieces such as "Four Beasts in One" (1833). Blackness and bondage are for Poe more than incidental gothic trappings or abstracted symbols of evil. From the very start of his prose career, Poe addresses the presence of Africans in America as a national problem.

"Metzengerstein" is also distinctive in that its political logic seems to me fairly coherent and specific relative to Poe's later works. Racial fears and slavery tropes run amok in many Poe texts often, collapsing allegorical structures into ideological chaos. "Metzengerstein" certainly reaches its

---

21 See "How to Write a Blackwood Article" (PT 291–92); Poe's 1845 review of Longfellow (ER 762); and the disputed Paulding-Drayton review. Note that these insults accused white female abolitionists of sexual desire for black men, but in "Metzengerstein," the horse is male, recalling Eric Lott's claim that antebellum racist anxiety is marked by the conflicted attraction and repulsion of white men for black male bodies (*Love and Theft: Blackface Minstrelsy and the American Working Class* [New York: Oxford University Press, 1993], 53–55, 120–22, 161–68).

22 *Constitutional Whig*, Richmond, Virginia, 29 Aug. 1831, in *The Southampton Slave Revolt of 1831: A Compilation of Source Material*, ed. Henry Irving Tragle (Amherst: The University of Massachusetts Press, 1971), 53.

own frantic end; but its political structure is sustained, revealing subtle though recognizable patterns of anti-abolitionism and registering, not only racial horror, but a possible position on civic events. Such political engagement need not entirely conflict with Whalen's account of the career. Even if a savvier, market-driven Poe shied away from the slavery controversy, the partisan and provincial "Metzengerstein" comes at the outset of Poe's professional life – before he was embroiled in the publishing world, and before he formulated ambitious plans for a national literary magazine.[23] There is no indication that "Metzengerstein" was criticized for its politics, yet Poe's subsequent fiction is more circumspect. For Whalen, Poe's obtuseness is governed by the strictures of political economy, but "Metzengerstein" suggests that Poe is not a passive conduit for racist ideology, nor is his racism, average or otherwise, so easily separated from the slavery crisis. There remains another explanation for Poe's tortured treatment of slavery and race: Poe struggles to integrate his politics and metaphysics, a problem of double consciousness evident in "Metzengerstein," if only in nascent form.

RACIAL METEMPSYCHOSIS

To read "Metzengerstein" in light of the slavery crisis is not to say that the story is philosophically flat. Joan Dayan has written separately on Poe's politics and metaphysics; and though her lines of inquiry do not often cross, she links Poe's writings on color and servitude to "mysteries of identity" and "the riddle of body and mind."[24] Can one ever know one's self? Is the self a stable entity? To what extent does the subject's mind constitute objective reality? Such questions premise Poe's discussions of American slavery and race, just as race and slavery impinge upon his metaphysical speculations. This dialectical relationship, so fundamental to American romanticism, points Poe toward a synthesis in which subject and object, white and black, master and slave become One. "Metzengerstein" imagines this troubling unity when the intimations of slave revolt suggest also a philosophical subtext – a fable of the racially violated mind.

By mentioning metempsychosis at the outset of his tale, Poe hints that the horse that dooms Metzengerstein embodies the soul of the deceased

---

23 Whalen argues that Poe's writings were governed by political economy *before* Poe entered the publishing industry. This may be so, though such claims seem stronger the further Poe advances in his career.

24 Joan Dayan, "Poe, Persons, and Property," in *Romancing the Shadow*, 121.

Count Berlifitzing, which can explain the animal's human intelligence and vindictive drive. This makes for a fairly totalized tale of crime and retribution in which Poe uses a spiritualist gimmick to invoke a fantastic cheap thrill. Yet Poe's allusion to metempsychosis is neither simple nor cheap. Nineteenth-century spiritualism, including animal magnetism, mesmerism, and metempsychosis, put forth laws that governed the workings of spirit in the material world. Typically spirit affects only spirit, will works on will, mind connects with mind. Only through limited invisible forces analogous to electricity and magnetism can otherworldly energies cause earthly disturbances such as rapping and flickering lights. Scholars have shown that antebellum spiritualism has affinities with transcendental idealism.[25] Not only are both extra-rational discourses historically intertwined, their cosmologies tend to segregate transcendental and material realms while at the same time granting occasional confluence through carefully delineated means.

At times Poe is willing to play by these rules. "The Facts of the Case of M. Valdemar" (1845) presents a mesmerized dead man whose eternal consciousness can move his tongue but cannot stop his body from rotting. As unlikely as the story seems, "Valdemar" abides by spiritualist logic. Because the material power of Valdemar's spirit is restricted to his tongue and is finally fleeting, some readers mistook Poe's fictional transcript for a factual account. This was not, however, the case with "Ligeia," a story that caused one of Poe's correspondents to complain about the tale's concluding "violation of ghostly proprieties."[26] The problem is not that Ligeia's spirit potentially inhabits the body of Rowena. The hitch is that Ligeia's spirit alters Rowena's color and height, ascribing too much corporeal agency to the incorporeal will. Poe once called "Ligeia" his best story; and as David Leverenz wonderfully shows, Poe's loose treatment of spiritualist law blurs the lines between matter and spirit, body and mind, black and white.[27] Such transgressions also cross the line between citizen and slave, for political subjectivity in America required the abstraction – that is, the disembodiment – of the rational citizen-self.[28] Thus when

---

25 Bret E. Carroll, *Spiritualism in Antebellum America* (Bloomington: Indiana University Press, 1997), 25–26; Maria M. Tatar, *Spellbound: Studies in Mesmerism and Literature* (Princeton: Princeton University Press, 1978), 46–9.
26 P. P. Cooke to Poe, 16 Sept. 1839, in *The Poe Log*, 271.
27 Leverenz, "Spanking the Master."
28 Michael Warner, "Mass Public and Mass Subject," in *Habermas and the Public Sphere* (Cambridge: MIT Press, 1992), 377–401; Bruce Burgett, *Sentimental Bodies: Sex, Gender, and Citizenship in the Early Republic* (Princeton: Princeton University Press, 1998); Castronovo, *Necro Citizenship*.

denying African-Americans political agency, pro-slavery arguments dwelled upon the brutish bodies of blacks and, conversely, emphasized the abstracted reason of whites.

In "Metzengerstein," Poe challenges this duality when pushing metempsychosis to an extreme. By implying that the spirit of Count Berlifitzing inhabits the body of his horse, Poe envisions a slaveholder literally taking the place of a slave. As we will see with Stowe, this is not unlike sentimental abolitionists – many of whom asked their readers to imagine themselves as slaves, and some of whom switched the status of whites and blacks as in Lydia Maria Child's "The Black Saxons" (1833) and Richard Hildreth's *Archy Moore, The White Slave* (1836). Other reformers like Daniel O'Connell, William Wilberforce, and Garrison invoked "white savages" to argue that white and black differences were culturally, not racially, determined. Abolitionists also pointed to instances where whites citizens were enslaved and, at least in one case, soaked in dye to make them look African.[29] The trope of racial interchange, however, was not only available to abolitionists. Though multilayered in meaning, blackface minstrelsy often voiced a virulent racism, while masters and mistresses cast themselves, howsoever unconvincingly, as slaves to their slaves. Less ironically and largely inspired by Nat Turner's Rebellion, Dew and others fixated on the dangers of white slavery, predicting that in southern society, "One [race] must rule the other" and that any "commingling of the races" would inevitably bring about "barbarism."[30]

Robert Montgomery Bird's *Sheppard Lee* (1836) is a fascinating example of how interracial metempsychosis can be put to pro-slavery ends. Lee is a slave-holding metempsychosist whose consciousness transmigrates to "Nigger Tom" in whose body he joins a slave revolt for which he is eventually hung. In 1836, Poe reviewed *Sheppard Lee* for *The Southern Literary Messenger*, praising the novel's "very excellent chapters upon abolition and the exciting effects of incendiary pamphlets and pictures, among our slaves in the South" (ER 399). Here Poe recalls an important moment in which Lee-as-Tom watches his illiterate fellow slaves study an abolitionist book. Struggling to understand the text, two of the slaves act out its picture of a slaveholder whipping his chattel. Thus a white

---

29 Garrison quotes O'Connell in his prefatory letter to Frederick Douglass's *Narrative* (1845). The quote is from Wilberforce, *An Appeal to the Religion, Justice, and Humanity of the Inhabitants of the British Empire* (1823), in *Slavery, Abolition, and Emancipation, Vol. 3: The Emancipation Debate*, ed. Debbie Lee (London: Pickering and Chatto, 1999), 64. For "tanned" whites, see Jonathan Walker, "A Picture of Slavery, for Youth" (Boston: J. Walker and W. R. Bliss, 184[?]), 27–28.
30 Dew, "Abolition of Negro Slavery," 47.

slaveholder in a slave's body witnesses an African slave represent abolitionist views by pretending to be a white master. To further confuse antebellum formations of mastery and race, Lee-as-Tom increasingly loses his
grip on his white subjectivity. He begins to think of himself as a slave and
falls under the spell of abolitionism, "[T]hat fatal book infected my own
spirit. . . . It is wonderful, that among the many thoughts that now
crowded my brain, no memory of my original condition arose to teach me
the folly of my desires." Memory, culture, loyalty to race – none seem to
ground Lee's self. His confusion lasts until the revolt when he refuses to
kill a white child, and it is not until the rebellion is quelled that he fully
re-possesses himself, "I was, in reality, *not* Tom the slave, but Sheppard
Lee the freeman."[31] After Lee-as-Tom is lynched, Lee finally returns to his
original body and life with his slave, Jim Jumble. Pro-slavery order is re-
established with little lingering doubt about the justice of chattel bondage
or the essential status of the self.

Like *Sheppard Lee*, "Metzengerstein" uses interracial metempsychosis to
play upon antebellum fears of white slavery and black revolt. The crucial
difference is that Poe denies any smooth return to *normality* (ironically
enough, a word he coined in 1848). One reason for this is that Poe is
unsure about the stability of selfhood, a fact indicated by a curious
complaint he brings against *Sheppard Lee*. In his review of the novel,
Poe approves of metempsychosis as a literary device, though he writes,
"The chief source of interest in such narrative is, or should be, the
contrasting of [its] varied events, in their influence upon a character
unchanging" (ER 401). Poe rightly charges that Sheppard Lee "very
awkwardly, partially loses, and partially does not lose, his identity,"
suggesting that Poe, a writer who at times plays with the fluidity of
selfhood, in this instance advocates a stable, essential, and unchanging
sense of self. Stories such as "The Man That Was Used Up" and "The
Man of the Crowd" (1840) show that Poe is sensitive to the contingency of
selfhood. Other tales – from "Ligeia" to "How to Write a Blackwood
Article," to the angelic dialogues – depict identities that are stubbornly,
hermetically, and often grotesquely essential. In "Morella" (1835), another
tale of metempsychosis, the speaker cites Locke to define the self as
"the sameness of a rational being," but by the end of the story he
can only shudder at the "too perfect *identity*" of his revenant bride (PT
235, 238).

31 Robert Montgomery Bird, *Sheppard Lee*, vol. 2 (New York: Harper, 1836), 179, 192–3, 211.

Fitting for a man who re-invented himself but was ceaselessly borne back to a never-ending past, Poe is torn. He knows that opium, amnesia, dreams, and demons can destabilize the self, while he also imagines in frantic reaction impregnable identities. Metempsychosis in "Metzengerstein" saves the self in a terrifying way, potentially retaining the soul of Count Berlifitzing in the body of a brutish slave. Unable or unwilling to reestablish the duality of master and chattel, Poe does not conclude his story on the sunny porch of *Sheppard Lee* but rather in the shadow of amalgamation and by the fiery light of slave revolt, a terror intensified by the fact that the transmigration of souls not only undermines enlightenment order but (as Olaudah Equiano shows) is a belief of African spiritualism.[32] By destabilizing personal identity, Poe destabilizes racial distinctions. He cannot seem to separate race and philosophical speculation, a complication that helps to shape his peculiar transcendentalism.

HIDEOUS SYNTHESIS

Thus far we have seen what might be called the objective terror of "Metzengerstein": Black rebellion and white slavery take embodied, physical forms. However, Poe's best terror lies, not in the material facts of death, upheaval, and bondage, but rather in the subjective perception and narration of such facts. Poe's strongest voice is the first-person for, as Henry James would demonstrate in "The Turn of the Screw" (1898), the witnessing and telling of a horrible thing can be more affective than the thing in itself. As a projected piece of Poe's aborted story sequence, "The Folio Tales," "Metzengerstein" has a first-person frame that quickly gives way to third-person narration, a perspective that limits the tale and one Poe would learn to eschew. "Metzengerstein" is probably not the text to frighten listeners around a campfire; and yet it offers in rough fashion its own subjective terror executed, not in formal practice, but by philosophical theme. Here again the tale's ambiguous steed plays a central role, for among its many manifestations the horse can be a creature of transcendental idealism representing a threatening blackness immanent in the white mind.

---

32 Olaudah Equiano *The Interesting Narrative* (1794), in *Pioneers of the Black Atlantic: Five Slave Narratives from the Enlightenment, 1772–1815*, ed. Henry Louis Gates Jr. and William Andrews (Washington, DC: Civitas Counterpoint, 1998), 205. See also Thomas, *Romanticism and Slave Narratives*, 167–200.

Kant famously theorizes a subjectivity that constitutes external reality in that structures of the mind organize, reveal, and – in this sense – make-up the phenomenological order. This seems the case when Baron Metzengerstein, "buried in meditation," fixates on the tapestry horse, seemingly bringing it into the natural world:

The longer he gazed, the more absorbing became the spell – the more impossible did it appear that he could ever withdraw his glance from the fascination of that tapestry. . . . To his extreme horror and astonishment, the head of the gigantic steed had, in the meantime, altered its position. The neck of the animal, before arched, as if in compassion, over the prostrate body of its lord, was now extended, at full length, in the direction of the Baron.

Simply considered, this summoning scene enacts a general transcendentalist claim. Reality is not passively perceived by the subject but actively constructed by it, so much so that it is impossible to separate subjective perceptions from objective truths. As we shall see, Poe's theory of race relies on this Kantian conviction, particularly as advanced by Schelling and disseminated by Coleridge, who together propound two ideas that are of special importance to Poe – absolute identity, a reality concept that synthesizes subject and object; and unconscious production, the means by which subjects unknowingly create the phenomenological world. First, however, some words on critical history and source are needed, for Poe's relation to transcendentalism is complicated.

Poe is most often taken to be a critic of transcendental idealism who satirizes the cant of Kant and the croaking of what he called the Concord "Frogpondians." Poe certainly makes light of romantic philosophy and feuds with Emerson and his followers.[33] However, some scholars find affinities between Poe and transcendentalism, in part because they go to transatlantic influences without passing through the confines of Concord.[34] Which sources one studies makes a difference when pursuing Poe's philosophy, though how Poe got his transcendentalism is difficult to say, especially in 1831 – prior to Frederic Hedge's essays on Kant and the stirrings of the Frogpondians, prior to Poe's occasional and at times misinformed direct references to German romanticism. Poe probably lacked the skill and opportunity to read German philosophy in its original, but by 1831 he was reading Coleridge and may have learned some version

---

33 Evan Carton, *The Rhetoric of American Romance: Dialectic and Identity in Emerson, Dickinson, Poe, and Hawthorne* (Baltimore: The Johns Hopkins University Press, 1985), 36–42,101–5.
34 Thompson, *Poe's Fiction*, 19–38; Leon Chai, *The Romantic Foundations of the American Renaissance* (Ithaca: Cornell University Press, 1987), 128–38.

of transcendentalism from Carlyle, Cousin, De Quincey, and De Staël.[35] There is also another possible source indicated by "Metzengerstein," for as the story itself suggests by footnoting "D'Israeli," Poe may take some philosophical direction from Benjamin Disraeli's *Vivian Grey* (1826).[36]

In the novel, Grey meets a German Prince who wars with a bordering estate and obsesses over a painting of a horse that seems to spring into life. Parallels to the plot of "Metzengerstein" are evident enough, but what has not been discussed is a subsequent scene in which Grey attends a party where he refers to the German states as the "country of Kant." His host then points to another guest:

The leader of the Idealists, a pupil of the celebrated Fichte! To gain an idea of his character, know that he out-herods his master. . . . The first principle of his school is to reject all expressions which incline in the slightest degree to substantiality. . . . Some say that he dreads the contact of all real things, and that he makes it the study of his life to avoid them. Matter is his great enemy.[37]

The joke is that this student of Fichte is gorging himself on beer soup, demonstrating that even committed idealists must live in the material world. For his part, Baron Metzengerstein suffers from a similar antinomy. Though prone to reflective meditation, he is also a "temporal king" whose appetites, like those of Disraeli's idealist, have "out-heroded Herod." At the same time, the Baron will not touch the horse to whom he is so passionately attached, and none of his servants can recall having "placed his hand upon the body of the beast." On the one hand, then, the horse is unreal, a phenomenon of the Baron's transcendental subjectivity. On the other hand, the horse is too real, embodying a savage materiality that overcomes Metzengerstein's mind. Is the horse an objective brute or a subjective nightmare? How does Poe mediate what Emerson would call the "wild contrast" of double consciousness, a dialectic Plato's *Phaedrus* compares to being torn apart by two horses, one material and the other ideal?[38]

35 Thomas Hansen and Burton Pollin, *The German Face of Edgar Allan Poe: A Study of Literary References in His Works* (Columbia, SC: Camden House, 1995). For early (and occasionally unflattering) references to *Biographia Literaria*, see Poe's "Letter to Mr. B——" (1831).
36 Poe's reference to Disraeli was probably not added until 1849 (*Tales and Sketches*, 2: 17). Poe mentions Disraeli and *Vivian Grey*, both positively and negatively, in multiple reviews. See also Lambert A. Wilmer's 1866 recollection of Poe, "Disraeli was his model" (*The Poe Log*, 125).
37 Benjamin Disraeli, *Vivian Grey: A Romance of Youth*, 2 vols. (1826; New York: M. Walter Dunne, 1904), 2: 251.
38 Plato, *Phaedrus*, trans. R. Hackforth (New York: Bobbs-Merrill, 1952), 69. In a later, related formulation of double consciousness, "Fate" (1860), Emerson more explicitly invokes the two horses of the *Phaedrus*.

By eliding potentially determinative evidence with disclaimers and narrative gaps, "Metzengerstein" refuses to settle the metaphysical status of its steed. This has the familiar Poe effect of collapsing dualisms as the horse-shade remains both subject and object, both spirit and matter, both human and beast. Poe does more, however, than only indulge an iconoclastic urge to cast the shadow of dark romanticism over enlightenment order. For Poe, such skepticism is the obverse of a serious transcendentalist effort to imagine the synthesis of subject and object in an absolute identity. In this way, Poe resists enlightened duality, not with a materialist critique that Jonathan Elmer associates with Horkheimer and Adorno, nor with a proto-post-structuralism as suggested by Lacan and Derrida, nor even with a kind of African epistemology hinted at by Dayan and Morrison.[39] Rather, Poe's urge to smudge distinctions between subjectivity and objectivity is a project he takes up in the language and logic of a specific transcendentalism.

The hungry idealist of *Vivian Grey* is a caricature of Schelling, the pupil of Fichte who during his phase of so-called "identity philosophy" sought to incorporate the material world into his transcendental system. For De Staël, "Schelling refers every thing to nature." Hedge called him, "the ontologist of the Kantian School." More recently, Emil Fackenheim describes Schelling as an idealist "who has been struck, almost physically, by brute facticity. . . . [I]f he is an empiricist of sorts, his is, as he himself on occasion calls it, a 'metaphysical empiricism.'"[40] This description is eerily appropriate for Poe, whose writings respond to both material and speculative modes of inquiry, and whose tales careen between idealism and a brute facticity often figured as race.

More than any German romantic, Schelling had an early and abiding, though probably indirect, influence on Poe.[41] "Loss of Breath" (1832) and "How to Write a Blackwood Article" refer to Schelling by name, and Poe's resistance to dualistic order in "Metzengerstein" and beyond dramatizes what "Morella" calls "*Identity* as urged by Schelling" (PT 235) – that is, identity not simply as self, but rather as a unified,

39 Elmer, *Reading at the Social Limit*, 187–92; *The Purloined Poe*; Dayan, "Amorous Bondage," 206–7; and Morrison, *Playing in the Dark*, 31–59.
40 Madame De Staël, *Germany*, trans. Murray (1810; Boston: Houghton Mifflin, 1859), 196; Frederic Henry Hedge, "Coleridge's Literary Character" (1833), in *Transcendentalism: A Reader*, ed. Joel Myerson (Oxford: Oxford University Press, 2000), 92; Emil L. Fackenheim, *The God Within: Kant, Schelling, and Historicity*, ed. John Burbidge (Toronto: University of Toronto Press, 1996), 51–2.
41 For Poe's references to Schelling and the availability of Schelling in English, see Hansen and Pollin, *The German Face of Edgar Allan Poe*, 80.

absolute truth that Schelling's *System of Transcendental Idealism* (1800) formulates as "the coincidence of an objective with a subjective."[42] Poe was likely exposed to this concept through Coleridge's *Biographia Literaria* (1817), a book that praises Schelling's massive influence and pays homage to the point of plagiarism. Borrowing from *System of Transcendental Idealism*, Coleridge posits absolute identity: "All knowledge rests on the coincidence of an object with a subject. . . . During the act of knowledge itself, the objective and subjective are so instantly united, that we cannot determine to which of the two the priority belongs."[43] This is precisely the challenge of Metzengerstein's steed. Because it is both a phenomenon produced by the mind of Frederick Metzengerstein and a brutish, material horse from the stables of Wilhelm Berlifitzing, subjectivity and objectivity are joined in an inseparable union that represents the absolute identity of Friedrich Wilhelm Schelling.

But whereas Schelling and Coleridge see absolute synthesis as harmonious, beautiful, and true, for Poe the yoking of subject and object is a horse of a different color:

[T]he Baron's perverse attachment to his lately-acquired charger – an attachment which seemed to attain new strength from every example of the animal's ferocious and demon-like propensities – at length became, in the eyes of all reasonable men, a hideous and unnatural fervor. In the glare of noon – at the dead hour of night – in sickness or in health – in calm or in tempest – the young Metzengerstein seemed riveted to the saddle of that colossal horse, whose intractable audacities so well accorded with his own spirit.

Poe cannot celebrate a transcendentalism that synthesizes black and white. Just as the narrator of "William Wilson" (1839) murders himself and the twin whose "absolute identity" nearly "enslaved" him, "Metzengerstein" recoils from a master-slave pairing by killing both subject and object (PT 355–56). Unlike the ecstatic, lyrical flights that characterize synthesis in Schelling and Coleridge, Poe renders the union of subject and object in an idiom of racial horror as absolute identity becomes an analog for amalgamation and slave revolt.

Even worse, Poe hints that this awful synthesis originates in Metzengerstein's unknowing mind, a possibility also suggested by transcendental

42 F. W. J. Schelling, *System of Transcendental Idealism*, trans. Peter Heath (1800; Charlottesville: University Press of Virginia, 1978), 5.

43 Samuel Taylor Coleridge, *Biographia Literaria; or, Biographical Sketches of My Literary Life and Opinions*, in *The Collected Works of Samuel Taylor Coleridge, Vol. 7*, 16 vols., ed. James Engell and W. Jackson Bate (Princeton: Princeton University Press, 1983), 7(I): 252, 7(I): 255.

idealism. The concept of unconscious production was first explored by Fichte, who addressed a paradox of Kantian subjectivity: If consciousness does in fact make up the world, why does not consciousness always know it? Fichte responded to this challenge by proposing that reality is created unconsciously, that the subjective production of phenomenon precedes the subject's knowledge of it. This explains why radical subjectivity is so counter-intuitive to the uninitiated. Because our minds do not know that our minds spontaneously make-up reality, only guided philosophical reflection can discover the truth-making process. Absolute identity is thus revealed when unconscious production becomes conscious, when subjectivity recognizes that it is indistinguishable from objectivity, a realization that effectively abolishes subject/object dualism.[44]

For Schelling and Coleridge, art is the means for recognizing such absolute unity. Schelling writes in *System of Transcendental Idealism*, "[A]rt is at once the only true and eternal organ and document of philosophy, which ever and again continues to speak to us of what philosophy cannot depict in external form, namely the unconscious element in acting and producing, and its original identity with the conscious.[45] Following Schelling, Coleridge posits "a *philosophic* (and inasmuch as it is actualized by an effort of freedom, an *artificial*) *consciousness*, which lies beneath or (as it were) *behind* the spontaneous consciousness natural to all reflecting beings." By extolling artistic expression as an aid to freely willed reflection, Schelling and Coleridge conflate metaphysics, psychology, and aesthetics. The creation and appreciation of beauty bring unconscious production to light, revealing absolute identity through what Coleridge calls art's "synthetic and magical power."[46]

The prospects of unconscious production would later appeal to New England transcendentalists, even if Emerson and his circle do not explore the destructive possibilities of the unconscious as relentlessly as Poe. In *Prose Writers of Germany* (1840), Hedge selected and translated a telling passage from Schelling, "It was long ago perceived that, in Art, not everything is performed with consciousness; that, with the conscious activity, an unconscious action must combine; and that it is of the

---

44 My sense of unconscious production has been aided by Roger Hausheer, "Fichte and Schelling," in *German Philosophy Since Kant*, ed. Anthony O'Hear (Cambridge: Cambridge University Press, 1999), 1–24; Andrew Bowie, *Schelling and Modern European Philosophy: An Introduction* (London: Routledge, 1993), 45–54; and Paul Redding, *The Logic of Affect* (Ithaca: Cornell University Press, 1999), 123–26.
45 Schelling, *System of Transcendental Idealism*, 231.
46 Coleridge, *Biographia Literaria*, 7(I): 236, 7(II): 16.

perfect unity and mutual interpenetration of the two that the highest in Art is born." Emerson echoed this thinking in "Intellect" (1844) when he claimed that "[o]ur spontaneous action is always the best" and that the productive (or "constructive") power of the mind "exists prior to reflection." Emerson would further write in "Beauty" (1860), "[A]ll beauty points at identity," which leads to "an all-dissolving Unity, – the first stair on the scale to the temple of the Mind."[47] Whitman, too, turned to Schelling (and Fichte) when describing what he called that "identity between himself subjectively and Nature objectively":

What is the fusing explanation and tie – what the relation between the (radical, democratic) Me, the human identity of understanding, emotions, spirit, etc., on the one side, of and with the (conservative) Not Me, the whole of the material objective universe and laws, with what is behind them in time and space, on the other side? . . . Schelling's answer, or suggestion of answer, is . . . that the same general and particular intelligence, passion, even the standards of right and wrong, which exist in a conscious and formulated state in man, exist in an unconscious state, or in perceptible analogies, throughout the entire universe of external Nature, in all its objects large or small, and all its movements and process – thus making the impalpable human mind, and concrete Nature, notwithstanding their duality and separation, convertible, and in centrality and essence one.[48]

From Shelling and Coleridge to Hedge, Emerson, and Whitman, art reveals the latent greatness of subjects who, in popular transcendentalist tropes, are like gods suddenly aware of themselves or drunks who awaken to find themselves king.

But for Poe newly self-conscious immortals suffer pain and disorientation, while topers awake to find themselves bloody, lost at sea, or simply hung-over. The unconscious-made-conscious-through-art is finally horrific in Poe's writings, not so much because the Kantian and Burkean sublimes can be implicated in terror and racism, but because a dangerous blackness emerges from the unsuspecting white mind.[49] When Metzengerstein first

---

47 Frederick Henry Hedge, *Prose Writers of Germany* (1840; Philadelphia: Porter and Coates, 1847), 512. The passage Hedge chooses is from Schelling's "On the Relation of the Plastic Arts to Nature" (1807). Emerson, "Intellect," in *Essays and Lectures*, 418, 425; and "Beauty," in *Essays and Lectures*, 1111–12.

48 Walt Whitman, *Specimen Days* (1882), in *Walt Whitman: Complete Poetry and Collected Prose* (New York: Library of America, 1982), 809, 895 (ellipses are mine). Note that later in the passage, Whitman turns to Hegel for a "fuller statement," reflecting the general rise of Hegelian thought in America after the Civil War (895).

49 Laura Doyle, "The Racial Sublime," in *Romanticism, Race, and Imperial Culture*, ed. Alan Richardson and Sonia Hofkosh (Bloomington: Indiana University Press, 1996), 15–39; Erkkila, "Poetics of Whiteness," 65–67.

glances at the tapestry horse, he does so "without his consciousness"; and he cannot quell the "overwhelming anxiety" that makes it "impossible" to avert his gaze as he "mechanically" stares at the object of art that becomes the "uncontrollable" horse-shade. In a frightening synthesis, the mono-maniacal subject unconsciously produces the object of its demise, creating a self-generated, self-annihilating nightmare culminating in the Baron's last ride, "The agony of his countenance, the convulsive struggle of his frame, gave evidence of superhuman exertion: but no sound, save a solitary shriek, escaped from his lacerated lips, which were bitten through and through in the intensity of terror."

Schelling called the unconscious-made-conscious "the holy of holies" that "burns in eternal and original unity, as if in a single flame."[50] "Metzengerstein" ends with the unholy union of white master and black slave, a union that perishes in an inferno of unnamable absolutism. "Metzengerstein" can carefully play on the fear of slave revolt, while metempsychosis figures the threat of whites becoming black. Absolute identity and unconscious production turn the screw once more. Distinc-tions of color and servitude become metaphysically untenable, for an uncontrollable, bestial blackness lurks in the white mind, ready to spring into hideous synthesis through an irresistible and distinctly transcendental process of coming-to-consciousness.

This conflation of black and white subjectivity may recall another pupil of Fichte, Hegel, whose dialectic of lord and bondsman frames the celebrated argument that the subject can only know itself through a subordinate or dominant other.[51] Like Hegel, Poe is sensitive to the dynamics of power and contingent selves. And just as Hegel's *Phenomen-ology of Spirit* (1809) derides Schelling's absolute identity as a night in which all cows are black, Poe at times will mock the monistic vision of transcendental Oneness. Nonetheless, the threat of subsuming blackness seems quite real to Poe, and Schelling and Coleridge remain more likely influences on his thought. Calvin Stowe, Harriet Beecher's husband, suggested as much in 1845 when he reviewed the "*four great pillars of the Modern Transcendentalism*" – Kant, Fichte, Schelling, and Hegel. Stowe writes of Schelling, "It was from him immediately that Coleridge drew, and the transcendentalism of this country probably owes its existence to

---

50 Schelling, *System of Transcendental Idealism*, 231.
51 Carton, *The Rhetoric of American Romance*, 15–18. Carton doubts that Poe studied Hegel but argues that this "only enhances the significance" of their relationship (15), a position from which I dissent.

a great extent to the influence of his writings." Stowe then offers what he believes to be the first American translation of Hegel, adding "I have never been able, I must frankly confess it, to find out what the man means by any thing which he says."[52] Stowe is right to doubt his expertise, but his confusion is indicative. In the antebellum era, particularly during the formation of transcendentalism in the early 1830s, Schelling was more accessible, better understood, and more broadly discussed than Hegel – despite an early interest in Hegel by James Marsh, Frederick Rauch, Theodore Parker, and others; despite the growing popularity of Hegel that would culminate after the Civil War.[53]

Antebellum philosophical contexts, thematic affinity, and textual allusion all suggest that "Metzengerstein" treats subjectivity with the help of Schelling and Coleridge. The tale probably errs when describing subjectivity in a third-person voice, for like many precocious works of fiction, it generally tells but does not show the protagonist's state-of-mind. For this reason, "Metzengerstein" is instructive – and also powerfully predictive – as a kind of component tasting in which political commentary and transcendental idealism are not formally integrated. Later, Poe's distasteful politics are more carefully blended in first-person texts characterized by racist anxieties and wild transcendental imaginings. Such narratives are often more dramatic and psychologically nuanced than "Metzengerstein," even though slavery and race refuse to be entirely assimilated as romantic subjectivity unconsciously creates the blackness it fears most. From Dupin's re-enactment of an orangutan's violence, to Roderick Usher's darkly haunted mind, to "The Raven" and its speaker's semi-conscious conjuring of a shadowy demon, a number of moments in Poe's work hint at the subjective production of race. Here three texts from 1838 more explicitly point to Poe's transcendental racism.

Critics have shown how *The Narrative of Arthur Gordon Pym* reveals the social constructedness of race.[54] From characters like the murderous

---

52 Calvin Stowe, "The Teutonic Metaphysics, or Modern Transcendentalism," *The Biblical Repository and Classical Review* (Jan., 1845), 65, 75, 79.

53 For Hegel in America, see Bruce Kuklick, *A History of Philosophy in America*, 75–94. Thomas Cooley has also suggested that, if anything, Hegel's *Philosophy of History* may be more relevant than *Phenomenology of Spirit* to antebellum discussions of slavery and race (*The Ivory Leg in the Ebony Closet: Madness, Race, and Gender in Victorian America* [Amherst: University of Massachusetts Press, 2001], 55–60). Poe's only explicit references to Hegel, to my knowledge, are neither early nor particularly telling: 1842 review of Rufus Dawes (ER 495), and "Marginalia" of 1849 (ER 1459).

54 Rowe, *At Emerson's Tomb*, 42–62; Dana Nelson, *The Word in Black and White: Reading "Race" in American Literature, 1638–1867* (New York: Oxford University Press, 1993), 90–108.

black cook and the half-breed Dirk Peters to the island of Tsalal where Poe enacts an allegory of a slave revolt, the novel exploits racist anxieties of the antebellum era. While doing so, *Pym* also subtly describes the phenomenological production of racial others. As Pym drifts from a unified white subjectivity to that of a prisoner, that of a cannibal, and finally that of a fugitive slave, he is repeatedly lost in the depths of his mind, figured by Poe in scenes of drunkenness, insanity, and interment. The generative powers of the unconscious become terrifyingly clear when a hunted, hungry, cliff-hanging Pym discovers his "fancies creating their own realities" (PT 1170). In this fugitive state, he attempts to define a superior white subjectivity over and against the jet-black Tsalalians, who act as his hunters and masters. Pym appears to succeed when escaping their island and sailing toward an all-white South Pole, particularly when his Tsalalian captive dies from over-exposure to whiteness, suggesting that blacks have no place in the "perfect whiteness" at the end of the book (PT 1179). Unlike most victims of the middle passage, however, the dead Tsalalian remains in the bottom of the boat. Inassimilable and inescapable, the corpse suggests that racial others are fundamental to Pym's subjectivity, a subjectivity terrorized by dark bodies it spontaneously creates and cannot cast behind.

A similar dynamic is at work in "Ligeia." Ligeia is a maven of "transcendentalism" and also a figure of amalgamation, whose physical features, as critics have shown, conjure images of Africa and Arabia (PT 266).[55] Like Metzengerstein's steed, Ligeia can symbolize the possibilities of absolute identity insofar as she is both a material other and a product of the narrator's opium-addled mind. Synthesizing objectivity and subjectivity under the narrator's transcendentally influenced eye, Ligeia's struggle to return from the dead models a process of unconscious production when her resurrection as dark phenomenon is simultaneously enacted in the natural world and in the irrepressibly associative mind of the narrator. In the end, she lives, but the taint of race remains to make her absolute identity horrific. The narrator's subjectivity is finally subsumed by the gaze of Ligeia, whose "black" eyes are "far larger than the ordinary eyes of [his] own race" (PT 264). Is Ligeia an embodied African figure or the figment of a racist unconscious? The transcendentalism of Schelling and Coleridge suggest that the answer is *yes*, for "Ligeia"

55 Among others, Dayan discusses race and "Ligeia" in "Amorous Bondage," 200–07.

shows how object and subject collapse in the process of unconscious production.

Even an aggressively satirical piece like "How to Write a Blackwood Article" does not eschew race when trying to "[s]ay something about objectivity and subjectivity" (PT 282). The story's narrator, Psyche Zenobia, is told to adopt "the tone transcendental" and shun "the tone heterogeneous," to praise the harmony of "Supernal Oneness" while avoiding "Infernal Twoness" (PT 283). Poe associates such absolutism with both "Coleridge" and a "pet baboon" (PT 281), and he further conflates transcendentalism and race mixing in Zenobia's tale, "A Predicament." Not only is the bluestocking Zenobia a reformer in the Frogpondian mode, Poe links her philosophy to amalgamation when her grotesque black servant crashes into her breasts. Poe responds to this bawdy union by slowing decapitating Zenobia, which she describes in sensational detail as she wonders whether her head or body represents her "proper identity" (PT 295). Faced with an absolute identity entailing the threat of racial unity, Poe retreats to an epistemology in which the division of subject and object is explicitly, violently demarcated. "How to Write a Blackwood Article" is clearly a burlesque; yet Poe's caricature of transcendental writing aptly describes some of his best work. Under the influence of Schelling and Coleridge, Poe desires the supernal truth and beauty of absolute oneness. At the same time, he does not let go of dualistic formulations of slavery and race, making transcendence a philosophically attractive but politically pernicious prospect.[56]

Teresa Goddu has shown how Cold War critics took the blackness of classic antebellum texts, not as an indication of race, but as a metaphysical cipher.[57] The case is quite the opposite now as race and slavery seem everywhere in Poe, though the politics and philosophy of blackness in his writings seem to me inextricably linked. In the case of Poe, dark romanticism is appropriately named. Hawthorne, Melville, and Dickinson know how to read Calvin against Concord. For Poe, race and slavery remain fearsome facts that resist any blithe absolutism. There are, of course, many good reasons why transcendentalism never took root in the South. As the Virginian-born transcendentalist convert Moncure Conway learned, slave states did not take to the perfectionist politics that characterized Concord idealism. Lewis Simpson shows how Emerson

---

56 For a compatible reading, see Leverenz, "Spanking the Master," 116–17.
57 Goddu, *Gothic America*, 7–8.

and the South made a kind of peace after the War, but he also points out that Quentin Compson could not survive at Harvard, for Faulkner knows that the heavy legacy of slavery is out of place in transcendental realms.[58]

Which is not to say that philosophical idealism could not and did not accommodate racism. Kant maintained a racist hierarchy, as did Coleridge and Emerson, while romanticism – European and American – can be profoundly implicated in racialist thought.[59] This did not prevent almost all American transcendentalists from supporting abolitionism, from being part of the racism problem and part of the slavery solution. In Poe, however, the threat of blackness is too ominous a concern. Poe retains a racist anti-abolitionism that mars his potentially transcendental plots, pushing him toward a terrifying synthesis in which absolute identity and unconscious production belie the mastery of white subjectivity, an embattled political and philosophical formation after Nat Turner.

POE KNOWS

Poe reportedly once leapt twenty feet in the running broad jump. To move from "Metzengerstein" to *Eureka* (1848) may require a similar stunt. The preceding section schematically offers some sense of the long middle ground. Poe's formal technique matures. Professional pressures and plans for a national magazine restrict his comments on slavery. At the same time, the Longfellow War and Poe's disastrous reading at the Boston Lyceum bring a more personal, polemic hostility to his views of abolitionism and New England reform. The vagaries of Poe's career make for a tragic and fascinating story. Yet it remains hard to index his fictions according to the shifting fortunes of his life, in part because Poe tends to revisit earlier topics and narrative strategies, prompting some scholars to organize his texts thematically, not chronologically. This makes sense in the case of slavery and race, for Poe's literary treatment is not inconsistent. Although the political subtext of "Metzengerstein" seems especially cogent, absolute identity and unconscious production when

---

58 Lewis Simpson, *Mind and the American Civil War: A Meditation on Lost Causes* (Baton Rouge: Louisiana State University Press, 1989), 96–105.
59 Mills, *The Racial* Contract, 69–72 ("Kant"); Thomas, *Romanticism and Slave Narratives*, 89–104 ("Coleridge"); Anita Haya Patterson, *From Emerson to King: Democracy, Race, and the Politics of Protest* (New York: Oxford University Press, 1997), 129–38 ("Emerson").

combined with color and servitude continue to cause ungovernable horror from "Metzengerstein" to *Pym* to Poe's major writings of the early- and mid-1840s. Race, slavery, and transcendentalism are often entangled in Poe's imagination, though a singular departure may be *Eureka*, his seldom-loved "Prose Poem" whose rhapsodic cosmology potentially invokes an absolutism free from the anxiety of race (PT 1257). How sustainable such freedom is for Poe is the subject of this final section, which ultimately examines the extent of Poe's political intentions.

In his "Marginalia" of 1849, Poe celebrated his skeptical prowess, "It is laughable to observe how easily any system of Philosophy can be proved false" (ER 1458). Poe, however, immediately betrays a lingering desire for rational certitude, "[I]s it not mournful to perceive the impossibility of even fancying any particular system to be true?" For all his doubting, Poe never abjures the rational dream of coherence, and nowhere is this clearer than in *Eureka*, his best effort to expound a philosophical system. Poe announces at the start of the text, "I design to speak of the *Physical, Metaphysical and Mathematical – of the Material and Spiritual Universe: – of its Essence, its Origin, its Creation, its Present Condition and its Destiny*" (PT 1261). The hubris here may rival that of some university mission statements, but if Poe becomes increasingly unbalanced toward the end of his life, there is no reason to take *Eureka* less seriously than any other Poe text. Indeed, considering Poe's long-standing commitment to speculation, and considering the metaphysical maxims of his "Marginalia" (1844–49) and "Fifty-Suggestions" (1849), his attempt to construct a system of philosophy comes as no surprise.

Not unlike William James's attempt to "embrace monistic pantheism on non-mystical grounds," *Eureka* draws from a dizzying number of thinkers, including Newton, Laplace, Leibniz, Kepler, and Alexander von Humboldt.[60] Much of the text discusses the physical sciences, which Poe pushes to metaphysical extremes. In this way, *Eureka* is a work of synthesis, for though the treatise dismisses "Transcendentalists" as canters and "divers for crotchets" (PT 1263), its overarching dialectal structure draws from transcendentalism in general and Schelling and Coleridge in particular.[61] Poe begins by positing "Material" and "Spiritual" aspects of the universe (PT 1261), and he derides the division of object and subject

---

60 William James, *Varieties of Religious Experience* (1902), in *William James: Writings, 1902–1910*, 459.
61 For *Eureka* and transcendentalism, see Chai, *Romantic Foundations of the American Renaissance*, 132. Richard Gravil makes connections between *Eureka* and Schelling in *Romantic Dialogues: Anglo-American Continuities, 1776–1862* (New York: St. Martin's Press, 2000), 129–38.

that vexes the history of Western thought. Poe's goal is to formulate what he variously calls "*absolute truth*" (PT 1269), "absolute oneness" (PT 1280), and "absolute homogeneity" (1279). He aspires to find a "return to unity" (PT 1278), which is reached through the "tranquility of self-inspection" and the "cool exercise of consciousness" (PT 1356). One contemporary review of *Eureka* identified such yearnings as transcendental.[62] And Poe's unity of object and subject in reflection sounds a lot like Schelling and Coleridge, for whom absolute truth reveals itself in an ecstatic coming-to-consciousness. This moment of knowledge announces the climactic synthesis of *Eureka*. "[C]onscious intelligences" learn "proper identity" through an effort of reflection, and in doing so return to an "identity with God" in which "myriads of individual Intelligences become blended – when the bright stars become blended – into One" (PT 1358). In this way, Poe moves toward absolute identity with an emphasis on self-knowledge, showing that the subject must be reunited with its original unconscious productions.

What is stunning is how happy this synthesis is; for once Poe is not shaken but stirred. In the vast majority of his writings, self-inspection is not tranquil, nor is self-consciousness cool, nor is the absolute blending of egos cause for transcendental joy. When the narrator in "Loss of Breath" is lynched, he mocks romantic absolutism, "Schelling himself would have been satisfied with my entire loss of self-identity."[63] In *Eureka*, however, "*perfection*" is the "plot" (PT 1342). Even evil is "intelligible" and "endurable" (PT 1357). The union of self and other in God is not a violation of the mind, for though Poe feels the "pain of the consideration that we shall lose our individual identity," assurance arrives with the conviction that "*each* must become God" (PT 1359). Like many transcendentalist texts, *Eureka* faced charges of pantheism. The main point that it proves may be James's claim in "The Compounding of Consciousness" (1909) that "the only thing that ever drives human beings insane is logic."[64] Poe, however, is unfazed. Absolute oneness is "agglomeration," not amalgamation, while Poe's predicted "revolution" of knowledge is not figured as a revolt (PT 1306, 1262). Thus *Eureka* seemingly frees transcendentalism from the trammels of bondage and blackness. To come to ecstatic consciousness

---

62 Silverman, *Edgar A. Poe*, 341.
63 This line does not appear in the Library of America version of "Loss of Breath." See *Tales and Sketches*, 2: 79.
64 James, *A Pluralistic Universe*, 721.

and realize absolute identity is to leave behind the dualistic vision that *Eureka* calls "mental slavery" (PT 1269).

And yet the very mention of slavery can summon the specter of the national sin. Given the intense racial fears that appear in so much of Poe's work, *Eureka* and its inset text, supposedly lifted from a "Nubian geographer," only tenuously banishes political anxiety from the paradise of absolute identity (PT 1263). Unity is a crucial concept in transcendental metaphysics, but it was also important to ethnologic debates of the antebellum era. Monogenesists argued that all races came from a single origin, a conclusion that was readily adapted to abolitionist ends. For their part, polygenesists and slavery advocates denied the unity of races, often citing the pseudoscientific work of writers like Samuel George Morton. Morton's work on mummies and skulls has been shown to inform racist ideology in *Pym* and "Some Words with a Mummy" (1845).[65] *Eureka,* however, is dedicated to Alexander von Humboldt, whose influential *Cosmos* (1845) came to dispute Morton's polygenesist views.[66] Following Humboldt, *Eureka* holds that all matter comes from a "common parentage" (PT 1286); and so if the text speaks to slavery at all, it seems to speak against it, even as Poe forecloses this possibility in a subsequent tale, "Mellonta Tauta" (1849).[67]

Presented as a series of letters from a balloonist in the year 2848, "Mellonta Tauta" quotes copiously from *Eureka* as it mocks the double consciousness of previous eras and celebrates the "absolute truth" recognized in the twenty-ninth century (PT 878). In this sense, "Mellonta Tauta" is an accurate rendering of *Eureka*. The difference is that the story is also an explicit political satire that takes "Amriccans" to task for reformist ignorance and government by mob (PT 879). The heavy-handed politics of the story are combatively conservative, sending up such republican practices as voting and the "queerest idea" that "all men are born free and equal" (PT 879). The story's commentary can be so extravagant as to seem at times capricious, yet Poe's complaint about equality has poignant social relevance. From Thomas Dew, Robert Montgomery Bird,

---

65 Jared Gardner, *Master Plots: Race and the Founding of an American Literature, 1787–1845* (Baltimore: Johns Hopkins University Press, 1998), 125–59; Dana Nelson, *National Manhood: Capitalist Citizenship and the Imagined Fraternity of White Men* (Durham: Duke University Press, 1998), 206–16.

66 Menand, *The Metaphysical Club*, 144.

67 For a compatible political reading of *Eureka* that focuses on constitutional theory, see W. C. Harris, "Edgar Allan Poe's *Eureka* and the Poetics of Constitution," *American Literary History* 12: 1 (spring 2000), 1–40.

and William Harper in the 1830s to James Henry Hammond, John Calhoun, and George Fitzhugh in the decades that followed, pro-slavery thinkers repeatedly denied that "all men are born free and equal," in part because the phrase was long a rallying cry for abolitionists.[68] Unable or unwilling to keep race and slavery out of *Eureka's* transcendental speculations, "Mellonta Tauta," like so many Poe texts, cannot reconcile race and romantic absolutism. In an 1847 article, "Bad News for the Transcendental Poets," an author in the *Literary World* crowed, "[T]he transcendental balloon is rapidly suffering collapse."[69] "Mellonta Tauta" ends when the narrator announces that her "balloon has collapsed" (PT 884–85). As it plummets toward the sea, Poe presents a familiar (if sanguinely reported) apocalypse in which transcendentalism yet again cannot bear the burden of antebellum politics. *Eureka* is the exception that proves the rule represented by "Mellonta Tauta": Poe's ambivalence toward transcendentalism constitutes and is constituted by his views on slavery and race. What remains unclear is why Poe continues to conflate metaphysics and politics. Why do his texts so stubbornly dwell on so tense and disruptive an antinomy?

In 1923, D. H. Lawrence hinted at a powerful explanation, "Moralists have always wondered helplessly why Poe's 'morbid' tales need have been written. They need to be written because old things need to die and disintegrate, because the old white psyche has to be gradually broken down before anything else can come to pass." Lawrence recognized that "Poor Poe" subverted white subjectivity; and though he sometimes sees Poe doing such work "*consciously*," he more often attributes the impulse to a primitive, irresistible, and almost pathological "need." Harry Levin and Leslie Fielder described this need more explicitly as an unconscious "racial phobia," a view that continues to dominate Poe scholarship in more sophisticated forms. Though Thomas Cooley has recently situated Poe in terms of nineteenth-century faculty psychology, John Carlos Rowe,

---

68 Dew, "Abolition of Negro Slavery," 28; Bird, *Sheppard Lee*, 187; Harper, "Memoir on Slavery" (1837), in *Ideology of Slavery*, 83; Hammond, "Letter to an English Abolitionist" (1845), in *Ideology of Slavery*, 176; Calhoun, *A Disquisition on Government and Selections from the Discourse* (1853; New York: The Liberal Arts Press, 1953), 44; George Fitzhugh, *Sociology for the South, or the Failure of Free Society* (1854; New York: Burt Franklin, 1965), 177–79. It is worth noting that in an 1836 review in *The Southern Literary Messenger*, Poe referred to the "iniquities" of Jefferson's progressive thought (ER 565).

69 "Bad News for the Transcendental Poets," *Literary World* (Feb. 20, 1847), 53. Based on content, style, and Poe's friendly relationship at the time with the *Literary World's* editor, Evert Duyckinck, Poe seems a likely candidate for the author of this piece. Note, too, that Emerson compared transcendentalism to a "wild balloon" in "The Transcendentalist" (194).

Dana Nelson, David Leverenz, and J. Gerald Kennedy are among the scholars who depict Poe as both in and out of control insofar as the vision of his "semiconscious" texts remains obscured by his racism. Even Whalen, who ascribes to Poe a significant amount of intention, does not consistently formulate Poe's conscious relation to social conditions. Whether the method is Marxist or psychoanalytic, whether the agency is ideology or id, for scholars who entertain questions of intention, Poe's literary treatment of slavery and race seems to operate beyond his authorial will.[70]

As Poe's detective Dupin suggests when contemning the "blundering idea of *motive*" (PT 421), there is always space for the unconscious psychologically, politically, or materially understood. The depiction of Poe as a man at the mercy of some hidden perversity is not utterly untrue. Henry James, no stranger to the dramatic potential of coming-to-consciousness, associated the vulgar pleasures of Poe with a "primitive stage of reflection," a judgment indulged by subsequent critics and generations of readers who prefer to think of Poe as driven by urges he neither knows nor controls.[71] Perhaps we like Poe best this way. Bodies under the floorboards, beasts in the jungle, madwomen in the attic – it is gripping to watch a subject in the throes of their unconscious, especially when the unconscious threatens to stun us by degrees. The contention here is that Poe knows, that for him, as for Schelling and Coleridge, the dialectical process of coming-to-consciousness is a necessary element of art premised on an aesthetic theory based in transcendentalism.

In 1842, a British critic wrote of German romantics in the *American Eclectic*, "They consider, that as Art is a production, a creation of the mind of man, the real way to set about its examination must be the investigation of those laws of the mind from whence it proceeds. . . . Thus it becomes itself a branch of psychology. . . . *They* [the Germans] examine the producing mind; *we* the work produced."[72] Poe's aesthetics often linger

---

70 Lawrence, *Studies in Classic American Literature*, 65, 71; Leslie Fiedler, *Love and Death in the American Novel* (1960; New York: Anchor, 1992), 391–400; Cooley, *The Ivory Leg*, 150–54; Levin, *The Power of Blackness*, 121. Rowe, "Edgar Allan Poe's Imperial Fantasy and the American Frontier," in *Romancing the Shadow*; Leverenz, "Spanking the Master"; Nelson, *The Word in Black and White*, 90–108; J. Gerald Kennedy, "Trust No Man: Poe, Douglass, and the Culture of Slavery," in *Romancing the Shadow*, quoted 253. Meredith L. McGill points out inconsistencies in Whalen's treatment of Poe's "authorial agency" in "Reading Poe, Reading Capitalism," *American Quarterly* 53.1 (March 2001), 145.

71 Henry James, *French Poets and Novelists* (New York: MacMillan, 1893), 60.

72 "Hegel's Aesthetics: The Philosophy of Art, Particularly in Its Application to Poetry," *American Eclectic: or, Selections from the Periodical Literature of All Foreign Countries* 4 (July 1842), 71.

on the form of the object of art, a preference prefiguring French symbol-
ists, high modernists, and New Critics. However, as much as any antebellum thinker, Poe follows the Germans in focusing on the subjectivity
of the artist. As he suggests when calling *Biographia Literaria* "an important service to the cause of psychological science," Poe's aesthetics are
closely related to his sense of the operations of the mind (ER 188).

Part of Poe's fame as a cryptologist and critic came in 1842 when his
review of Dickens's *Barnaby Rudge* correctly predicted some features of
the ending before the novel was entirely serialized. When doing so, Poe
pointed to the unconscious production of literature: "This is clearly the
design of Mr. Dickens – although he himself may not at present perceive
it. In fact, beautiful as it is, and strikingly original with him, it cannot be
questioned that he has been led to it less by artistical knowledge and
reflection, than by that intuitive feeling for the forcible and the true. (ER
222–23). Here Poe does more than present himself as an expert reader
of texts and minds. He implies a theory of authorial production that
relies, not on conscious "knowledge" or "reflection," but on an "intuitive"
mental faculty that the author "may not at present perceive." Such claims
undermine the omnipotent intention Poe ascribes to the poet in "The
Philosophy of Composition" (1846), a work that seems especially
specious in light of other Poe texts. In "MS. Found in a Bottle" (1833),
the narrator "unwittingly" paints "DISCOVERY" on a canvas, suggesting
in both production and product that writing is a kind of graphic automa-
tism revealing the author's unconscious (PT 195). Moreover, in an 1836
review and in later critical pieces, Poe celebrates artistic effects that "arise
independently of the author's will" (ER 263).[73]

Unconscious production is a consciously theorized aspect of Poe's
thought – both in his metaphysics of race and in his thinking on art.
This does not, of course, exclude psychoanalytic or ideological readings of
Poe, but it does suggest that Poe can be a remarkably canny subject whose
texts are acutely sensitive to the play between the known and unknown
mind. Considering the political position of "Metzengerstein," and considering Poe's continued attention to the unconscious production of
beauty and blackness, writings that may seem haunted by Poe's buried

---

73 For racial readings of "MS. Found in a Bottle," see Leland Person, "Poe's Philosophy of
Amalgamation: Reading Racism in the Tales," in *Romancing the Shadow*, 205; and Albert von
Frank, "'MS. Found in a Bottle': Poe's Earliest Debt to Tennyson," *Poe Review* 34: 1 (2001), 1–5.
For other examples of Poe and the authorial unconscious, see his 1836 review of Daniel Defoe (ER
202) and his 5 April 1845 sally in the Longfellow War (ER 759).

racial phobias can be taken as complex dramatizations of a psychology of mastery and racism, dramatizations driven by Poe's abiding refusal to integrate the differences of racial others into an absolute Oneness. In this way, Poe rises from the couch and moves toward the analyst's chair. The story of many of his stories, and a narrative in the history of Poe criticism, is the gradual coming-to-consciousness of American slavery and racism.

The problem is that such acute self-consciousness fails to raise Poe's moral conscience. How can an author so committed to race and subjectivity deny in his literary theory and practice, as well as in his more explicitly political writings, the subjectivity of racial others who become for Poe literal images of blackness in the white mind?[74] Clearly theoretical sophistication need not lead to convincing truth-claims or humanist convictions. Clearly Poe can suffer and spread what Paul Gilroy calls the "racial terror" of enlightenment.[75] One might also read Poe's theory of race as a kind of sublimation or ideological formation, thus re-inscribing Poe's psychological insights within a larger unconscious plot. Such arguments might invoke some version of the intentional fallacy, though there are also more specific, more historical grounds for retaining what Dana Nelson calls "psychopolitical imperatives" as an explanatory factor in the structure and practice of antebellum racism.[76]

Addressing the fear of slave revolt in the post-Turner South, Tocqueville claimed that the white man "hides it from himself."[77] Douglass, Melville, and Jacobs also discuss the white repression of blackness, though the very fact that these writers recognized a "deep" psychology to the slavery crisis suggests that Poe himself had access to similar conclusions. There is always space for consciousness when the evidence interpreted by the analyst is also available to the subject of analysis, even if the subject's sense of psychology is not phrased in a modern idiom. One way to determine authorial intention is to look for patterns of reflection and recognition that indicate an extended, self-conscious examination into the recesses of the mind. If my reading of Poe is right, Poe knows that race operates unconsciously. A difference between him and his knowing contemporaries is that he does not follow this insight toward a

---

74 Poe grants virtually no subjectivity to his stereotypical African-American characters or his African-American figurations; and in his reviews of such novelists as Bird, Simms, and Beverly Tucker, he applauds Sambo stereotypes. In "The Literati of New York City" (1846), Poe specifically objects to Catherine Sedgwick's more humanized characterizations of blacks (ER 1203).

75 Gilroy, *The Black Atlantic*, 56.

76 Nelson, *National Manhood*, 206.

77 Tocqueville, *Democracy in America*, 1: 329.

progressive politics. One reason for this is that Poe's thinking is so aggressively phenomenological that for him to conclude that the horror of blackness is "only" a mental construction may not subvert that construction as such but rather establish it as the most reliable indication of a reality that is only maintained through fierce denials of intersubjectivity that mark the limits of Poe's truth-claims, ethics, and imagination.

Toni Morrison has asked how American authors elide the subject of slavery and race, how they use "strategies for maintaining the silence" that surrounds Africans in America.[78] Poe's peculiar strategy derives from his understanding of the *unconscious,* which brings together two implications of the word – the modern sense of the unrecognized mind, and the etymological connotation that signals the negation ("un") of shared ("con") knowledge ("science").[79] In Poe, race precludes intersubjectivity, driving narrators into the depths of their minds. As in "The Masque of the Red Death" (1842), the artist figure can lock the doors, but the contagion of color still enters in – not so much because racism is for Poe an irrational superstition, but because its terror exists within the walls of his rationally formulated system.

As morally suspect as Poe's writings can be, their outcome is often affective. Applying Elmer's sense of sensationalism, one might formulate race in Poe's works as an inassimilable and therefore compelling Lacanian "leftover" or "slag." Slavoj Žižek supports such claims in a general discussion of American racism when he associates race with an "unfathomable remainder" that simultaneously drives and defies the search for absolute truth. That Žižek makes this point while forging connections between Schelling and Lacan suggests that Poe's appeal to both transcendental and psychoanalytic criticism may not be entirely coincidental or inherently at odds.[80] Most histories of modern American psychology begin with either William James or the importation of Freud.[81] Earlier, however, transcendental idealism helped invent the modern unconscious

78 Morrison, *Playing in the Dark,* 51.
79 For the historically shifting connotations of "conscience," see Jean Hagstrum, *Eros and Vision: The Restoration to Romanticism* (Northwestern University Press, 1989), 3–28.
80 Elmer, *Reading at the Social Limit,* 125; Slavoj Žižek and F. W. J. von Schelling, *The Abyss of Freedom/Ages of the World: An Essay by Slavoj Žižek with the Text of Schelling's Die Welater (second draft, 1813),* Judith Norman (Ann Arbor: The University of Michigan Press, 1997), 27.
81 See, for instance, John Demos's "Oedipus in America: Historical Perspectives on the Reception of Psychoanalysis in the United States," in *Inventing the Psychological: Toward a Cultural History of Emotional Life in America,* ed. Joel Pfister and Nancy Schnog (New Haven: Yale University Press, 1997), 63–64.

when it located the source of absolute truth beyond the subject's immediate reflection. This claim is borne out by various accounts of the deep
psychology of British romanticism; and the philosopher Paul Redding has
further argued that "Schelling's development of Fichtean ideas . . . gave
rise to pre-Freudian ideas about the nature of unconscious mental function."[82] In this way, Poe can be a stop on the road from Kant to Lacan.
Influenced by unconscious production and attentive to layered psychological states, Poe writes about the fraught relation between the hidden
and recognized mind, dramatizing his fear of and his desire for transcendental unity. Which is to say that Poe is less a passive subject of psychoanalysis and more a thinker who participates in a history of subjectivity.

In 1800, Coleridge first used "unconscious" to indicate what the self
does not know of itself. In 1822, he coined "subjectivity" to signify the
consciousness of one's mind engaged in the act of perception. Coleridge
did not invent these concepts, but he brought them to the United States
with the help of other romantics who moved, among others, Poe. In 1831,
Carlyle proclaimed, "Unconsciousness is the sign of creation." In 1832,
De Quincey coined the related term "subconscious."[83] That same year,
Poe published "Metzengerstein," commencing a prose career that would
use romantic theories of the unconscious to explore the metaphysics of
slavery, race, and art. Poe's philosophy is not systematic, entirely coherent, or analytically rigorous. Yet as Stanley Cavell has argued, Poe is
perversely attuned to the skeptical potential of romantic philosophy,
revealing "the recoil of a demonic reason, irrationally thinking to dominate the earth . . . not to reject the world but rather to establish it."[84] Like
other authors treated in this book, Poe's creativity relies in part on his
understanding of the limits of philosophy, particularly its failure to bring
order to the slavery crisis.

In this sense, Poe plays the unfamiliar role of a representative antebellum writer, though his political tendencies continue to make him
something of an anomaly in American literary history. On the margins
of southern gentility, Poe's treatment of race is too radically troubled
for pastoral plantation fiction. Fearing transcendence, he could not join
in the perfectionist projects of Concord. Such skepticism can leave him in
the usual company of Hawthorne and Melville, the later of whom attested

---

82 Redding, *The Logic of Affect*, 4.
83 Thomas Carlyle, "Characteristics," in *John Stuart Mill and Thomas Carlyle*, ed. Charles W. Eliot
(New York: P. F. Collier, 1909), 347. All first usages based on the *OED*.
84 Stanley Cavell, *In Quest of the Ordinary: Lines of Skepticism and Romanticism* (Chicago:
University of Chicago Press, 1988), 138.

to Poe's quarrel with New England transcendentalism. In *The Confidence-Man* (1856), Melville's Cosmopolitan talks idealism with an Emerson figure; and when a "crazy beggar" with "raven curls" interrupts to peddle a "rhapsodical tract" written in "the transcendental vein," we recognize *Eureka* and the down-and-out Poe whose derelictions were becoming legendary. To the bemusement of Melville and his Cosmopolitan, the Emerson figure gives Poe the cold shoulder, calling him a "scoundrel" and a "vagabond" who yet possesses "a damning peep of sense."[85] Melville thus names the tense relationship between Poe and New England transcendentalism. Attuned to the social hostility of the parties, Melville knows that Poe and the Frogpondians share a peep of philosophical commonality.

A tendentious syllabus for American romanticism might sketch a three-pronged attack on Concord: Hawthorne doubts transcendental theology; Melville subverts transcendentalist reform; Poe derides the metaphysics of Emerson and his circle. A crucial difference, however, is that Poe remains a more insistent idealist, repeatedly returning to absolute identity and unconscious production and, with *Eureka,* offering a vigorous if ultimately tenuous synthesis. When Hawthorne and Melville task transcendentalism, they are often overly conscious of Concord, so much so that their writings tend toward satires such as Melville's episode in *The Confidence-Man* and Hawthorne's "The Celestial Railroad" (1843). "How to Write a Blackwood Article" is similarly derivative. Poe, however, pursued romantic philosophy before the founding of the Transcendental Club. He would eventually meet the Frogpondians in polemic, defensive, and not always earnest ways, but this was after he initiated an original relation to transatlantic romanticism. Poe's understanding of transcendental oneness is not premised on a transparent eye, for his dramatic depictions of absolutism are occluded by slavery and race, and his thinking is too intensely fixated on the productive opacity of the unconscious mind.

One exceptional aspect of American transcendentalism is its abiding, problematic and, in some ways, irreconcilable relationship with antebellum politics. For De Staël, German idealists lacked a social impetus, "The enlightened men of Germany . . . give up, without difficulty, all that is real in life to the powerful."[86] Margaret Fuller, like the transcendentalist historian Octavius Brooks Frothingham, also believed that German intellectuals were "relieved by their position from the cares of government"

85 Melville, *The Confidence-Man* (New York: Library of America, 1984), 1049–50.
86 De Staël, *Germany,* 42.

(interestingly enough, a claim Fuller made when applauding what she took to be the carefree genius of blackface performers).[87] In America, however, transcendentalist thinkers were profoundly committed to social questions, particularly the intractable problem of chattel bondage in freedom's land. Such is the case with the first transcendentalist to theorize American slavery and race, though the example of Poe does not fit the profile of the New England transcendental abolitionist. Imported from Germany, translated in England, and shaped by the American slavery crisis, Poe's philosophy details a metaphysic, aesthetic, and psychology that for all their sophistication form a conscious and unconscionable system of transcendental racism.

It may be tempting to think of racism as irrational, unconscious, unenlightened, and therefore open to reform through education and reflection. However, to take this too much for granted is to make a Poe-like mistake, to maintain a separate, masterful subjectivity by so radically distancing the racist other as to render their thinking alien. It is probably comforting to think of Poe as politically, morally, and philosophically different. His popular image is all too alluring – wine bottle in one hand, opium pipe in the other, lusting after relatives and shamelessly plagiarizing while muttering slurs and dying in the gutter. Poe may be a pathological figure, but the point that his writings make so well is that perversity is never too far from reason and that racism retains a stubborn relation to more humane aspects of "civilized" thought. Ivan Hannaford has made the case that the Enlightenment invented modern racism.[88] Poe further suggests the limited ability of Western philosophy to combat slavery, at least insofar as his urge for transcendence cannot overcome his desire for difference and even helps to reduce black subjects to projections of the white mind. Habermas has insisted that the historical coincidence and structural connections between enlightenment and oppression "should not mislead us into denouncing the intentions of an intransigent Enlightenment as the monstrous offspring of a 'terrorist reason.'"[89] Antebellum American philosophy, including its strain of

---

87 Margaret Fuller, "Entertainments of the Past winter," *Dial* 3: 2 (1842), 52 (quoted in Lott, *Love and Theft*, 16); Octavius Brooks Frothingham, *Transcendentalism in New England: A History* (New York: 1876), 105.

88 Hannaford, *Race: The History of an Idea.*

89 Jürgen Habermas, "Modernity: An Unfinished Project" (1980), trans. Nicholas Walker, in *Habermas and the Unfinished Project of Modernity: Critical Essays on The Philosophical Discourse of Modernity*, ed. Maurizio Passerin d'Entreves and Seyla Benhabib (Cambridge: MIT Press, 1997), 50.

transcendentalism, certainly led to emancipating views and progressive political ends. Such democratic possibilities will occupy the chapters that follow, though Poe reminds the rational reader that good intentions are by no means foregone, especially in the antebellum period where plenty of racists thought hard about race and where the project of emancipation remained stubbornly unfinished. A marginal Southerner and anti-abolitionist who died before the Civil War, Poe – as is so often the case – is something of a foil in this book. But even as Poe's writings take an early and politically regressive stand, his inability to leave philosophy behind proves to be predictive, even of someone as radically different as Harriet Beecher Stowe.

CHAPTER 2

"Lord, it's so hard to be good": affect and agency in Stowe

Thinkers sometimes champion beliefs that they themselves cannot confidently hold. Intellectual projects are sometimes driven, not by conviction, but rather the desire for conviction. The dogged search for definite knowledge becomes especially compelling when the shortcomings of a philosophical system form a kind of fortunate flaw. Barred from the paradise of coherence and unable to verify truth-claims, theories that struggle against their own limitations point to both the fall of rational authority and the hope for redemption, for order. As we have seen, Poe cannot or will not reconcile his urge for a unified transcendental design with the political leveling it implies. Indeed, Poe's narratives of slavery and race rely on this disjunction, which Poe sometimes bemoans but more often exploits with a sensational and transfixed glee. Like Poe, Stowe is unable to ignore the incongruities of her philosophy. But while Poe revels in his collapsing systems, the more constructive, more perfectionist Stowe tries harder to salvage her logic. Stowe, that is, oftentimes appears as a writer utterly convinced of her rightness, yet she remains profoundly self-critical in her self-contradictions. Her precarious poise makes her an especially insightful theorist of affect precisely because she does not back away from the problems inherent to her thought. These problems involve both the accuracy and agency of sympathy, both the challenge of determining moral truth and of enacting that truth in the world. In her antebellum writings, Stowe finally fails to reconcile her sentimental theory and practice; but in an era when irresistible enlightenment optimism met the unmovable impediment of slavery, she became all the more dedicated to achieving a workable philosophy of reform.

There are some precedents for regarding Stowe in a philosophical light. While occasional Cold War critics studied Stowe's theological commentary, others examined the confusion, hypocrisy, and naïveté of her politics, depicting Stowe as an instinctive and unselfconscious writer who reflected the contradictions of her culture better than she reflected upon them.[1] Revisionist scholars of the 1980s and 1990s found in Stowe a more cogent sentimental design as the reclamation of *Uncle Tom's Cabin* (1852) and of American sentimental literature in general proceeded in the name of cultural work, not the history of ideas.[2] The social consequences of sentimentality continue to generate debate, though critics are increasingly moving away from questions of political rectitude, in part because the concept of sentimentality remains insufficiently defined.[3] Among other things, American sentimental literature needs to be situated within and against broader philosophical narratives that explore the psychological operations and moral authority of the emotions. The work thus far has almost exclusively involved eighteenth-century moral philosophy, particularly traditions of Scottish commonsense most often exemplified by Adam Smith's *Theory of Moral Sentiments* (1759).

In the powerfully representative case of Stowe, the results of such inquiry have been rewarding and stand further elaboration. As Gregg Camfield, Elizabeth Barnes, Marianne Noble, and Glenn Hendler have shown, Stowe draws upon a widely circulating discourse of sentimentality that posits intersubjective affect as the basis for moral truths.[4] What is less apparent is how precisely and how strategically Stowe argues her position – how she formulates the laws of sympathy using specific philosophical sources; how she resists opponents of her sentimentality such as Hobbes, John Calhoun, and (more selectively) Hume; how she negotiates patriarchal opposition to female philosophers; and how her work in surprisingly dynamic ways confronts deep-seated metaphysical problems deriving from her own sentimental assumptions. As an ambitious and

1   For early accounts of Stowe's religious thought, see Charles Foster, *The Rungless Ladder: Harriet Beecher Stowe and New England Puritanism* (New York: Cooper Square, 1970); Alice Crozier, *The Novels of Harriet Beecher Stowe* (New York: Oxford University Press, 1969); and Lawrence Buell, "Calvinism Romanticized: Harriet Beecher Stowe, Samuel Hopkins, and *The Minister's Wooing*," *Emerson Society Quarterly* 24 (1978): 118–32. Early political critics include James Baldwin, "Everybody's Protest Novel," in *Notes of a Native Son* (Boston Beacon Press, 1955), 13–23; and Ann Douglas, *The Feminization of American Culture* (New York: Doubleday, 1977), 64–66, 244–55.

2   Jane Tompkins, *Sensational Designs: The Cultural Work of American Fiction, 1790–1860* (New York: Oxford University Press, 1985), 122–46; Philip Fisher, *Hard Facts: Setting and Form in the American Novel* (New York: Oxford University Press, 1985), 87–127.

3   June Howard, "What is Sentimentality?" *American Literary History* 11: 1 (1999): 63–81.

4   Gregg Camfield, *Sentimental Twain: Samuel Clemens in the Maze of Moral Philosophy* (Philadelphia: University of Pennsylvania Press, 1994), 22–59; Elizabeth Barnes, *States of Sympathy: Seduction and Democracy in the American Novel* (New York: Columbia University Press, 1997), 91–99; Marianne Noble, "Sentimental Epistemologies in *Uncle Tom's Cabin* and *The House of the Seven Gables*," in *Separate Spheres No More: Gender Convergence in American Literature, 1830–1930*, ed. Monika M. Elbert (Tuscaloosa: The University of Alabama Press, 2000), 261–81; Glenn Hendler, *Public Sentiments: Structures of Feeling in Nineteenth-Century American Literature* (Chapel Hill: University of North Carolina Press, 2001), 3–11.

self-critical thinker, Stowe suffers from and intervenes in philosophical conundrums as she seeks fundamental mechanisms with which to settle the slavery crisis. In doing so, her writings engage richly related theories of emotion, including not only Adam Smith's system of moral sentiments, but Catharine Beecher's sentimental psychology and Puritan notions of disinterested benevolence.

At least two benefits come from reading Stowe in terms of these intersecting contexts. First, Stowe's sentimentality appears in fuller historical complexity once it is shown to adopt, adapt, and mediate diverse theories of affect. Secondly, Stowe's antebellum career, which has in many ways escaped explanation, makes sense as a philosophical narrative in which paradoxes manifest in Stowe's metaphysics push her toward a quarrel with Calvinism. These paradoxes center on the challenge of affective correctness; for though *Uncle Tom's Cabin* famously posits right feeling as the solution to slavery, Stowe comes to doubt the possibility of knowing and changing the heart. Much of Stowe's skepticism comes from her failure to mitigate the slavery crisis and her inability to move her sentimental convictions from theory into practice. The irony is that Stowe's writings become less focused on the issue of slavery at the very moment the United States verge on civil war. This shift is evident in Stowe's work after *Uncle Tom's Cabin*, particularly as *Dred* (1856) and *The Minister's Wooing* (1859) struggle with the epistemology of affect and the freedom of the will. What to make of this drift away from chattel bondage is a necessary question that exposes Stowe's failure to implement a coherent system of sentimental reform.

"THOROUGHLY METAPHYSICATED"

In many ways, Stowe was well prepared to talk about slavery in philosophical terms. Metaphysical debate and speculative analysis were part of growing up in the Lyman Beecher family, and Stowe's schooling at Connecticut's Litchfield Academy included moral philosophy. When her sister, Catharine Beecher, left home to establish the Hartford Female Seminary in 1822, Stowe followed to become a pupil and teacher in one of the most ambitious women's schools of the day. Catharine, who published on faculty psychology, theology, and moral philosophy, left a lasting influence on her younger sister's mind. Stowe wrote proudly at the age of nineteen that Catharine had her "thoroughly metaphysicated"; and she studied such thinkers as William Paley, Hugh Blair, and Archibald Alison, standard purveyors of philosophy and rhetoric at Hartford as well as Harvard. After completing her formal education, Stowe continued to be embroiled in metaphysics as Catharine, Lyman, and Stowe's minister-brothers engaged in speculative discussion, as did her husband Calvin Stowe who, in addition to his biblical scholarship, studied transcendental idealism. Like Margaret Fuller, Elizabeth Palmer Peabody, Sarah Helen Whitman, Julia Ward Howe, Augusta Evans Wilson, and others, Stowe was an antebellum woman versed in the philosophy of her day.[5]

This is not to say that Stowe was free to publicly indulge in metaphysics, for although Nina Baym has emphasized the diversity of nineteenth-century women's writings, antebellum women were often discouraged from philosophical pursuits.[6] The Hartford Seminary encountered resistance from parents on this very point, and Catharine learned to publish her most analytical work circumspectly and in some cases anonymously as a result of what she carefully called "the not unreasonable prejudice which has existed against *learned ladies.*"[7] Even John Brace, Stowe's progressive instructor at the Litchfield Academy, felt compelled to apologize for his curriculum, assuring his listeners in a commencement address that his goal was "not to make learned ladies, or skilful metaphysical reasoners."[8] When Stowe discovered a painful gap between her catholic education and the limited prospects of post-graduate life, she experienced a problem not uncommon among educated antebellum women who suffered from what Fuller described in 1840 as "unemployed force."[9] Stowe's predicament reflects the larger cross-purposes of women's education as the American Enlightenment moved toward the Victorian age.[10] On the one hand, female education flourished as domesticity became increasingly institutionalized and women entered new professions such as teaching and nursing. On the other hand, females were typically dissuaded from analytic study, particularly in fields such as

---

5 Stowe quoted in Kathryn Kish Sklar, *Catharine Beecher: A Study in American Domesticity* (New Haven: Yale University Press, 1973), 145. For Stowe's education and early intellectual interests, see Joan Hedrick, *Harriet Beecher Stowe: A Life* (New York: Oxford University Press, 1994), 17–66.

6 Nina Baym, "Women's Novels and Women's Minds: An Unsentimental View of Nineteenth-Century America's Women's Fiction," *Novel* 31: 3 (summer 1998): 335–50.

7 Catharine Beecher, "Suggestions Respecting Improvements in Education" (1829), in *The Limits of Sisterhood: The Beecher Sisters on Women's Rights and Woman's Sphere*, ed. Jeanne Boydston, Mary Kelley, Anne Margolis (Chapel Hill: University of North Carolina Press, 1988), 44. See also Sklar, *Catharine Beecher*, 94.

8 Quoted in Nina Baym, *Feminism and American Literary History: Essays* (New Brunswick, NJ: Rutgers University Press, 1992), 106.

9 Fuller to William Henry Channing, March 22, 1840, *The Letters of Margaret Fuller*, ed. Robert Hudspeth, 3 vols. (Ithaca: Cornell University Press, 1983), 2: 126.

10 Baym, *Feminism and American Literary History*, 105–20; Ostrander, *Republic of Letters*, 39–43, 190–99.

philosophy, which were considered unnecessary and downright dangerous to delicate constitutions, as the Scottish realist Dugald Stewart suggested in "The Sexes" chapter of *The Elements of the Philosophy of the Human Mind* (1792).[11] Stowe's friend and biographer Annie Fields took pleasure from the verve of the Beecher sisters; but she also indicated the general resistance to female metaphysicians when she quoted the reaction of a German professor to one of Catharine's essays, "You have a woman that can write an able refutation of [Jonathan] Edwards on 'The Will?' God forgive Christopher Columbus for discovering America!"[12]

Hostile reactions to *Uncle Tom's Cabin* display a similar opprobrium, deriding both Stowe's political views and her mode of argumentation. Taking up what Charlotte Brontë called the "weapon of personality" wielded against women, George Frederick Holmes's chauvinistic review in *The Southern Literary Messenger* linked Stowe's novel with "'unsound philosophy'" and invidiously compared Stowe's efforts to the "intellectual devotion" of her sister. Holmes further fumed in a later article that *Uncle Tom's Cabin* "unsexed" the "female mind," and he did not resist an unfortunate pun when he charged that the "Stowe-ic philosophy is a fatal contamination to woman."[13] In order to recover this philosophy – which, truth be told, is some way from stoic[14] – we should recognize that as an intellectually driven, liberally educated woman of her day, Stowe had ample training but restricted opportunities to participate in public metaphysical debates, a complication she addresses in "The Young Lady Philosopher" chapter of *My Wife and I* (1871).[15] A radical and feminist like William Lloyd Garrison could praise *Uncle Tom's Cabin* for its "philosophical acumen."[16] Yet patriarchal constraint was a salient

---

11 Dugald Stewart, *Elements of the Philosophy of the Human Mind* (1792), in *The Works of Dugald Stewart, Vol. III* (Cambridge: Hilliard and Brown, 1829), 228–34.

12 Harriet Beecher Stowe, *Life and Letters of Harriet Beecher Stowe*, ed. Annie Fields (Boston: Houghton and Mifflin, 1897), 64.

13 Charlotte Brontë, 1850 preface to Emily Brontë, *Wuthering Heights* (1847; New York: Penguin, 1995), xliv; George Frederick Holmes, "*Uncle Tom's Cabin*," *The Southern Literary Messenger* 18: 10 (Oct. 1852), 630, 637; Holmes, "A Key to Uncle Tom's Cabin," *The Southern Literary Messenger* 19: 6 (June, 1853): 323.

14 Classical stoicism understood emotions as bearing on moral questions, but they saw the influence as pernicious and advocated the repression of affect. Stowe agrees with the first premise but departs from stoicism's normative response (Martha Nussbaum, *Upheavals of Thought: The Intelligence of Emotions* [Cambridge: Cambridge University Press, 2001], 3–7).

15 This chapter may respond to a chiding review of Stowe's *The Chimney Corner* (1868): "[Stowe's] chair of philosophy stands in its proper place, we think, when it stands in the chimney corner" (*The Nation* [23 April 1868], 334).

16 William Lloyd Garrison, "Review of Harriet Beecher Stowe's *Uncle Tom's Cabin*," *The Liberator* (26 March, 1852): 50.

challenge to Stowe's rhetorical task; for just as her novels often recast political questions in domestic terms, they subtly advance philosophical positions that avoid formal argumentation and require an amount of close reading.

INTEREST, SYMPATHY, AND PASSION

As Edmund Wilson once wrote, "Let us begin with *Uncle Tom's Cabin,*" the novel that brought Stowe sudden fame and first established her sentimental system.[17] Stowe writes in the preface that her object is to "awaken sympathy and feeling for the African race," a mission that she favorably contrasts to the efforts of male politicians who are too often confounded by "conflicting tides of interest and passion."[18] The basic design of Stowe's sentimentality is widely recognized: She aspires to govern the public sphere by domestic rules, lifting the authority of feminine feeling over that of masculine logic. Stowe does not, however, simply phrase her claims in a generalized idiom of heart and home. Rather, she carefully formulates a philosophy of reform built around the central concepts of interest, sympathy, and passion.

Uncle Tom's Cabin condemns self-interest in no uncertain terms, but the scope and coherence of Stowe's objections are subject to debate. As Gillian Brown and others have shown, Stowe's sentimentality does not escape the egoistic ideology of liberal individualism, a discourse based on autonomous, acquisitive and, by some accounts, over-developed notions of the self. In many ways, Stowe's sentimentality is powerfully self-interested and stolidly middle-class. Though ostensibly offered in the service of the weak, it often empowers the sympathizing subject at the expense of abject others; and though supposedly defined against capitalist greed, it understands individual subjectivity as a function of property and possession.[19] In *The Minister's Wooing,* Stowe will dwell more critically on the hegemonic capacities of sentimental selfhood. For now, it is important to note that while *Uncle Tom's Cabin* does not free itself from

17 Edmund Wilson, *Patriotic Gore: Studies in the Literature of the Civil War* (New York: Oxford University Press, 1962), 3.
18 Harriet Beecher Stowe, *Uncle Tom's Cabin: Or, Life among the Lowly* (New York: Signet, 1966), v–vi. Hereafter cited parenthetically in the text.
19 Critics of sentimentality include Gillian Brown, *Domestic Individualism: Imagining Self in Nineteenth-Century America* (Berkeley: University of California Press, 1990); Sadiya Hartman, *Scenes of Subjection: Terror, Slavery, and Self-Making in Nineteenth-Century America* (New York: Oxford University Press, 1997); Lauren Berlant, "Poor Eliza," in *American Literature* 70: 3 (Sept. 1998): 635–68; and Lori Merish, *Sentimental Materialism: Gender, Commodity Culture, and Nineteenth-Century American Literature* (Durham: Duke University Press, 2000), 135–90.

liberal individualism, Stowe does offer a trenchant critique of social systems built on self-interest.

On the Shelby plantation, Stowe presents Sam, a slave who speaks "like a philosopher" (55) and acts like a "politician" (87). When describing Eliza's recent escape, Sam brags about his role in the plot, explaining to his fellow slaves the "principles" of his actions (88). "[Y]er see, now what dis yer chile 's up ter, for 'fendin' yer all," he says, "For him as tries to get one o' our people, is as good as tryin' to get all." Sam styles himself a defender of his people and selfless champion of their common interests, even as he gorges on chicken and tosses the bones to his audience. Sam's literally self-serving performance exposes his comic hypocrisy, which is especially evident when he illustrates the principles of his political philosophy:

I'm a tryin to get top o' der hay. Wal, I puts up my larder dis yer side; 't an't no go; – den, 'cause I don't try dere no more, but puts my larder right de contrar side, an't I persistent? I 'm persistent in wantin' to get up which any side my larder is; don't you see? . . . Yes, my feller-citizens and ladies of de other sex in general, I has principles. . . . [H]ere I comes to shed my last blood fur my principles, fur my country, fur der gen'l interests of s'ciety. (89–90)

How "gen'l" Sam's "interests" actually are is a question Stowe invites. Climbing to the top of the hay is a pejorative metaphor for political ambition, particularly because the opportunistic Sam does not care on which side he ascends. In this sense, his political principles, purportedly founded on communal concerns, are in truth only consistent in advancing his own interests, a point Stowe repeats in her next chapter involving Senator Bird. In his sputtering defense of the Fugitive Slave Law, the controversial statute requiring Northern states to return runaway slaves to the South, the Senator can only justify his position by appealing to his wife, "But Mary . . . there are great public interests involved . . . we must put aside our private feelings" (93). Like Sam, the good-hearted Senator will ultimately help the fugitive slave Eliza, and in doing so he exposes the faulty claims of what Stowe calls "great state interests" (102).

In debunking the logic of Sam and the Senator, Stowe handles with a light, ironic touch a sensitive political issue. From *Cato's Letters* (1720) to *The Federalist Papers* (1788) to Tocqueville's *Democracy in America* (1835) to frequent antebellum complaints about partisan and sectional strife, "interests" implied a longstanding problem for many republican theorists who, having reluctantly admitted the difference between state and personal interests, attempted to restrain self-centered motives within systems of checks and balances.[20] Moreover, as Habermas finds in the middle of the nineteenth century in Europe, the problem of interests also threatened the enlightened public sphere where ideas were supposed to be objectively evaluated according to rational merits.[21] However, with the rise of sectional animosity and the flourishing of liberal individualism, antebellum Americans feared that their nation, more than ever before, lacked the capacity to rationally reconcile its contentious concerns. Seeking to establish what Amy Schrager Lang calls the "harmony of interests," Daniel Webster pleaded in his 1850 defense of the Fugitive Slave Law, "Can this country, with one set of interests at the South, and another set of interests at the North, and these interests supposed, but falsely supposed, to be at variance; can this people see . . . that this Union is their main hope and greatest benefit, and that their interests in every part are entirely compatible?"[22]

For Stowe and radicals on both sides of the slavery conflict, the answer was *no. Uncle Tom's Cabin* denies the principles of Webster and other compromising men who invoke the rhetoric of great state interests to salvage both nation and bondage. Stowe writes, "[T]emptations to hardheartedness" will "always overcome frail human nature . . . with no heavier counterpoise than the interests of the helpless and unprotected" (19). Such hard-heartedness is painfully evident in Simon Legree's distopian polity, whose organizational structure is a brutal satire of American republican theory. Pitting Sambo, Quimbo, and his other slaves "one against another," Legree "governed his plantation by a sort of resolution of forces" (370). The problem is that the balance of interests is inherently unjust, for the plantation-state is founded upon "unrestricted animal selfishness" (372), and no institutional mechanism checks the desires of the "tyrant" Legree (421). For Stowe, self-interests cannot be balanced in any moral sense, a challenge that *Uncle Tom's Cabin* extends into the related realm of economics.

In the eighteenth and nineteenth centuries, interest came to imply not only a locus of political power but also of economic motivation.[23] The

---

20 For discussions of interests and republican theory, see J. G. A. Pocock's classic *The Machiavellian Moment: Florentine Political Thought and the Atlantic Republican Tradition* (Princeton: Princeton University Press, 1975).

21 Jürgen Habermas, *The Structural Transformation of the Public Sphere: An Inquiry into a Category of Bourgeois Society,* trans. Frederick Lawrence (1962; Cambridge, Mass: The MIT Press, 1991), 129–140.

22 Daniel Webster, "The Compromise Measures" (1850), in *The Works of Daniel Webster, Vol. V* (Boston: Little, Brown, and Co., 1890), 437. Amy Schrager Lang, *The Syntax of Class: Writing Inequality in Nineteenth-Century America* (Princeton: Princeton University Press, 2003), esp. 69–71.

23 Albert O. Hirschman, *The Passions and the Interests: Political Arguments for Capitalism before Its Triumph* (Princeton: Princeton University Press, 1977), 38.

most powerful formulation of economic interest came from Adam Smith, who (in)famously argued that society advances when individuals pursue selfish ends. In *The Wealth of Nations* (1776), greed is good – a conclusion that made even Smith uneasy, but one that was less troublesome to most antebellum political economists. Southerners such as Jacob Cardozo and Thomas Dew invoked Smith to defend chattel bondage, while Henry Carey, a Northern unionist and leading proponent of *laissez faire*, downplayed the antislavery sentiments of *The Wealth of Nations*, naming "*self-interest*" the "most important motive power" and relying upon the master's "*own interest*" as a sufficient guarantee for the welfare of slaves.[24] For her part, Stowe rejects such logic with the wicked example of Legree. She also points to the inefficiency of slavery when George Harris, a valuable factory slave and inventor of a "labor-saving machine" (23), takes his talents out of America to escape the scourge of bondage. For Smith, labor-saving invention was the single best way to swell the wealth of a nation, and so George's master betrays a shocking ignorance of political economy when he condemns George's "saving work" as a sign of "nigger" laziness.

Not content, however, to refute the practicality of slavery, Stowe goes on to dispute the principle of beneficial self-interest, a radical project with a neglected background in antebellum economic thought. Stowe may have read Orestes Brownson's socialistic "The Laboring Classes" (1840), though a more likely influence is Daniel Raymond's *Elements of Political Economy* (1821), a book Matthew Carey called "far superior" to *The Wealth of Nations*.[25] The antislavery congressman John Quincy Adams was also an admirer, and he started a skirmish in the House of Representatives by attempting to enter Raymond's book into the Library of Congress. The controversy stemmed from Raymond's aggressive abolitionism:

[W]hen we consider what oceans of blood have been shed – how many human beings have been butchered – how many nations of brave, high minded men have been exterminated; and when we add to this the mass of human suffering which has been already caused by negro slavery, the philanthropist is almost

---

24 Henry Carey, *Principles of Political Economy* (Philadelphia: Lea and Blanchard, 1840), 208. Note that Carey was later willing to entertain abolitionism as an economic, but not moral, problem.

25 For Brownson, see Foster, *The Rungless Ladder*, 50–55. Carey quoted in Charles Patrick Neill, *Daniel Raymond: An Early Chapter in the History of Economic Theory in the United States* (Baltimore: Johns Hopkins University Press, 1897), 29. See also Allen Kaufman, *Capitalism, Slavery, and Republican Values: Antebellum Political Economists, 1819–1848* (Austin: University of Texas Press, 1982), 37–81.

ready to drop the tear of regret, and exclaim, alas, that America was ever discovered![26]

There is no direct evidence that Stowe read Raymond's work; but Raymond lived in Cincinnati between 1842 and his death in 1849, years in which Stowe lived in the city and associated with its intellectuals. Raymond also attended the Litchfield law school of Stowe's beloved hometown, and an edition of his *Political Economy* came out in 1840, the year that Catharine Beecher was writing her *Treatise on Domestic Economy* (1841). Most poignantly, *Uncle Tom's Cabin* dramatizes an objection that Raymond brings against Smith, "[T]he interests of a nation, and the interests of individuals . . . are often directly opposed."[27]

Stowe turns this point against Senator Bird and his brethren by demonstrating that great state interests do not account for the interests of slaves; and just as Raymond resisted the *laissez faire* policies of Jacksonian America, the injustice of selfish economic motivation is everywhere in *Uncle Tom's Cabin*. This does not mean that Stowe rejects capitalism in total. Subscribing neither to Smithian economics nor to nascent forms of socialism, Stowe – like Raymond – most strenuously objects to the market revolution, the aggressive spread of free-market forces into every corner of life.[28] Stowe and Raymond nostalgically laud the intimacy of local exchanges in which economic relations are tempered with charity and community mores. *Uncle Tom's Cabin* trusts the "hand of benevolence" (v), not Smith's invisible hand, for just as Stowe belies the "gen'l" interest of politicians like Sam, Bird, and Webster, she denies that unrestrained economic motives advance the public good. Or as Tom preaches to Cassy when he refuses to murder Legree, "[G]ood never comes of wickedness. I'd sooner chop my right hand off!" (423), a lesson also taught by the moral philosopher William Paley, who after admitting "occasions in which the hand of the assassin would be very useful," instead recommends "the Divine economy" as a guide to proper behavior.[29]

26 Daniel Raymond, *The Elements of Political Economy, Vol. II* (1823; New York: Augustus M. Kelley, 1964), 356.
27 Ibid., 35.
28 Charles Sellers, *The Market Revolution: Jacksonian America, 1815–1846* (New York: Oxford University Press, 1991); James Livingston, *Pragmatism and the Political Economy of Cultural Revolution, 1850–1940* (Chapel Hill: University of North Carolina Press, 1994), 24–31.
29 William Paley, *The Principles of Moral and Political Philosophy* (1785; London: Baldwyn and Co., 1821), 46, 48.

That Stowe prefers Christian benevolence to free-market avarice comes as no surprise. Indeed, part of the power of *Uncle Tom's Cabin* resides in such seemingly simple convictions. Stowe's claims, however, are far from simple when applied to political questions, for self-interest in many antebellum minds was the first principle of social organization. Stowe rebuts such dominant views in an antislavery speech of Augustine St. Clare. Like the sentimental philosopher Francis Hutcheson, who denounced "false Views of Interest," St. Clare proclaims, "[T]he majority of our world . . . have n't even an enlightened regard to their own interest" (239).[30] By revealing the tyrannous political imbalance and exploitive economics of slavery, St. Clare argues that the institution has no place in American life. More challenging, however, is Stowe's larger point that theories of self-interest are flawed, that no just system of earthly governance – be it liberalism or *laissez faire* – can be built on the premise that individuals naturally and even rightfully pursue selfish ends. Stowe condemns these prevailing beliefs, but what does she offer instead? If not upon principles of self-interest, how is the nation to run?

In her "Concluding Remarks" to *Uncle Tom's Cabin*, Stowe names her solution to the slavery problem: To properly deploy their "sympathetic influence," readers should "see to it that *they feel right*" (472). This classic formulation of sentimentality, like many British and American sentimental novels, draws upon a philosophical tradition that grounds moral claims in emotion. Following the work of Lord Shaftesbury and Hutcheson, Adam Smith's *Theory of Moral Sentiments* resists Hobbes and Bernard Mandeville, who put self-interest at the center of human motivation and, consequently, civil society.[31] Despite potential conflicts with the coming *Wealth of Nations* (the so-called "Adam Smith problem"), Smith's *Theory of Moral Sentiments* posits sympathy as the basis for his moral philosophy. His oft-quoted chapter, "Of Sympathy," begins, "How selfish soever man may be supposed, there are evidently some principles in his nature, which interest him in the fortune of others," an opening salvo squarely aimed at theories that privilege self-interest. Smith argues that humans can understand and share the concerns of others, though to do so he must answer

---

30 Francis Hutcheson, *Inquiry into the Original of Our Ideas of Beauty and Virtue*, 252, quoted in Charles Taylor, *Sources of the Self: The Making of Modern Identity* (Cambridge: Harvard University Press, 1989), 262.
31 Antebellum moral philosophers did not always endorse Smith's *Theory of Moral Sentiments* (Howe, *The Unitarian Conscience*, 52–53). However, it was popular among abolitionists such as John Greenleaf Whittier in "Justice and Expediency" (1833) and Horace Mann in "Speech on the Institution of Slavery" (1852).

the skeptical objection that "we have no immediate experience of what other men feel." For Smith, this problem of intersubjectivity is distinctly Lockean. He worries, "Every faculty in one man is the measure by which he judges of the like faculty in another . . . I neither have, nor can have, any other way of judging." Smith fears that there is no sure way to verify experiences; and he solves the problem with "moral sentiment," a faculty by which humans feel "sympathy" for others and so can know "what we ourselves should feel in the like situation."[32]

Uncle Tom's Cabin names "moral sentiment" as a principle of Stowe's abolitionism, a claim dramatized when two white women debate slavery aboard *La Belle Riviéra* (121). The first woman condemns chattel bondage for "its outrages on the feelings" and, noting a nearby family of slaves, asks her interlocutor, "Suppose, ma'am, your two children . . . should be taken from you, and sold?" (137–38). This appeal assumes that one can feel in the like situation of others, though Stowe's pro-slavery character denies such claims in the case of blacks, "We can't reason from our feelings to those of this class of persons." Here Stowe addresses a hostile argument raised by, among others, John Calhoun (sometimes known as "The Metaphysician"). In his posthumously published *Disquisition on Government* (1851), an opus of pro-slavery political theory, Calhoun invoked Hobbes to argue that Man is "so constituted that his direct or individual affections are stronger than his sympathetic or social feelings." He also drew from Hume, who believed in moral sense but proscribed its sentimental power, "[T]he sympathetic or social feelings are not so strong between different communities, as between individuals of the same community."[33] This insistence on what Gregg Crane calls "resemblance" as a crucial factor in ethical and legal traditions is shared by the slavery apologist of the *Belle Riviéra*, whose denial of interracial sympathy is repeatedly countered by Stowe.[34]

Most memorably, this happens at the home of the Birds. There is an initial, uneasy distance between the white family and the fugitive slaves who suddenly appear in their kitchen. But when Eliza asks Mary if she has ever lost a child, her words elicit a "hearty sympathy" from the entire household (97) – a sympathy that bridges the Humean gap between people of different communities, and one that recalls an example from

32 Adam Smith, *The Theory of Moral Sentiments*, ed. Knud Haakonssen (Cambridge: Cambridge University Press, 2002), 11, 23, 11.
33 John C. Calhoun, *A Disquisition on Government*, in *Calhoun: Basic Documents*, ed. John M. Anderson (State College, Penn.: Bald Eagle Press, 1952), 4, 35.
34 Crane, *Race, Citizenship, and Law*, 19–27.

Smith, who pointed to the emotional "pangs of a mother" as a universally understood feeling.[35] Even Calhoun conceded that "a mother and her infant" are intimately connected by sympathy, but he called the case an "extraordinary" one irrelevant to matters of government.[36] A central goal of *Uncle Tom's Cabin* is to show that sympathy is not extraordinary, that feelings are intensely relevant, not only to motherhood and moral philosophy, but to politics as well. In this sense, Stowe extends the reach of Smith's sentimental theory, though as an astute, self-critical practitioner of a self-critical genre, Stowe also revises troubling aspects of Smith's sentimentality.

For Smith, sympathy is a powerfully affective and therefore highly subjective feeling that requires what he calls an "impartial spectator" to maintain objectivity. Smith writes, "We can never survey our own sentiments and motives, we can never form any judgment concerning them; unless we remove ourselves, as it were, from our own natural station, and endeavour to view them at a certain distance from us." Smith is especially worried about "the fury of our own passions" under whose influence "every thing appears magnified and misrepresented by self-love."[37] To guard against such embodied, self-interested passion, Smith – like so many eighteenth-century thinkers including Kant and Thomas Reid – presents two components to right feeling: an unmediated acceptance of emotion that allows us to sympathize with others, and a disembodied, impartial spectator that distinguishes sympathy from passion. Particularly interesting (and often neglected) is that Smith explicitly genders these components:

Humanity is the virtue of a woman, generosity of a man. . . . Humanity consists merely in [an] exquisite fellow-feeling. . . . The most humane actions require no self-denial, no self-command, no great exertion of the sense of propriety. They consist only in doing what this exquisite sympathy would of its own accord prompt us to do. But it is otherwise with generosity. We are never generous except when in some respect we . . . sacrifice some great important interest of our own to an equal interest of a friend or of a superior.[38]

Like Stowe, Smith associates competing interests with the calculating world of men. For him, male morality ("generosity") must rationally weigh the interests of others before deciding to sacrifice one's own

---

35 Smith, *Theory of Moral Sentiments*, 15.
36 Calhoun, *A Disquisition on Government*, 31.
37 Smith, *Theory of Moral Sentiments* 30, 128, 182.
38 Ibid., 223.

interest, while female virtue ("humanity") does not entail objective mediation. But whereas Smith reduces female affect to a "merely" intuitive urge, Stowe describes feminine feeling as the very foundation of justice, not only for Smith's "friend" and "superior," but for the lowly as well.[39] Carefully, Stowe privileges feminine humanity over the balanced interests of masculine generosity, essentially accepting Smith's gendered distinction but inverting his patriarchal hierarchy and applying it more democratically.

In doing so, Stowe also subordinates Smith's judicious spectator, for she worries that the demands of objectivity can suppress one's sympathy. Speaking of himself, St. Clare wonders, "[W]hat shall be said of one whose own heart, whose education, and the wants of society have called in vain to some noble purpose; who has floated on, a dreamy, neutral spectator of the struggles, agonies, and wrongs of man?" (336). Deep down where a man really hurts, St. Clare feels right about slavery. But he also exemplifies an affective failing noted by Frederick Douglass, "The grim and bloody tragedies of outrage and cruelty are rehearsed day by day to the ears of the people, but they look on as coolly indifferent as spectators in a theatre."[40] St. Clare is indeed a "neutral spectator" whom Stowe likens to the stoic Cicero, for although he is aware of the brutality of slavery, he is hindered by a logical "scepticism" (300). St. Clare confesses, "I've got the habit of doubting. . . . Who knows anything about anything?" He even questions his affection for Eva, "Was all that beautiful love and faith only one of the ever-shifting phases of human feeling, having nothing real to rest on?" (324–25).

St. Clare is vexed by a Humean argument that Emerson called an "outrage upon the feelings."[41] In opposition to his Scottish peers, Hume argued that inconsistent perceptions preclude objective truth, reducing experience, including emotions, to a series of shifting impressions. Hume sought relief from his disbelief in material enjoyments, "I dine, I play a game of backgammon, I converse, and am merry with my friends."[42] Like

39 For the historical shift in sentimentality from relations between equals to those based on gendered inequality, see Julie Ellison, *Cato's Tears and the Making of Anglo-American Emotion* (Chicago: University of Chicago Press, 1999), 10–20.

40 Frederick Douglass, "The Prospect in the Future" (1860), in *Frederick Douglass: Selected Speeches and Writings*, ed. Philip S. Foner, abridged and adapted by Yuval Taylor (Chicago: Lawrence Hill Books, 1999), 398–99.

41 Ralph Waldo Emerson, "The Present State of Ethical Philosophy" (1821), in *Ralph Waldo Emerson: Together with Two Early Essays of Emerson*, Edward Everett Hale (Boston: American Unitarian Association, 1902), 122.

42 David Hume, *A Treatise of Human Nature* (1739), in *David Hume: The Philosophical Works*, ed. T. H. Green and T. H. Grose (1886; Darmstadt, Germany: Scientia Verlag Aalen, 1964), 548.

Hume, St. Clare retreats from doubt into frivolous pleasure when dinner bells truncate his talks with Ophelia and when he and his brother play a game of backgammon to escape an impasse in their slavery debate. St. Clare finally makes clear that a person's emotions should rightfully supersede logic; for when he dies after interceding in a brawl, after setting aside his newspaper and literally renouncing his role as a spectator, he finds redemption as he passes away with the cry of "*Mother!*" on his lips (342). After this famous deathbed conversion, the texture of *Uncle Tom's Cabin* changes. Instead of carefully engineered debates, there is the ranting of Legree. Rather than reason with pro-slavery logic, Stowe turns toward Tom's untutored Christianity and the gothic machinations of Cassy, strategies of resistance that do not emphasize rationality. Nonetheless, Stowe's preference for the heart remains a complicated matter as *Uncle Tom's Cabin*, like so many efforts to theorize sentimentality, struggles to conceive an extra-rational system in more or less rational terms.

From romanticism to spiritualism to evangelism and sentimentality, diverse antebellum discourses both objected to and partook of logical modes of analysis. Stowe's childhood friend Sarah Willis Parton has the heroine of *Ruth Hall* (1855) say of sympathy, "I shall not stop to dissect the philosophy of that feeling, lest . . . I should lose the substance."[43] Likewise, Stowe reacted against the murderous dissection of emotion, writing to her brother Edward in 1827, "Your speaking so much philosophically has a tendency to repress confidence. We never wish to have our feelings analyzed down."[44] *Uncle Tom's Cabin* also remains uneasy about systematizing sympathy not only because social conventions dissuade Stowe from explicit metaphysical argument, but also because she resists what she calls "cold, definite, intellectual rationalism."[45] This can point toward the antinomian Stowe who subverts patriarchal logos. Yet Stowe remains intensely committed to the rationality she delimits, an ambivalence indicated in *Uncle Tom's Cabin* by the example of the slave cook Dinah. "Like a certain class of modern philosophers," Dinah "perfectly scorned logic and reason in every shape, and always took refuge in intuitive certainty; and here she was perfectly impregnable" (225). Dinah is a formidable, emotional character, though no perfect model for Stowe,

43 Sarah Willis Parton, *Ruth Hall: A Domestic Tale of the Present Time* (New York: Mason Brothers, 1855), 310.
44 Charles Edward Stowe and Lyman Beecher Stowe, *Harriet Beecher Stowe: The Story of Her Life* (Boston: Houghton Mifflin, 1911), 56.
45 Harriet Beecher Stowe, *Sunny Memories of Foreign Lands, Vol. I* (Boston: Phillips, Sampson, and Co., 1854), 56.

in part because her affective certainty can be flat-out wrong. In anticipation of the abolitionist Thomas Wentworth Higginson, who saw blacks as "natural transcendentalists,"[46] Stowe uses Dinah to remind "modern philosophers" that intuition can fail. But if Stowe, like her husband,[47] directs this caveat toward Emersonian enthusiasts, she also admits a potential problem with her own sentimental philosophy. How can one judge the accuracy of convictions based on affect? How can one know for certain if one does in fact feel right? Or as suggested by an anti-abolitionist cartoon titled "What's sauce for the goose is sauce for the gander" (1851), if an abolitionist can liberate slaves under a higher law discerned through the feelings, what precludes someone from "liberating" bolts of cloth from a store when so moved by personal affections?[48]

Nowhere is this question so troubling as in the case of passion. Just as interest is a rational manifestation of selfishness, passion is its emotional correlative. While republican thinkers feared that interest led to faction and conspiracy, they worried that passion brought on violence, corruption, and mobocracy. In the antebellum era, the South was caricatured as a region of unrestrained passion – for drinking, gaming, duels, and cruelty against defenseless slaves, particularly females. For the most part, passion in *Uncle Tom's Cabin* is a tragic symptom of slavery seen in Marie St. Clare's false sympathy, in Legree's lascivious rages, and in Henrique St. Clare, the fiery youth who gives "too free scope to [his] passions," causing his Uncle Augustine to remark, "They that cannot govern themselves cannot govern others" (291). The passion inherent in the slavery system leads to personal and national crimes, yet in *Uncle Tom's Cabin* passion is not an entirely brutal affection. George Harris's "passion" cannot be separated from his heroic appeal (27). The same is true of the passionate Cassy, whose emotional intensity leads to both violence and freedom. It is also the "passion" of Mary Bird that helps her regenerate her world, even if such passion is difficult to distinguish precisely from her sympathy (92).

Affective intensity can, for Stowe, save or ruin a person, a quandary that Smith's *Theory of Moral Sentiments* answers by setting masculine objectivity over feminine feeling. When Stowe, however, dispenses with Smith's impartial, judicious spectator, she leaves no mechanism with

---

46 Thomas Wentworth Higginson, "Leaves from an Officer's Journal," *Atlantic Monthly* 15 (Jan. 1865), 70.
47 Calvin Stowe, "The Teutonic Metaphysics, or Modern Transcendentalism," 64–97.
48 Edward Williams Clay, "What's sauce for the goose is sauce for the gander," Library of Congress Prints and Photograph Division.

which to evaluate the transports of emotion. Charles Taylor shows that "the word 'sentiment' itself, partly replaces 'passion'" in eighteenth-century philosophy, though as "partly" implies the difference between passion and moral sentiment is extremely difficult to stabilize, a central (if not *the* central) concern of American sentimental novels that dramatize the question of love versus lust in domestic and national terms.[49] *Uncle Tom's Cabin* does not rely on the trope of marriage as national union. Nonetheless, Stowe's characters and, through them, her readers must learn to correctly identify emotions in order for them to save themselves and, by extension, their country. How to tell sympathy and passion apart, how to master the epistemology of right feeling, will remain a crucial problem for Stowe, though it is not the only one.

WANTING AGENCY

In *Uncle Tom's Cabin*, Stowe feels as she feels, and no logic will convince her otherwise. By insisting, however, that the readers of her novel "can see to it that *they feel right*," Stowe faces a challenge that the passionate Topsy voices to Eva St. Clare, "Oh, Miss Eva, I *is* tryin'! . . . but, Lor, it 's so hard to be good!" (312). This could be the chorus of a country-western song or more likely the theme of a Calvinist sermon. When Stowe bemoans inconstant human nature, when Ophelia admits that she cannot leave her sins, when the "tempted" (240) Augustine goes "up to heaven's gate in theory" but "down in earth's dust in practice" (253), Stowe shows that seeing to our feelings is never a simple task, for the will is weak, the heart untoward, and humans fall easily to sin. When holding that correct emotion is the best way to save the nation, *Uncle Tom's Cabin* must also theorize a means for feeling right. Stowe addresses this duty in a mix of Christian and secular idioms that cannot quite mediate her father's Calvinism and her sister's sentimental work.

In addition to an education steeped in secular learning, Stowe was also raised within a less sanguine metaphysical tradition that in its own impressive right pursues correct affection. Stowe's father Lyman was a renowned evangelist cut from a Calvinist cloth. Her brothers answered congregational calls, and she married a biblical scholar. Her sister Catharine published on theology, if somewhat circumspectly. And Stowe herself followed debates in religious tracts and journals, while also familiarizing herself with the systematic Calvinism of Samuel Hopkins, Joseph

49 Taylor, *Sources of the Self,* 283.

Bellamy, and the eminent Jonathan Edwards. Calvinist doctrine is explicitly at issue in *The Minister's Wooing* (1859) and *Oldtown Folks* (1869), novels in which Stowe quarrels at length with the legacy of New England Puritanism. The intention here is not to establish Stowe's exact position on Edwardean Calvinism, a concept that by the nineteenth century may have reached the limits of definitional use.[50] Rather, to explicate Stowe's theory of emotional reform is to consider Puritan influences in her culture, family, and writings, particularly as such influences pertain to feeling right.

Calvinist theology and secular philosophy were diversely and often uneasily intertwined in New England intellectual life. From as early as Edwards in the mid-eighteenth century and with increasing intensity, Calvinists developed what Bruce Kuklick calls a "love-hate relationship" with Old World philosophy, including the sentimental theories of Shaftesbury, Hutcheson, and Adam Smith.[51] Even forward-thinking divines such as Henry Boynton Smith worried about the integration of sacred and secular thought. Smith complained in 1849, "We see the orthodox system, and Christianity itself, superseded by ethical, by social, and by metaphysical systems. . . . [Religion's] sacred language is converted to profane and philosophical use."[52] One year later, Edwards Park, another Edwardean Calvinist and the head of Andover Theological Seminary, published "The Theology of the Intellect and that of the Feelings," an essay more open, though still resistant, to the incursions of sentimentality (as Elizabeth Stuart Phelps would later suggest by using Park as a model for the rational Dr. Bland in *The Gates Ajar* [1868]). Park focused on a ministerial style he considered moving but dangerous, "[T]he theology of feeling aims to be impressive, whether it be or not minutely accurate. Often it . . . forces its passage through or over rules of logic, and presses forward to expend itself first and foremost in affecting the sensibilities." Park called such preaching an "outpouring of sentiments" that can "rouse the sympathies of the populace." It remained, however, insufficiently

---

50 Foster calls Stowe's theology "Edwardean Calvinism" (*Rungless Ladder*, x), a claim Alice Crozier challenges (*The Novels of Harriet Beecher Stowe*, 19–22). Buell's reading of *The Minister's Wooing* emphasizes Stowe's adaptation of the Edwardean tradition. Douglas Sweeney further complicates matters by demonstrating that Edwardean Calvinism was a hotly contested concept in the antebellum era ("Edwards and His Mantle: The Historiography of The New England Theology," *New England Quarterly* 71 [March 1998], 97–119).

51 Bruce Kuklick, *Churchmen and Philosophers: From Jonathan Edwards to John Dewey* (New Haven: Yale University Press, 1985), 28.

52 Henry Boynton Smith, "Faith and Philosophy" (1849), in *Faith and Philosophy* (1877 rpt.; New York: Garland, 1987), 2.

"dispassionate" to dispel Park's fears of antinomianism.[53] As with Adam Smith's distinction between female humanity and male generosity, Park maintained a patriarchal hierarchy that subordinated the heart to the head. Park recommended that ministers cultivate "the sensibility of a woman without becoming womanish," for "reason has an ultimate, rightful authority over the sensibilities."[54] Practically predicting the passionate sins of the effeminate Arthur Dimmesdale, Park argued that the theology of feeling excites but cannot manage the affections, a popular charge against emotive evangelists such as Park's friend, Lyman Beecher.

Lyman, according to his son Henry Ward Beecher, practiced an "alleviated Calvinism"; and just as Lyman during his life was compelled to defend his Calvinism as such, scholars have taken him to task for doctrinal laxity.[55] Following his mentor Timothy Dwight, Lyman mitigated but did not deny important orthodox tenets of Calvinism such as predestination, natural depravity, and original sin. Lyman also wondered how a benevolent God could create a world in which His subjects cannot help but damn themselves, a problem of theodicy that he traced to the slippery status of the will. In keeping with orthodox Calvinism, which largely meant keeping with Edwards, Lyman retained a Puritan horror of the Arminian presumption that privileged the efficacy of human agency over God's sovereign power. At the same time, Lyman's evangelical urge insisted that "men are free agents, in the possession of such faculties . . . as render it practicable for them to do whatever God requires."[56] For Lyman, these faculties operate during states of intense emotion. But though at times he shared the language and logic of sentimental philosophy, his theology of feeling never strayed beyond the margins of the Calvinist fold.

Such was not the case with his daughter, Catherine, who quarreled with her father's faith early in her adult life after the unexpected death of a

---

53 Edwards A. Park, "The Theology of the Intellect and that of the Feelings" (1850), in *Selected Essays of Edwards A. Park*, ed. Bruce Kuklick (New York: Garland, 1987), 536, 534, 538, 563.
54 Ibid., 535, 561, 567. Note, too, that in 1850 Park offered Calvin Stowe a position at Andover. After *Uncle Tom's Cabin*, Harriet and Calvin became cordial neighbors with Park, and Stowe would borrow his biography of Samuel Hopkins for *The Minister's Wooing* (Hedrick, *Harriet Beecher Stowe*, 207, 277–76).
55 Henry Ward Beecher quoted in Thomas F. Gossett, *Uncle Tom's Cabin and American Culture* (Dallas: Southern Methodist University Press, 1985), 13. Lyman defends his orthodoxy in *The Autobiography of Lyman Beecher, Volume I*, ed. Barbara Cross (1864; Cambridge: Belknap Press of Harvard University Press, 1961), 415–18. For criticisms of Lyman's rigor, see Cross's introduction to *The Autobiography*, xxx; and Kuklick, *Churchmen and Philosophers*, 106.
56 Lyman Beecher, *Autobiography*, 412.

pious but unregenerate suitor. According to her father's lights, the nice young man was damned. What troubled Catharine most, however, were two features of his Calvinism that Stowe herself would later resent in her New England novels. The first is that Calvinism restricts human agency while still demanding conversion, a paradox bedeviling writers from Anne Bradstreet to Benjamin Franklin to Hawthorne and Dickinson. Secondly, even ministers of feeling (in Catharine's case, her father) pushed the claims of rational argument beyond the tolerance of human hearts. In the words of Kathryn Sklar, Catharine came to emphasize "morality over piety." Though she continued to share her father's belief in affective transformation, she established the power of correct emotion on more secular and more feminine ground.[57]

Catharine's philosophical work most notably breaks with Calvinism by rejecting the mental philosophy expounded by Jonathan Edwards. In eighteenth-century faculty psychology, the mind was typically split in three parts: the will, the understanding, and the affections. Edwards agreed that the mind has understanding, which perceives in the Lockean sense. More radically, he collapsed the will into the affections by showing that humans cannot control their emotions, which he formulated in terms of desire. In this bipartite model of the mind, the will cannot be viewed independently of the affections and, consequently, some exterior motive force must always direct our feelings. For Edwards, this prime mover was God. While humans may enjoy the power to execute their preferences, in the end they do not control those preferences and so lack free will as it is generally understood. Edwards's logic is compelling but also hard to take. Determinism combined with natural depravity and an irritable, punishing God can offend one's earthly sense of justice, as it did in the young Catharine.

In the nineteenth century, Unitarians answered Edwards with moral arguments against his determinism. But for Calvinists who did not cut the cord – and such were the antebellum Beechers[58] – there was the New Haven Theology of Nathaniel Taylor, who returned to a tripartite mental philosophy to reclaim the freedom of the will. By retaining Edwards's sense of understanding but detaching the will from the affections, Taylor posited a motivational faculty with which to control the emotions, an

---

57 Sklar, *Catharine Beecher*, 49. Sklar treats Catherine's speculative work, as does Camfield (*Sentimental Twain*, 39–42). My reading of Catharine's influence on Stowe is compatible with Camfield, though the emphasis here is on agency.
58 Both Catharine and Stowe became Episcopalians in the early 1860s.

account of the mind that drew heavily from Scottish sentimental philosophers and also paralleled advances by antebellum psychologists such as Thomas Upham (a family friend of the Beechers whose experience with a fugitive slave may have inspired Stowe's depiction of Senator Bird).[59] By synthesizing liberal Calvinism with popular secular thought, Taylor's system dominated American psychology up through the nineteenth century. Moreover, and to trace patiently this intellectual genealogy toward Stowe, Taylor was a close friend of the Beechers whose theories influenced Catharine's *Elements of Mental and Moral Philosophy* (1831).

"Man is a voluntary agent," Catharine writes, turning to the challenge of Edwards. She concedes to Edwards that "[e]motions arise *involuntarily* in the mind," though she quickly adds an important exception, "[T]he will cannot control the emotions in any other way, but by the selection of different modes of enjoyment."[60] This ability to willfully cultivate feeling, limited though it is, forms a fundamental premise of Catharine's mental and moral philosophy. Catharine grounds her motivational principle in the seeking of pleasure and avoidance of pain, a premise that Smith (following Hutcheson) treats at length in *The Theory of Moral Sentiments*. In general, improper behavior and emotions result from unfortunate associations of ideas, though such bad habits can be improved by the vigilant pedagogue. This mode of socialization can be seen as a utilitarian or proto-behaviorist process, but Catharine distinctly describes its workings in Smith's sentimental terms. For her, a discerning education awakens "affection in the human mind" by deploying, not donuts and electrical shocks, but rather the *"power of sympathy,"* an intensely intersubjective faculty that causes the student to share the same pain and pleasure as the instructor.[61]

59 Kuklick, *Churchmen and Philosophers*, 97–109; Thomas Upham, *Abridgement of Mental Philosophy: Including the Three Departments of the Intellect, Sensibilities, and Will* (New York: Harpers and Bros., 1861). For Upham's assistance to a fugitive slave, see Hedrick, *Harriet Beecher Stowe*, 205–6. See also Cooley, *The Ivory Leg*, 21–26 on the bipartite vs. tripartite mind in America.

60 Catharine Beecher, *The Elements of Mental and Moral Philosophy, Founded upon Experience, Reason, and the Bible* (1831 rpt.; Ann Arbor, Mich.: University Microfilms, 1969), 369, 421. Edwards might answer that the seemingly voluntary "selection" of enjoyment is itself governed by involuntary drives. Thus Catharine's formulation does not escape Edwards's infinite regression of desire. Catharine generally expresses her proto-behaviorism under the auspices of "habit," a term Norman Fiering discusses in both Edwards and sentimental philosophy [*Jonathan Edwards's Moral Thought and Its British Contexts* (Chapel Hill: The University of North Carolina Press, 1981), 308–13]. *Uncle Tom's Cabin* also emphasizes this word, particularly in relation to St. Clare's skepticism (324, 326).

61 Beecher, *Mental and Moral Philosophy*, 300.

Appropriately enough, Catharine formulated this theory while running the Hartford Seminary. What teacher has not motivated, or attempted to motivate, students by communicating joy or displeasure? Richard Brodhead has described such pedagogy as a mode of Foucauldian discipline, and he names Catharine's *Domestic Economy* as an exemplary middle-class project that attempts to internalize social control within the student-subject.[62] Catherine, however, presented her pedagogy in social and metaphysical terms. Having established a theory of the mind a decade before her *Domestic Economy*, she continued to buttress her mental philosophy in "An Essay on Cause and Effect, in Connection with the Doctrines of Fatalism and Free Agency" (1839). More explicitly replacing Edwardian psychology with the concepts of Taylor and Smith, Catharine's philosophical writings grant the burgeoning and increasingly professionalized ranks of female teachers the power to alter the hearts of their students and, hence, the conscience of the country. Catharine dedicates a later edition of *Mental and Moral Philosophy*, "To Woman, as the Heaven-Appointed Educator of Mind." In teacherly fashion, she shows "How one Mind causes Volition in Another," a chapter that is distinctly Smithian in both its logic and language. By rewarding good and punishing evil through the faculty of "*Sympathy*," defined as "the power the mind possesses of experiencing such emotions as . . . exist in another mind," Catharine posits a model in which the instructor shapes the emotions of her charges.[63]

Derived as it is from Taylor and Smith, Catharine's philosophical work is not particularly original; its contribution lies in its application of ideas to antebellum culture. Catharine's philosophy is also important in that it bears on Stowe in at least two ways. In the interests of source study, it serves as a link between Stowe and Smith's *Theory of Moral Sentiments*, suggesting that Stowe does not vaguely circulate in a generalized discourse of sentimentality, but rather with Catharine revises Smith's thinking toward more feminist and reformist ends. Catharine also provides a psychological basis for the sentimental power of *Uncle Tom's Cabin*,

---

62 Richard Brodhead, "Sparing the Rod: Discipline and Fiction in Antebellum America," *Representations* 21 (1988): 67–96. See also Laura Wexler, "Tender Violence: Literary Eavesdropping, Domestic Fiction, and Educational Reform," in *The Culture of Sentiment: Race, Gender, and Sentimentality in Nineteenth-Century America*, ed. Shirley Samuels (New York: Oxford University Press, 1992), 9–38.

63 Catharine Beecher, *Commonsense Applied to Religion: Or, the Bible and the People* (New York: Harper, 1857), ix, 158–59, 15. This 1857 book is essentially a revised version of *The Elements of Mental and Moral Philosophy*.

which seems to me best understood, not as a novelistic dramatization of Garrison's moral suasion, but as a fully-articulated sentimental pedagogy grounded in a theory of the mind. In the serialized version of *Uncle Tom's Cabin*, Stowe describes Tom as a "psychological phenomenon"; and later she discusses emotional reform in terms of the "law of mind" (424). Most poignantly, Topsy's education serves as a kind of case study that demonstrates the psychological principles set forth in Catharine's work. St. Clare calls Topsy a "fresh-caught specimen" (259) and compares her mind to "virgin soil" (263). He tells Ophelia, "[P]ut in your own ideas, – you won't find many to pull up." The lesson that Topsy demonstrates is that teaching requires sympathy, for it is only after Ophelia opens her heart that "she acquired an influence over the mind of the destitute child" (321). This result is exactly predicted by Catharine's central premise that sympathy is the single best way to shape the mind of the subject. That Topsy seems bereft of ideas can indicate Stowe's racist tendency to figure slaves as primitive, emotional, and largely dependent on whites. At the same time, affection is a crucial element of Stowe's mental philosophy in which the heart and the head are both part of the mind, whether possessed by a black or a white. In this sense, *Uncle Tom's Cabin* resists somatic interpretation, for when Topsy's schooling overcomes her decidedly African body, Stowe points to a universal human mind psychologically understood.[64]

In *Uncle Tom's Cabin*, mental cultivation is open to everyone, so much so that the road to right feeling, though not always smooth, seems assured. Despite the far-reaching evil of slavery, Stowe maintains a perfectionist faith in the education of everyone to a point where even the devil himself seems capable of waking to the good: "Legree had had the slumbering moral element in him roused by his encounters with Tom" (427). Granting even Legree a moral sentiment, Stowe's first novel is optimistic about the chances for human improvement, a conviction shared by Adam Smith, Catharine Beecher, and other sentimental philosophers who held that everyone has free will and an intersubjective, affective faculty open to

---

64 For *Uncle Tom's Cabin* and body theory, see Noble's "Sentimental Epistemology"; and Lora Romero, *Home Fronts: Domesticity and Its Critics in the Antebellum United States* (Durham: Duke University Press, 1997), 70–88. I agree, however, with Barnes's position that in *Uncle Tom's Cabin* "bodies are treated as primarily affective rather than material" (*States of Sympathy*, 96), even if it is important that Ophelia must embrace Topsy. From Smith and Hartley to Beecher and Stowe, associationists saw bodily pleasure and pain as means to shape the affections, but it is not until William James's dynamic "field of consciousness" that associationism came to emphasize the biology of body structures over the connections between ideas. See also Crane, *Race, Citizenship, and Law*, 58.

sympathetic influence. Smith says of moral sentiment, "The greatest ruffian, the most hardened violator of the laws of society, is not altogether without it."[65] *Uncle Tom's Cabin* suggests as much, even as Stowe retains a counter-impulse that, like Lyman's lingering Calvinism, threatens any abolitionist program based on moral sentiment.

In a scene when Legree tortures Tom, Legree is unmoved by his victim's appeal to the "invisible voice" of God (362). Stowe then comments, "Legree heard no voice. That voice is one he never shall hear." This moment suggests that Legree lacks the faculty ever to know God's word, that his wicked soul is "past repentance, past prayer," and even "past hope" (441). Can everyone see to it that they feel right? Stowe answers *yes* and *no. Yes* receives more emphasis in the pages of *Uncle Tom's Cabin* – whether the plot is the coming millennium or the ameliorist progress of a destined nation, whether the agent is God's love or a humanly cultivated sympathy. Yet despite all the positive modeling, doubt comes creeping in. *Uncle Tom's Cabin* does not dwell on natural depravity or predestination, but much of Stowe's rhetoric and imagination is steeped in what James Baldwin called the "theological terror" of Calvinism.[66] Stowe remains intensely attuned to hypocrisy, backsliding, presumption, self-love, and unregenerate hearts, while her conflation of personal and national salvation is indebted to Puritan notions of the self.[67] Evil is real in Stowe's world. Chattel bondage is its most powerful manifestation. And as Hawthorne knows, neither confident science nor liberal Christianity say quite enough about sin, for abiding iniquity is a damaging fact to anyone predicting that a Christian enlightenment precipitates heaven on earth. In 1852, Stowe and many others had not grasped the full stubbornness of slavery. There seemed no reason why all Americans could not see to it that they felt right. Perfectionist hopes largely remain in the fore of *Uncle Tom's Cabin*, and the Hawthornian doubter can blithely be answered, *A better world is just over this hill; come walk with me and see.* This is the tautology of the jeremiad. Present sins, religious and political, become signs of future grace. In this manner, Stowe represses the *no* if only for one novel.

Desperately holding to the promise of a providential nation, *Uncle Tom's Cabin* ultimately offers a sophisticated theory of sympathy that Stowe sets over and against the dangers of interest and passion. Stowe,

65 Smith, *Theory of Moral Sentiments*, 11.
66 Baldwin, "Everybody's Protest Novel," 18.
67 Bercovitch, *The Puritan Origins of the American Self.*

however, struggles to reconcile the influences of her father's Calvinism and her sister's mental philosophy, generally privileging the latter's faith in the sentimental power of right teaching. Of course, Stowe's sentimentality has significant limitations. For all the talk of sympathy, of feeling the feelings of others, Stowe's characterizations of African Americans can be extremely insensitive. Martin Delany named this failing in 1853 when, frustrated with moral suasion in general and sentimentality in particular, he took aim at the heart of *Uncle Tom's Cabin*, "[Stowe] *knows nothing about us* . . . neither does any other white person" (a complaint also voiced by Romney Leigh in Elizabeth Barrett Browning's *Aurora Leigh* [1856]).[68] *Uncle Tom's Cabin* is also vulnerable to other political complaints. Stowe lacks the egalitarian breadth of more *ultra* antebellum figures, for her racialist abolitionism, domesticated feminism, and bourgeois critique of capitalism all fall short of radical positions she might have advocated. Stowe's specific views on gender and race probably do not offer modern progressives a model for social reform. What remains provocative is Stowe's belief that intersubjective emotions might best govern the world.

Which returns us to a pair of related difficulties that *Uncle Tom's Cabin* touches upon but does not finally resolve. The first is the epistemological problem of differentiating sympathy and passion. A modern reader can share Stowe's conviction that chattel bondage is wrong. Yet Stowe remains susceptible to the charge she brings against Dinah; for howsoever cogently Stowe presents her sentimental design, it rests in the end on

---

68 M. Delany to F. Douglass, *Frederick Douglass's Paper*, March 23, 1853, reprinted in *Martin R. Delany: A Documentary Reader*, ed. Robert S. Levine (Chapel Hill: University of North Carolina Press, 2003), 224. In the May 6 edition of *Frederick Douglass's Paper*, Delany softened his comment: "They knew nothing, comparatively, about us" (*Martin R. Delany: A Documentary Reader*, 232). Stowe would later respond to Delany's critique in the conclusion to *Dred*, "We shall never have all the materials for absolute truth on [slavery], till we take into account, with our own views and reasoning, . . . the feelings and reasoning of the slave" (556). For the relationship of Delany and Stowe, see Robert S. Levine, *Martin Delany, Frederick Douglass, and the Politics of Representative Identity* (Chapel Hill: The University of North Carolina Press, 1997), 143. In *Aurora Leigh*, Romney charges:

> "None of all these things,
> Can women understand. You generalize
> Oh, nothing! – not even grief! . . .
> . . . You gather up
> A few such cases, and, when strong, sometimes
> Will write of factories and of slaves, as if
> Your father were a negro, and your son
> A spinner in the mills. All's yours and you, –
> All, coloured with your blood, or otherwise
> Just nothing to you.

self-evident truths that Stowe asserts but does not argue. Stowe strongly feels and therefore knows that slavery is wrong. Leading the reader to the same conclusion is her ambitious goal – a goal that met with little success below the Mason–Dixon line, where the affective intensity of female abolitionists was figured by Poe, Dew, Holmes, Calhoun, and others as passion, not sympathy.

The second problem of *Uncle Tom's Cabin* turns on the question of agency. If everyone possesses moral sentiment, a main premise of Stowe's system, how does one account for abiding iniquity, for the *no* that *Uncle Tom's Cabin* represses even as the novel's polarized reception made the failure of sympathy more palpable? In addition to the transformative miracles wrought on an incredible number of readers, Stowe's novel failed in equal magnitude to convert many hearts, a fact that seems predictable today but surprised and discouraged Stowe.[69] *Uncle Tom's Cabin* estranged the South as sympathy led to antagonism, while stage productions of the novel slipped into partisan violence.[70] Stowe does excuse the physical resistance of George Harris and Phineas Fletcher, and she even celebrates violent retribution when young George Shelby knocks down Legree. But if Abraham Lincoln did indeed call Stowe the little woman who made a great war, *Uncle Tom's Cabin* ultimately supports intersectional right feeling, not strength of arms. After *Uncle Tom's Cabin*, Stowe lamented, "the moral sense becomes more and more blunted" by slavery, a fear also shared by Lydia Maria Child, Harriet Jacobs, and Ralph Waldo Emerson.[71] The thesis, however, of Stowe's first novel is that sympathy is stronger than bondage, that in theory nothing on earth can stop correct affections.

Here Stowe reaches the limitations of a philosophical system that will come to face the darker predictions of a less alleviated Puritanism. Liberal Calvinists like Lyman Beecher may speak the language of sentimentality, and theologians like Park can name the change a matter of ministerial style. There remain, however, gaps between an eighteenth-century philosophy intent upon benevolent laws common to Man and a religion that, for all its declension, still instructs a chosen people how to live among

---

69 Gossett, *Uncle Tom's Cabin and American Culture*, 306.
70 Lott, *Love and Theft*, 211–26.
71 Stowe, *A Key to Uncle Tom's Cabin* (Salem: Ayer, 1987), 255. Lydia Maria Child, "The Iron Shroud," in *A Lydia Maria Child Reader*, ed. Carolyn Karcher (Durham: Duke University Press, 1997), 216; Harriet Jacobs, *Incidents in the Life of a Slave Girl*, ed. Jean Fagan Yellin (Cambridge: Harvard University Press), 56; Ralph Waldo Emerson, "Address to the Citizens of Concord on the Fugitive Slave Law, May 3, 1851," in *Emerson's Antislavery Writings*, ed. Len Gougeon and Joel Myerson (New Haven: Yale University Press, 1995), 55.

differently predestined men. Maybe all humans are not created equal. Maybe some of them go to hell. But before they do, they sin on earth without compunction or even choice, and whom (or Whom) do we blame for that? *Uncle Tom's Cabin* does not directly address this crisis of theodicy. In 1852, the triumph of sympathy seemed entirely possible to Stowe – despite the dangers of self-interest and passion, despite even a moment with Legree in which Stowe concedes that some damned people can never be taught to feel right. That *Uncle Tom's Cabin* did not peacefully resolve the American slavery crisis does not discount the fact that Stowe's first novel was an important step toward emancipation. No one in antebellum America found a bloodless path to abolition, and no one solved the philosophical problem of establishing moral consensus. But if Stowe's sentimental system proved flawed, she had some time to redeem it, even if her efforts lead into deeper struggles.

FIXING UNCLE TOM'S CABIN

Uncle Tom's Cabin may rightfully dominate discussions of Stowe's work. The novel was a major event in nineteenth-century American literature and culture, and it continues to speak to scholarly interests across a range of fields. The problem is that *Uncle Tom's Cabin* tends to occlude Stowe's subsequent writings, so much so that her sentimentality becomes too monolithic, too static. In ambitious theory, Stowe aspires to be guided by unchanging laws; but over the course of the slavery conflict, she came to adjust her system of reform, especially as the tide of battle appeared to favor her pro-slavery foes. After the stunning but painfully incomplete success of *Uncle Tom's Cabin*, Stowe increasingly questioned in Calvinist terms the coherence of her sentimentality. Gregg Camfield has argued that Stowe comes to deploy secular philosophy against Calvinist doctrine, that she lifts the moral authority of affect over that of systematic theology.[72] The obverse, however, may also be true. Namely, that Stowe's antebellum writings after *Uncle Tom's Cabin* come to focus so intently on Calvinism precisely because Calvinism recognizes too well the flaws of her sentimentality.

The furor raised by *Uncle Tom's Cabin* immediately put Stowe on the defensive, forcing her to justify her entrance into politics and to consider the limits of sympathy. Among the slavery documents and interspersed commentary that make up *A Key to Uncle Tom's Cabin* (1853), Stowe

---

72 Camfield, *Sentimental Twain*, 52–58.

invokes Nathaniel Taylor to mitigate original sin, while also promoting her sentimentality in a familiar affective idiom. Stowe does not explicitly discuss the challenge of Calvinist determinism, but when she decries the "awful paralysis of the moral sense," she takes a tone of desperation that surpasses anything in *Uncle Tom's Cabin*. Stowe says of her country in *A Key*, "We *are* wrecking the ship – we *are* losing the battle. There is no mistake about it." She writes of slavery, "So, Church of Christ, burns that awful fire! Evermore burning, burning, burning, over church and altar; burning over senate-house and forum; burning up liberty, burning up religion!" Such evangelical imagery and cadence show Stowe to be her father's daughter; and Stowe's increasing exposure to abolitionist litera- ture takes further rhetorical effect, not only in her militancy and sarcasm, but also in her jeremiad pleas that ring louder than in *Uncle Tom's Cabin*. The final chapter of *A Key* dwells on the looming fear that America will not, and perhaps even cannot, attend to its salvation. As in her first novel, Stowe asks the Pauline question, "What is to be Done?" But after the expected praise of Christian "Pureness" and cultivated "Knowledge," she writes, "If we trust to our own reasonings, our own reform of abuses, we shall utterly fail. There is a power, silent, convincing, irresistible, which moves over the dark and troubled heart of man." *Too true, too true,* Hawthorne might reply to *A Key to Uncle Tom's Cabin* as a sterner sense of sin and fatalism begins to come over Stowe.[73]

As its title suggests, *Sunny Memories of Foreign Lands* (1854) mainly stands clear of discouraging shadows. Describing Stowe's tour of Britain and the Continent, the book has the itinerant structure typical of travel narratives. Nonetheless, into its curious mix of political agitation, aes- thetic speculation, and sightseeing pleasure, Stowe – like the minister Benjamin Babcock of Henry James's *The American* (1877) – discovers her Old World sojourn returning her to a Puritan state of mind. She recalls the journals of Jonathan Winthrop and praises Hawthorne's "gloomy power." She complains about her Calvinist upbringing on "the very battle field of controversial theology" in which "every religious idea [was] guarded by definitions, and thoroughly hammered on a logical anvil." Here Stowe begins a critique of Calvinism that she later pursues at length, yet the disturbingly attractive Catholicism of the Continent evokes from her a Puritan reaction. Stowe proclaims with sectarian and sectional pride, "[W]herever John Calvin's system of theology has gone, civil liberty has gone with it." She writes that "Calvinism in its essential features, never will cease from the earth, because the great fundamental facts of nature are Calvinistic." The phrase "essential features" allows Stowe to claim a measure of doctrinal latitude, to use Calvinism in a sense broad enough to include her liberal views. *Sunny Memories of Foreign Lands* does not stake out a specific Calvinist position. What matters is that Stowe's thoughts are turning more and more to her Puritan legacy as she attempts to reconcile her religious heritage and her sentimentality.[74]

Dred, Stowe's highly anticipated second novel published in 1856, more explicitly engages the fundamental facts of a fallen Calvinist world. After the controversy over *Uncle Tom's Cabin*, after civil warfare in Kansas, after the fugitive Anthony Burns was returned into bondage by federal troops, after the antislavery statesmen Charles Sumner was assaulted on the floor of the Senate, Stowe increasingly comes to doubt the peaceable triumph of sympathy. *Dred* presents a fairly traditional sentimental narrative as the white southerner Nina Gordon comes to love the antislavery southerner Edward Clayton, despite their temperamental differences and obstacles raised by the forces of slavery. In some ways, *Dred* follows the lead begun in *Uncle Tom's Cabin*. The book offers Anne Clayton's school for black children as a model of sentimental pedagogy, and Stowe recalls Catharine's philosophy when she describes the "sentiment of justice" as a "part of the moral constitution, which exists in some degree in us all."[75] "[M]oral sense" (43), "cultivation of [the] mind" (170), the "development of [a] child's mind" (273), the "development of Nina's moral nature" (423), the redemptive power of "educational association" (643) – all suggest Stowe's continuing commitment to a psychological form of sentimentality.

For all its continuities, however – and as Robert Levine has argued – *Dred* comes to curtail the relative optimism available in *Uncle Tom's Cabin*, presenting instead a more fatalistic, more polemic vision of the slavery conflict.[76] A pro-slavery mob torches Anne Clayton's school, indicating that Catharine's sentimental pedagogy is not in itself a sufficient solution. The partisan violence that erupts in the novel suggests that Edward Clayton is wrong to believe that "all that was necessary [to end slavery] was the enlightening of the public mind" (493). Unlike Stowe's first novel, abolitionist characters must finally flee the South in *Dred*, implying that only Northern intervention can redeem the slaveholding

---

74 Stowe, *Sunny Memories*, Vol. I: 93, 315; and Vol. II: 409, 277.
75 Harriet Beecher Stowe, *Dred: A Tale of the Great Dismal Swamp*, ed. Judie Newman (1856; Exeter: Edinburgh University Press, 1999), 617.
76 Robert Levine, introduction to *Dred: A Tale of the Great Dismal Swamp* (New York: Penguin, 2000), ix–xxxv.

states. Though *Uncle Tom's Cabin* includes physical resistance, slave revolt haunts *Dred*, suggesting that violence and not moral suasion might end the slavery crisis. It is true that Tom Gordon, the principal villain, retains a "sufficient perception of right" (71). But Stowe denies the faculty of moral sentiment to the pro-slavery lawyer Jekyl, who is "wholly inaccessible to any emotion of particular humanity" (227). Nina's "instinct" immediately recognizes Jekyl as a figure of unmitigated evil: "I never saw him before. But I hate him! He is a bad man! I'd as soon have a serpent come near me! . . . [T]his man don't even know what good is!" (209–10). Here Stowe returns with sustained attention to an unresolved problem of *Uncle Tom's Cabin*, for Jekyl comes to represent the conundrum of theodicy. How can an irredeemable sinner crawl on God's green earth? Or more specific to the project of sentimental reform: What can a sympathetic abolitionist do with those who cannot even recognize good?

In *Dred*, Stowe offers two responses to Jekyl's lack of moral sentiment, both of which restrict the purview of sentimental reform. Unlike Uncle Tom, the pious slave Tiff addresses the mystery of iniquity. He muses allegorically, "Bress if I know what de Lord want of so many weeds. 'Pears like dey comes just to plague us; but, den, we doesn't know. May be dere's some good in 'em. We doesn't know but a leetle" (424). Tiff knows enough to stop and say that the Lord can work in mysterious ways, but the very suggestion of necessary evil is antithetical to perfectionist theories of reform, suggesting a more Puritan, more deterministic world in which some people will never feel right. For his part, Clayton has an answer to evil. Referring to those who, unlike Jekyl, actually possess "moral sentiment," Clayton pronounces with abolitionist fire, "They *must* get the balance of power in the country" (581). This is sentimentality with a political strategy. Transform those who have moral sentiment and outvote the irredeemable remainder, a potential synthesis of sympathy and interest that indulges, for Stowe, a polemic spirit that reflects what Gregg Crane calls Stowe's "faltering confidence in consensual models of legal order."[77] As Stowe becomes more committed to partisan activism, both as an abolitionist and (later) as a suffragist, *Dred* shows a growing resignation to the limits of right feeling. In the uncertain world of *Dred*, Stowe concedes that sin may not be entirely susceptible to moral suasion, even as she indicates through Clayton's failed efforts that political solutions are also untenable.

---

77 Crane, *Race, Citizenship, and Law*, 76.

Facing up to another unresolved philosophical problem of *Uncle Tom's Cabin*, *Dred* discusses the difficulty of knowing moral authority. Stowe worries, "One might almost imagine that there were no such thing as absolute truth," admitting, "We all console ourselves too easily for the sorrows of others" (555–56). This represents a significant attempt to address the antinomianism of *Uncle Tom's Cabin*, particularly a possibility suggested by the worldly Frank Russell, namely that "moral sentiment, as you call it, is a humbug!" (581). Importantly, Russell is not the only rationalist in the novel. When Nina intuitively recoils from Jekyl, Clayton equivocates, "Instinct may be a greater matter than we think; yet it isn't infallible, any more than our sense. We try the testimony even of our eyesight by reason. It will deceive us, if we don't" (210). As a kind of impartial spectator, Clayton repeatedly voices the warning that Dinah only implies: Affective intensity needs objective restraint, a point also suggested by the slave-rebel Dred, whose "religious enthusiasm" and "absolute certainty" are inspired but not entirely trustworthy (616). Predictably, and like *Uncle Tom's Cabin*, *Dred* sides with emotion over logic. The difference is that *Dred* gives more credence to Clayton's rational caveats, for not only is Clayton more persuasive (and dashing) than Senator Bird, the slippery distinction between passion and sympathy is integral to *Dred's* plot.

Sentimental novels often trace a young woman's struggle to master her heart; and such is the case with the fiery Nina who, with some logical guidance from Clayton, grows beyond self-interested passion while coming to do God's work. Nina begins the novel as a self-absorbed young woman, but by the end of the book she can report, "Jesus is so good that he [made] me feel right" (441) – a victory predicating her beautiful martyrdom working with the sick (black and white), and one marked by her crucially selfless declaration, "I lost all thought of myself" (442). Nina finally achieves the selfless subjectivity naturally enjoyed by Eva and Tom, but in *Dred* Stowe lingers with dramatic, heuristic, and psychological attention over her heroine's vexing journey from self-interested passion to sympathy. Stowe describes in loving detail this struggle to feel right and in doing so broaches a Calvinist worry that *Uncle Tom's Cabin* largely neglects.

In *Dred*, the danger of self-interest returns in a particularly tenacious form, for the threat is not only manifest in liberal and *laissez faire* social structures, but also in the individual subject and the state of the soul itself. Whereas Adam Smith and Catharine Beecher saw pleasure as an acceptable motive force, *Dred* takes to heart the Calvinist fear that feeling right is not really feeling right if one feels for one's own benefit. This is the failure of Nina's self-centered Aunt Nesbit, who voices pious lines but hypocritically thinks too much on profiting her soul. Like William James's investigation of Calvinist conversion narratives, Stowe explores "the crisis of self-surrender" as both a religious and psychological topic.[78] Right feeling must lose all thought of the self – a dilemma at the core of the Puritan mind, and a challenge to sentimental abolitionism that *Dred* begins to confront when Nina worries with Topsy-like despair, "I know I am not good as I ought to be,! . . . but I don't know how to be any better" (336).

Modern scholars are hardly alone in doubting the efficacy of sentimentalism, nor are they the first to suspect self-interest lurking in sympathy. When attacking the supposedly disinterested philosophy of the Hutcheson school, Kant charged, "[W]e everywhere come upon the dear self, which is always turning up." In *The Blithedale Romance* (1852), Zenobia worries that reform is "nothing but self, self, self," while Melville suggests throughout his short fiction that charity is always self-aggrandizing. Dickinson further shares the concern that the "Fortress" of the "Heart" cannot be entered "Except by subjugating / Consciousness" and banishing "Me from Myself."[79] Antebellum reviews of *Uncle Tom's Cabin* also note the egoist potential of sympathy, accusing Stowe of profit motive, self-righteousness, and a lack of charity. *Dred* responds to these attacks with the selfless example of Nina, whose maturation from passion to sympathy endures a series of setbacks and victories that both follows the model of conversion experiences and preempts potential detractors. More than *Uncle Tom's Cabin*, *Dred* critically traces the uneven path toward correct affection. It dwells on the fear that achieving true sympathy is never a settled thing, for self-interest has a way of hiding behind seemingly benevolent motives. For many readers, Stowe's second novel is not as compelling as *Uncle Tom's Cabin*, in part because of structural flaws and the unrealized depiction of Dred. The novel also lacks some of the conviction that makes *Uncle Tom's Cabin* so powerful; for even as Stowe remains convinced that slavery is wrong, she examines more closely the problem of evil and the pitfalls of self-interest. Such

78 James, *Varieties of Religious Experience*, 196.
79 Immanuel Kant, *Groundwork of the Metaphysics of Morals*, trans. Mary Gregor (1785; New York: Cambridge University Press, 1997), 20. Nathaniel Hawthorne, *The Blithedale Romance* (New York: Norton, 1978), 201. Dickinson, "Me from Myself – to banish –" (1863), *The Poems of Emily Dickinson: Reading Edition*, ed. R. W. Franklin (Cambridge: Belknap Press of Harvard University Press, 1999), 317 (poem no.709).

equivocation may bring to *Dred* a measure of dramatic unevenness, though it can also make the novel more nuanced as a philosophical and political statement that identifies many of the difficulties that Stowe pursues in her third novel.

Published in 1859, *The Minister's Wooing* is often seen to begin a new episode in Stowe's career. Stowe turns from antislavery novels set mainly in the antebellum South to a historical romance focused on life and theology in eighteenth-century New England. Stowe continued to explore this subject in *The Pearl of Orr's Island* (1862), *Oldtown Folks,* and *Poganuc People* (1878). Yet as much as *The Minister's Wooing* looks forward to later developments in Stowe, it also culminates her first two novels as an attempt to formulate a system of reform by measuring the increasingly incompatible claims of sentimentality and Calvinism. In *The Minister's Wooing,* the heroine Mary Scudder must choose between her true love James Marvyn and her avuncular minister Samuel Hopkins to whom she is engaged. That is, she must choose between her heart and the rational dictates of covenant law. Mary aspires to make her decision with "disinterested benevolence," a term that Stowe might have associated with the sentimentality of Hutcheson, who set "disinterested benevolence" against the self-centered theories of Hobbes and Bernard Mandeville. Instead, *The Minister's Wooing* features a fictionalized version of Hopkins, the disciple of Edwards who put "disinterested benevolence" at the center of his Calvinist system. In *The Minister's Wooing,* Stowe's religious propensities exceed her interest in secular philosophy, in part because the Puritans have pride of place in her account of American history, but also because they offer a challenging way to think about affect and agency.

Stowe's novel is intensely concerned with "Views of Divine Government," exploring such abiding Calvinist puzzles as freedom of the will, evidence of salvation, and the willingness to be damned for the glory of God.[80] Though *The Minister's Wooing* repeatedly critiques the logical rigor of Calvinism, Stowe discusses the challenge of right feeling in rigorous Calvinist terms. Continuities do exist between *The Minister's Wooing* and Stowe's slavery novels. The self-interested slave-trader Simeon Brown plays a familiar – if surprisingly minor – role, as does the African-American Candace, who possesses a wealth of sympathy and, like Uncle Tom and Tiff, exemplifies a primitive Christianity. The

---

80 Harriet Beecher Stowe, *The Minister's Wooing* (Hartford: The Stowe-Day Foundation, 1978), 332. Hereafter cited in the text. The best account of New England theology in *The Minister's Wooing* remains Buell's "Calvinism Romanticized."

fictionalized figure of Aaron Burr links the danger of passion with that of secession, though his disruptive presence remains itinerant and something of a side plot. Slavery is one of many concerns in *The Minister's Wooing,* but while Stowe's previous novels are impossible to imagine without the slavery crisis, here the primary conflict of the book occurs, not between ideological positions, but within a single soul.

The soul in question is Mary, who falls in love with James just before he reportedly dies at sea. The crisis comes when she agrees to marry Hopkins only to discover (surprise!) that James is not actually dead. In the moral deliberations that follow, Stowe discusses with a Puritan dogged-ness the epistemology and agency of right feeling as Mary attempts to find and follow the path of disinterested benevolence, variously figured as "unselfishness" (12), "*self*-renunciation" (25), "self-oblivion" (25), "abso-lute self-abnegation" (88), and "perfect unconsciousness of self" (184). The committed Calvinists of *The Minister's Wooing* recognize how hard it is to achieve "that celestial grade where the soul knows self no more" (88). One character worries, "I'm 'fraid it's all selfish" (48); and even the well-intentioned Mary fears, "I am selfish, after all!" (80). Such inescapable selfhood can be seen as a basic feature of Cartesian metaphysics, liberal individualism, or romantic egoism, but Stowe examines the stubbornness of the self from a decidedly Calvinist perspective. Because selflessness is a cause (or at least a sign) of salvation and thus serves to profit (or at least ease) the soul, any self-consciousness of one's ostensible selflessness opens the door to self-interest. The mission is to be unselfconsciously selfless, an extremely vexing task for Puritans who believed in humankind's fallen nature and thus trained themselves in what Stowe calls "constant, unsleeping self-vigilance" (552). Small wonder that a divine from *The Minister's Wooing* believes in "no such thing as disinterested benevolence," though the character Hopkins, like his historical source, holds that selflessness can be reached when the self is lost unto God (277).

Stowe shows the hardships of this process through the travails of Mary. Before her crisis, Mary generalizes, "How very difficult it must be to know one's self perfectly!" (291). Later, she learns this truth first hand when she wonders if her preference for James is motivated by her selfish desire or by a selfless duty to Hopkins, who might or might not want to marry a woman who might or might not be able to abjure her love for another man. The simple solution would be to ask Hopkins, but the problem is that Hopkins himself is dedicated to disinterested benevolence. Thus Mary knows that if Hopkins knows that she is in love with James, Hopkins will probably release her from her promise, an acceptable and even joyous outcome as long as Mary herself is sufficiently disinterested and does not tell Hopkins of her true feelings in order to gratify her selfish desires. As if to test the limitations of her sentimental system, Stowe imagines a tangled case in which disinterested benevolence is so difficult to determine that it paralyzes agency. The irony in *The Minister's Wooing* is that everyone wants to do the selfless thing, a theoretical quandary that Calhoun predicted in his *Disquisition on Government*, "[I]f [everyone's] feelings and affections were stronger for others than for themselves . . . the necessary result would seem to be, that all individuality would be lost; and boundless and remediless disorder and confusion would ensue."[81] This is what happens at the start of Hawthorne's tale, "Roger Malvin's Burial" (1832), until self-interest comes to settle the paralysis of disinterested benevolence. This is also why it can take so long at a conference to decide where to go to dinner: Because people are concerned about the feelings of others, and because no one wants to be selfish, everyone ends up standing in the lobby saying, *Oh, I don't care, where do you want to go?*

The Minister's Wooing enacts such confusion in its dramatic and philosophical impasse, for Mary's generous share of sympathy provides her no moral or practical direction. In fact, her capacity for emotion literally incapacitates her when she claims at the climax of her uncertainty the irreducible ontology of affect, "My feelings . . . are feelings over which I have no more control than over my existence" (534). In the context of a courtship plot, such words reveal true love. In the Puritan mind, they demonstrate an Edwardean reliance on God. From a sentimental point of view, they establish the truth-claims of emotion. But if applied to social reform, if put in the mouth of a rake like Burr or a slave-trader like Brown, they become a justification for evil and can lead to a kind of quietism, for they admit no mechanism with which to alter the heart.

Here, then, is the paradox of *The Minister's Wooing*. Despite its resistance to Edwardean Calvinism figured by the too rational, too theoretical Hopkins, and despite its preference for a sentimental Christianity represented by Mary and Candace, the novel suggests that we cannot change our feelings when the epistemological authority of affect relies on the loss of human agency. That is, we can *see* – we can recognize – right feelings only when we cannot *see to* them, a logic suggesting that the emotions

81 Calhoun, *A Disquisition on Government*, 32.

and, hence, the nation cannot be guided (and a problem of the disjunction of the will and the perceptions that Dickinson alludes to in "I heard a Fly buzz" [c. 1863] when the speaker "could not see to see"). This formulation, anathema to Catharine Beecher's thinking and the program of *Uncle Tom's Cabin*, is in many ways borne out over the course of *The Minister's Wooing*. Simeon Brown never learns to feel right about slavery. Chattel bondage in the South is not directly addressed. And though Burr does have a perfunctory conversion, one lingering lesson of *The Minister's Wooing* is one also taught by that quasi-Puritan, occasional-sentimentalist Hawthorne: The human heart is hard to change, and the most demanding trial of life is learning to live with the feelings one has. The limitations of sentimental reform that remain recessive in *Uncle Tom's Cabin* become main features in the theory of affect expounded in *The Minister's Wooing*. Mary struggles mightily to distinguish self-interested passion from sympathy. Stowe wonders at length if people possess the power to better their hearts. Both Edwardean Calvinism and sentimental philosophy speak to the need for affective correctness, and the Puritans certainly had a streak of utopian optimism. But Calvinism, so distrustful of selfish delusions and human usurpations of God, explains the immutability of feeling better than eighteenth-century moral philosophy, which tends to elide such embarrassments as epistemological uncertainty and dependence on God. This is not to say that *The Minister's Wooing* advocates or even excuses what Stowe shows to be the overly-rational and demoralizing excesses of Calvinism. Rather, the novel cannot help but recognize the power of certain Puritan claims, even if that recognition takes the form of objection.

The Minister's Wooing does manage to find a kind of happy ending when the seamstress Miss Prissy intervenes to tell Hopkins the truth about Mary. As expected, Hopkins benevolently and disinterestedly releases Mary from her pledge, though not before assuring himself of Mary's own disinterested benevolence. This takes place in a closed-door meeting that can model a kind of sentimental politics in which well-intentioned parties convene to compare their intersubjective feelings. With Candace providing religious succor and Miss Prissy rendering practical service, the outcome is positive because the parties involved are good-souled, old town folk. Their world is eighteenth-century Newport, not antebellum America where disinterested discourse between differing parties was in short supply, and where neither side of the slavery debate was willing to release the other side from competing versions of a national contract that each side felt was right. Changing such sentiments looked highly unlikely in 1859, and so the lessons of *The Minister's Wooing* are difficult to apply to the slavery crisis, so much so that they seem less like instruction and more like wishful thinking. There were few meetings of the minds or hearts between antagonists before the Civil War. Estranged Americans could only look at their ideological others and say, *I can't, for the life of me, understand how you can feel that way.*

The trajectory of Stowe's antebellum novels can thus look something like this. *Uncle Tom's Cabin* advocates right feeling without directly confronting two troubling questions – What if some people lack the faculty to know correct affections? And what if the subject cannot come to right feeling even when she knows what it is? *Dred* addresses these issues more explicitly as Stowe faces up to political facts that defy her sentimentality. *Dred* handles with no little complexity irredeemable evil and inveterate selfishness, and *The Minister's Wooing* traces these topics into the labyrinth of Calvinist theology. Stowe does not renounce her sentimentality; rather the power of sympathy becomes increasingly qualified in her work as Calvinism exposes the theoretical flaws behind the practical failings of sentimental reform. Throughout *Uncle Tom's Cabin* and *Dred*, the path of righteousness is clearly lighted. For Stowe, sympathetic abolitionism is right, and self-interested slavery is wrong. However, in *The Minister's Wooing* matters are not so certain; for while the reader probably feels that Mary should wed the heroic James, there remains real poignancy in her cry, "I wish somebody would tell me exactly what is right!" (528). The epistemological limits of affect thus occupy *The Minister's Wooing*, even as the politically interested reader notes a debilitating irony. Stowe's third novel is hardly innocent of the slavery crisis, and Stowe herself was engaging more aggressively in organized reform. Yet the most necessary contexts for the book come from Perry Miller, not John Hope Franklin. Which might lead one to wonder how an abolitionist champion could write such a novel in 1859.

As the threat of civil war loomed and history seemed to catch up with America, Stowe turned her talents to historical romance, de-emphasizing in setting and theme the topic of chattel bondage. Perhaps Stowe's fictional imagination lost, or lost interest in, the battle over slavery. Perhaps *Dred's* flaws are signs of defeat, and *The Minister's Wooing* is a faint-hearted retreat from a fight that Stowe could not win. More pejoratively, despite her efforts in the abolitionist cause, perhaps Stowe the artist did not care enough to know people like Delany, a failing suggested by her callous interaction with Harriet Jacobs in 1857 and her racially over-determined portrait of Sojourner Truth in 1863.[82] Given such lack of sympathy for African-American subjectivity, *Uncle Tom's Cabin* in the final tally may be most about the souls of white folk and Stowe's most compelling interest in *Dred* can be indicated by the fact that the eponymous slave does not appear until the middle of the novel, which Stowe later and more appropriately titled *Nina Gordon*. *The Minister's Wooing* stubbornly dwells on the problem of right feeling, and problems of gender and marriage in the novel are not unrelated to the problem of chattel bondage. But does the story of Mary Scudder belong to the literature of slavery? If so, what about *Agnes of Sorrento* (1862) and *The Pearl of Orr's Island* – serialized novels that appear between Harper's Ferry and the Emancipation Proclamation, but both of which have little to say about America's national sin?

The obvious point is that the slavery crisis does not delimit Stowe's antebellum writings or her interests in sentimentality. The implication, however, is that slavery became an increasingly difficult topic as the country reached a terrible stasis in which no one knew what to say. As early as 1830, Garrison worried about the course of the slavery debate, "It is morally impossible, I am convinced, for a slaveholder to reason correctly on the subject of slavery." Conversely, Holmes warned abolitionists that the "fanatic may mistake for the laws of nature the suggestions of his own blind passions, and may assume as the immutable canons of right and wrong the hallucinations of his own diseased mind." Stowe herself was open to the charge of what Holmes called "reasoning *a priori*," and she witnessed a failure of logical argument in 1834 when she listened to a pro-slavery man "whose mode of reasoning consist[ed] in repeating the same sentence at regular intervals." Stowe is condescending here; *she* knows how to run a question to its root. But in 1851, after the passage of the Fugitive Slave Law, Stowe herself took part in a slavery argument "which consist[ed] in both sides saying over and over just what they said before."[83] Five years later, the beating of Sumner turned *Dred* toward a partisan conclusion in which both literal and prophesized violence

---

82 Jean Fagan Yellin, "Introduction" to *Incidents in the Life of a Slave Girl*, xix; Nell Irvin Painter, *Sojourner Truth: A Life, A Symbol* (New York: Norton, 1996), 154. Note, however, that Stowe's relationship with the black author Frank Webb seems to be more supportive (Eric Gardner, "'A Gentleman of Superior Cultivation and Refinement': Recovering the Biography of Frank J. Webb," *African American Review* 35: 2 [summer 2001]: 300).

83 Garrison quoted in *Against Slavery: An Abolitionist Reader*, ed. Mason Lowance (New York: Penguin, 2000), 109. George Frederick Holmes, "Observations on a Passage in the Politics of Aristotle Relative to Slavery," *Southern Literary Messenger* 16: 4 (April 1850): 196; Stowe quoted in Hedrick, *Harriet Beecher Stowe*, 93, 205.

overshadow moral suasion. The Sumner beating exemplifies one end of the slavery debate. Blows superseded words in the Senate, not only because Preston Brooks found best expression with a gutta-percha cane, but also because he retaliated for a speech in which even the intellectual Sumner abandoned deliberation for *ad hominem* attack. The Civil War was not simply caused by an inadequacy of language; deep-seated differences between the sections made rational mediation extremely unlikely. Still, Stowe's retreat from the literature of slavery just before the War reflects a larger cultural frustration with peaceful debate in the public sphere.

This frustration continued during the War. Scholars are reclaiming a body of literature written between Fort Sumter and Appomattox, but historical exigencies took a toll on the literary production of Stowe, who wrote in 1862, "The agitations and mental excitements of the war have in the case of the writer . . . used up the time and strength that would have been devoted to authorship."[84] As Louis Masur has demonstrated, this was a common complaint, yet it was not entirely accurate in the case of Stowe.[85] Stowe wrote two novels during the War, both of which avoided the topic; and even after Appomattox she wrote little on the conflict that she helped to start (a criticism that John De Forest leveled in 1868).[86] Instead, Stowe turned to sanguine fiction in her "House and Home Papers" (1864), which she called "gay, sprightly, [and] wholly domestic" prose that met her "need to write in these days, to keep one from thinking of things that make me dizzy and blind, and fill my eyes with tears."[87]

As much as the victory of the North confirmed the cosmology of many abolitionists, the bloodshed of war painfully demonstrated the limits of sentimental reform. Though (as Garrison worried) *Uncle Tom's Cabin* was not a pacifist novel, it hoped to persuade the South of slavery's evil by eschewing the violent, partisan rhetoric that marred the national debate. Stowe, however, remained a staunch abolitionist with her own incendiary agenda. No amount of literary care, no amount of sympathy for the ideological other, could make her message of intended good will palatable to slavery defenders. It is vexing to argue with an author of fiction who knows it is she, and not you, who feels right. It is hard to refute the moral

84 Charles Edward Stowe and Lyman Beecher Stowe, *Harriet Beecher Stowe*, 204.
85 Louis Masur, introduction to *The Real War Will Never Get in the Books: Selections from Writers During the Civil War*, ed. Louis P. Masur (New York: Oxford University Press, 1993), vii–x.
86 De Forest wrote of the post-*Dred* Stowe, "[S]tricken with timidity, the author shrank into her native shell of New England" ("The Great American Novel," *The Nation* [9 January 1868], 28).
87 Harriet Beecher Stowe, *Household Papers and Stories*, *The Writings of Harriet Beecher Stowe*, 16 vols. (New York: AMS Press, 1967), 8: ix.

authority of supposedly self-evident emotions whose tautological truth-claims, so problematic when trying to distinguish passion from sympathy, become in heated political forums formidable rhetorical strengths. Then as now, moral clarity based on gut feeling can be all too effective in democratic "debate."

No wonder that Stowe's sentimentality angered so many readers, some of whom accused *Uncle Tom's Cabin* of preempting meaningful discussion. William Gilmore Simms, on the verge of writing a novelistic refutation of Stowe, complained to fellow Southerner John Pendleton Kennedy in 1851 that abolitionist writers "have utterly subverted the only bond (that of sympathy) by which the people of our separate sections were ever truly held together." For his part, Kennedy also abhorred the "mawkish sentimentality which has been so busy of late in inventing sympathy for the pretended oppression of negroes"; and in 1851 he re-issued *Swallow Barn* (1832), a prototype of plantation fiction that painted slavery in pleasant domestic terms. Yet for all these words, no one seemed to be changing anyone's opinion, as an 1860 article in *The Southern Literary Messenger* suggests. Titled "The Difference of Race between the Northern and Southern People," the piece attributed sectional strife to "*ethnological* differences": "The Northern mind and character differ widely from the Southern mind and character" – sentiments echoed by Moncure Conway, who complained that slavery created a "gulf that yawned between the Northern and the Southern mind."[88]

As a writer committed to awakening intersubjective and intersectional mental faculties, Stowe proved unable to bridge the gulf and continued to wonder why. Struggling with the philosophical tensions of what Martha Nussbaum calls "Rational Emotions," Stowe resisted the systematizing of affection while still rationally, vigorously and, in many ways, systematically arguing her sentimental case to a point where perfectionist theories of sympathy became a quarrel with Calvinism.[89] Other factors no doubt influence the shape of Stowe's pre-Jubilee career – intellectual eclecticism, financial pressures coupled with market forces, the urge to address

---

88 Simms to John Pendleton Kennedy, May 12, 1851, *Letters of William Gilmore Simms, Vol. 3: 1850–1857*, ed. Mary Simms Oliphant and T. C. Duncan Evans (Columbia: University of South Carolina Press, 1954), 122–23; Kennedy to Simms, March, 1851, quoted in William Osborne's introduction to Kennedy, *Swallow Barn, Or A Sojourn in the Old Dominion* (New York: Hafner, 1962), xl. "The Difference between the Northern and Southern People," *The Southern Literary Messenger* 30 (1860), 402, 405; Moncure Conway, *Autobiography: Memory and Experiences, Vol. I* (1904; New York: De Capo Press, 1970), 224.

89 Martha Nussbaum, *Poetic Justice: The Literary Imagination and Public Life* (Boston: Beacon Press, 1995), 53–78.

religious doubts arising from personal tragedies. None of these reasons are particularly successful in explaining all of Stowe's pre-War novels. And none of them preclude the claim that Stowe came to understand slavery, not only as an atrocity suffered by African Americans, but as a manifest-ation – or more worrisome, a symbol – of evil in a providential plot. The arc of Stowe's antebellum writings can be one of encroaching provincial-ism as she turns toward local color and New England piety at the expense of a humanitarian mission. From a different perspective, Stowe's career becomes a story of broadening vision as she moves from temporal political questions toward more universal concerns.

Regardless of how much significance one grants the New England Mind, and regardless of how one defines the moral and political res-ponsibilities of literature, the slavery crisis became for Stowe a crisis of philosophy as the approaching Civil War undermined her confidence in sentimental reform. In this sense, Stowe speaks to a larger problem of nineteenth-century American thought, for some political conflicts are so intractable that they frustrate every solution short of war, revealing in traumatic specificity the limits of rational authority. Facing such limits, some post-War thinkers turned to pragmatism. If metaphysics could not govern experience, then experience would govern metaphysics. The first generation of pragmatists gave some credence to moral sentiment, though for them feelings indicated the various truth-claims available to individ-uals and did not grant special access to universal truths. Stowe, however, continued in her stubborn efforts to create from the ideas at her disposal what William James would call a "tender-minded" theory – one that posited absolute truths based on *a priori* arguments, one not explicitly presented and never entirely coherent, but one that when artistically advertised moved a multitude, if not quite a quorum, of hearts.[90] Finding even *Uncle Tom's Cabin* unable to redeem America, Stowe pursued her sentimental philosophy in subsequent antebellum writings whose connection to the slavery crisis became increasingly abstract. Stowe's theorizing may have become an end in itself – a deferral of more immediate political duties, and a dalliance some scholars may know. But such is a risk of putting faith in ideas near the end of enlightenment in America, particularly if the systematic urge pushes one to feel and think right.

---

90 James, *Pragmatism*, 491. For more positive discussions of affect from the pragmatists, see Peirce's "Evolutionary Love" (1893) and James's "The Sentiment of Rationality" (1897).

CHAPTER 3

Taking care of the philosophy: Douglass's commonsense

Thus far we have seen how Poe and Stowe enter into philosophical narratives: Poe helps to signal the rise of transcendentalism, while Stowe explores the theory of moral sentiments and its tense relation to Calvinism. Romantic, sentimental, and Puritan legacies are certainly important to antebellum literature. Yet the dominant philosophy in pre-Civil War America was Scottish commonsense, represented here by a literary figure not generally regarded in terms of philosophy. Looking back on leaders such as Alexander Crummell, Henry Highland Garnett, Sojourner Truth and "above all, Frederick Douglass," W. E. B. Du Bois wondered, "Where were these black abolitionists trained?"[1] Du Bois simply called Douglass "self-trained" and said little else on the matter, though subsequent scholarship more stubbornly traces Douglass's intellectual roots. For a time, Douglass's thinking appeared to be fairly representative of his era and not particularly profound, in part because of what David Blight sees as Douglass's strain of realism.[2] Douglass was indeed a politically savvy and remarkably effective abolitionist who first knew slavery as a physical atrocity, not a philosophical problem. Douglass's race and experience as a slave distinguish him from other main figures in this book, and yet as he pursued practical ends he, too, found both disillusionment and hope in the possibilities of philosophy.

As Henry Louis Gates, Jr. first pointed out, the issue is not whether Douglass deals with metaphysics, but rather how he views and deploys its emancipatory power. What Gates calls Douglass's "burden" of knowledge

---

1 W. E. B. Du Bois, "The Talented Tenth" (1903), in *W. E. B Du Bois: Writings*, 845–46.

2 See, for instance, Benjamin Quarles's claim that Douglass was "broad rather than deep" (*Frederick Douglass* [1948; New York: Atheneum, 1970], xv), and Waldo Martin's sense that Douglass's thought was "more often representative than novel" (*The Mind of Frederick Douglass* [Chapel Hill: The University of North Carolina Press, 1984], x). David Blight discusses Douglass's realism in *Frederick Douglass's Civil War: Keeping Faith in Jubilee* (Baton Rouge: Louisiana State University Press, 1989).

entails important questions.[3] Are universal ideals inherently prejudicial, ethnocentric, and oppressive? Are alternative epistemologies tenable? How do black thinkers adopt, adapt, and resist Western philosophical traditions? For the political philosopher Charles Mills, Douglass works too comfortably within "Modernist Enlightenment liberalism" insofar as he fails to recognize its deeply structured racism.[4] Somewhat differently, Paul Gilroy finds more radical potential in Douglass, who remains invested in enlightenment projects but still manages to mitigate the "totalizing power of universal reason."[5] Such arguments are ambitious in scope and generally justified to read Douglass in light of European philosophy. Yet they also stand serious qualification – in part because Douglass's philosophy requires firmer and more specific historical grounding, in part because his speculative performances are subtle and dialectical, making it hard to ascribe to him an unequivocal stance.

This chapter examines Douglass's use of Scottish commonsense philosophy, particularly as it relates to the slavery debate and Douglass's second autobiography, *My Bondage and My Freedom* (1855). Two main claims are at issue here – one methodological, one practical. The first is that the reconstruction of Douglass's metaphysics requires attention to the cultural conditions shaping his expression as a black intellectual who witnessed (in Hortense Spillers' words) an "ongoing crisis of life-worlds in historical confrontation with superior force."[6] The second claim is that Douglass draws on Scottish commonsense to vindicate African mental equality and authorize community activism. Whereas Poe denies or demonizes black subjects, and while Stowe attempts to imagine them, Douglass fights to establish his subjectivity in the logic of his era's dominant philosophy, though commonsense proves to be more a compromise than a panacea. Douglass learns first hand that metaphysics can be racially biased in practice, and he understands that discursive reasoning has political and philosophical limits. Nonetheless, with the help of a careful introduction from the black intellectual James McCune Smith, *My Bondage and My Freedom* seeks what it calls the "unchangeable laws of human nature," even as Douglass questions the utility of asserting

---

3 Gates, *Figures in Black*, 14.
4 Charles Mills, *Blackness Visible: Essays on Philosophy and Race* (Ithaca: Cornell University Press, 1998), 187. For a more positive view of Douglass's liberalism, see Bernard Boxill, "Radical Implications of Locke's Moral Theory: The Views of Frederick Douglass," in *Subjugation and Bondage*, 29–48.
5 Gilroy, *The Black Atlantic*, 69.
6 Hortense Spillers, "The Crisis of the Black Intellectual," in *A Companion to African-American Philosophy*, ed. Tommy Lott and John Pittman (London: Blackwell, 2003), 87.

transcendental truths.[7] In doing so, he operates less within idealistic romantic traditions and more within the Scottish Enlightenment and its American legacy.

The first step in recovering Douglass's philosophy is to examine his education, though what Douglass knew and when he knew it are difficult to say. Douglass cobbled his learning from books, meetings, lectures, and the popular press, as well as from the array of thinkers he met on his wide-ranging travels. There are, however, no journals, marginalia, or book lists with which to track Douglass's intellectual growth, in part because his personal papers and library were lost in an 1872 fire. What is known of Douglass's itinerant education is mainly derived from his public works, copious evidence that yet entails its own set of interpretive difficulties. Allusions in Douglass are hard to pin down, for his catholic penchant for paraphrase can drive even a musty disciple of source study into the fresh air of discourse. Additionally challenging is Douglass's tendency to fashion his public image for diverse audiences who brought to bear multifarious and often contradictory pressures. Most of Douglass's listeners doubted black reason and demanded proof of black mental achievement, while even friendly parties could constrict the latitude of African-American thinkers. Douglass has much to gain and lose by displaying his intellectual ambitions, and so he simultaneously disavows and pursues his commitment to metaphysics.[8]

As a kind of intellectual autobiography, *My Bondage and My Freedom* gives the fullest account of Douglass's rise as a fugitive philosopher. In what is probably the book's best-known chapter, "Introduced to the Abolitionists," Douglass recalls his antislavery work for William Lloyd Garrison in the early 1840s. After a season as a speaker relating his "personal experience" as a slave, the twenty-five-year-old Douglass tires of repeating "the same old story month after month" (367). At issue is the fact that he is "reading and thinking" and formulating "[n]ew views" of slavery. No longer content to "*narrate* wrongs," he "was growing, and

---

7 Frederick Douglass, *My Bondage and My Freedom* (1855), in *Frederick Douglass: Autobiographies*, 105.
8 For Douglass's education, see Martin, *The Mind of Frederick Douglass*; William McFeely, *Frederick Douglass* (New York: Norton, 1991), 29–34; and John Blassingame's introduction to *The Frederick Douglass Papers; Series One: Speeches, Debates, and Interviews: Volume 1–3*, ed. John Blassingame (New York: Yale University Press, 1979–85), 1: xxi–lxix (hereafter cited as *FDP*).

needed room." The problem is that Douglass's white fellow lecturers do not encourage his aspirations, a reaction that *My Bondage and My Freedom* recounts in accusatory detail. George Foster asks for a "simple narrative," while Garrison whispers, "Tell your story, Frederick." John Collins instructs him, "Give us the facts, . . . we will take care of the philosophy." That Douglass resents such condescension is to be expected; and when Collins tells him to retain "a *little* of the plantation manner . . . 'tis not best that you seem too learned," Douglass reveals racist capitulations within Garrison's American Antislavery Society, suggesting that the title of *My Bondage and My Freedom* and its explicit diptych structure disguise a measure of ambivalence and may be a *little* ironic.

Clearly many white abolitionists did not believe in racial equality or black leadership within the antislavery cause – a charge that Martin Delany lodged in *The Condition, Elevation, Emigration, and Destiny of the Colored People* (1852), and one that Douglass intimated in England as early as 1847, "[T]he hatred of the American [is] especially roused against the intellectual coloured man."[9] *My Bondage and My Freedom* more forthrightly condemns the proscription of black intellectuals, even as Douglass remains guarded about his progress beyond simple narrative. He acknowledges that, despite his own boredom, "[m]uch interest was awakened" by his early speeches (366). He also confesses with "some embarrassment" that – praise the crusade and bless its goals, but abolitionist projects aside – the popular success of his scripted performances failed to "entirely satisfy" him (367). Such a personal preference was a conspicuous fault in a movement obsessed with self-sacrifice. Thus Douglass knowingly opens himself to accusations of egotism, an indictment one white Garrisonian voiced in 1849, "[Douglass] is thinking more of his speech than of the end for which he professes to make it."[10] Such criticism is racially inflected (none of Garrison's followers attacked the white Wendell Phillips for aspiring to eloquence). But even as Douglass notes the hostility toward African-American intellectuals, and even as he admits the political efficacy of playing his limited antislavery role, he dismisses Garrisonian suppression with the unapologetic pronouncement, "I must speak just the word that seemed to *me* the word to be spoken *by* me" – as strong a claim for individual expression as any romantic might wish, and a formative conviction in Douglass's career. Assuming that we believe him.

9 Martin Delany, *The Condition, Elevation, Emigration and Destiny of the Colored People of the United States* (1852; Baltimore: Black Classic Press, 1993), 10; *FDP* 2: 5.
10 Ephraim Peabody, "Narratives of Fugitive Slaves" (1849), *Christian Examiner* 47: 1 (July 1849): 75.

According to *My Bondage and My Freedom,* Douglass's conflict with Collins and Garrison came after his first speech before a white audience in 1841 and prior to the publication of his first autobiography in 1845. However, some scholars argue that *My Bondage* retrospectively exaggerates Garrisonian censure by projecting 1855 quarrels onto Douglass's earlier life.[11] Douglass drifted from Garrison's non-resistance throughout the 1850s; and in 1853 the one-time friends engaged in bitter personal attacks, so much so that *My Bondage and My Freedom* can be read as Douglass's public separation from the American Antislavery Society and Garrison's overweening influence. This raises the more or less obvious point that Douglass willfully shapes his life in his second autobiography to present himself as, among other things, an embattled intellectual. Yet the progress of his struggle is not entirely clear, for though Douglass's encounter with abolitionist racism is a climactic chapter in *My Bondage and My Freedom,* it is hard to tell from the historical record precisely how early and how explicitly Douglass turns to philosophy.

The Narrative of the Life of Frederick Douglass (1845) offers a brilliant analysis of slavery, examining fundamental structures "within the circle" of bondage – the epistemology of slavery's "immutable certainty"; the psychology of the masters' "irresponsible power"; the problem of describing the brutality of slavery as "a witness and a participant."[12] Douglass's *Narrative* dramatically exposes the ideology of chattel bondage, revealing the complex social structures and psychological workings of slavery. Nonetheless, *The Narrative* does not argue in an idiom that an antebellum audience might recognize as philosophical. Nor for all its remarkable insight does *The Narrative* announce the metaphysical aim of *My Bondage and My Freedom* – "to enlighten the public mind, by revealing the true nature, character, and tendency of the slave system" (106). Doubtlessly, Garrison's powerful influence was of some sway in *The Narrative,* perhaps causing Douglass to restrain or defer his speculative ambitions.[13] Yet even afterwards in Britain where Douglass enjoys a larger measure of freedom, he does not unleash a sudden burst of previously stifled

11 Blassingame, introduction to *FDP* 1: xlviii; Gregory Jay, "American Literature and the New Historicism: The Example of Frederick Douglass," *Boundary 2* 17 (spring 1990): 229.
12 Frederick Douglass, *Narrative of the Life of Frederick Douglass, an American Slave* (1845), in *Frederick Douglass: Autobiographies* (New York: Library of America, 1994), 24, 29, 40, 18.
13 Wilson J. Moses, "Writing Freely? Frederick Douglass and the Constraints of Racialized Writing," in *Frederick Douglass: New Literary and Historical Essays,* ed. Eric J. Sundquist (Cambridge: Cambridge University Press, 1990), 66–83; John Sekora, "'Mr. Editor, If You Please': Frederick Douglass, *My Bondage and My Freedom,* and the End of the Abolitionist Imprint," *Callaloo* 17 (spring 1994): 608–26.

philosophy, but instead makes cautious, tentative moves beyond the facts of his personal history.

In 1846 Douglass told an English audience in the presence of his mentor Garrison, "I feel that my friend Garrison is better able to instruct you. . . . I never had a day's schooling in my life, and, therefore, any learned or eloquent language from me need not be expected. I come here to tell a simple tale of slavery, as coming under my own observation."[14] Douglass repeated similar disclaimers even after Garrison returned to America. Adopting the oratorical convention of diffident, genteel modesty, he invokes his absent education as a sign of slavery's wrong while also blunting potential resistance to his efforts as a black orator. Douglass, that is, has rhetorical reasons for underrating his mental accomplishments, but his lack of formal schooling is also a real concern. In Britain, Douglass is only twenty-seven-years old and a mere seven years out of bondage. Sharing the stage but not the learning of the intellectual elite, he enters a complicated slavery debate that was waged in diverse scholarly disciplines – historical, political, legal, theological, scientific, and philosophical. Douglass is not trained in these fields and must make the best of a fraught situation. On the one hand, he acknowledges a connection between intellectual and political power, "[O]verwhelming influence . . . must ever be exercised by superior intellect," a claim that helps to explain his desire for what he later calls "mental culture."[15] On the other hand, Douglass understands that the standards of scholarly discourse can seriously disadvantage a person who never had a day's schooling in his life. Douglass is cautious of the double-edged logic that equates book knowledge and truth, a logic that for a brilliant ex-slave in the process of self-education simultaneously promises future power and painfully present constraint.

This ambivalence toward enlightenment learning is an abiding feature of Douglass's thought. He said in Britain, "Truth needs but little argument, and no long drawn metaphysical detail," yet he later encouraged blacks to "ascend to the loftiest elevations of the human mind." Douglass further called on the "great truths of moral and political science." But while he emphasized the advantages of "moral philosophy" and "the enlightenment of the age," he also wrote in 1850 that to know the evil of slavery, "No argument, no researches into mouldy records, no learned disquisitions, are necessary."[16] Up to and beyond *My Bondage and My*

14 *FDP* 1: 399.
15 *FDP* 1: 172.
16 *FDP* 1: 108; *FDP* 2: 536; Douglass, *Selected Speeches and Writings*, 261, 277, 430; FDP 2: 261.

Freedom, Douglass continues to question the primacy of rational, forensic debate – even in his most scientific text, "The Claims of the Negro Ethnologically Considered" (1854); even in "The Anti-slavery Movement" (1855), one of his most philosophical works. Like the gothic Poe, the sentimental Stowe, the skeptical Melville, and the transcendental Emerson, Douglass delimits the power of reason while at the same time trying to rationally formulate a systematic understanding of the world.

While doing so, Douglass labors under the additional burden of race, for enlightenment philosophy, in Gilroy's words, was "both a lifeline and a fetter" for blacks who recognized the liberating potential of universalizing systems that not only accommodated but helped to invent invidious racial distinctions.[17] Many thinkers of Douglass's time affirmed natural rights, civil liberties, and broad conceptions of equality, though many also subscribed to scientific views that excluded blacks from such advantages. As David Goldberg has argued, the universal, abstract modern Subject at the center of the Enlightenment was in many ways defined over and against dehumanized racial others.[18] Douglass, then, is a careful thinker, not only as an African-American intellectual in a country that hated his presence, and not simply as an autodidactic ex-slave moving toward scholarly confidence, but also as a black philosopher suspicious of intellectual traditions that had the potential both to further and hamper his emancipatory goals. Given these factors, and not to forget that African-Americans could resent black intellectuals, how does Douglass come to speak the words to be spoken by him? How in the face of conflicting interests does he take care of the philosophy? It seems likely that any adequate answer must rely on textual explication that heeds the ironies, gaps, and subtexts of Douglass's fugitive self-presentations. Such is the case of *My Bondage and My Freedom* – a book that critics have increasingly called Douglass's "true" life story, and one in which more than ever before he offers in wary but willful fashion the story of a black thinker who discovers in his life and mind a liberating and limiting philosophy.[19]

17 Gilroy, *The Black Atlantic*, 30. See also Hannaford, *Race: The History of an Idea*.
18 David Goldberg, *Racist Culture: Philosophy and the Politics of Meaning* (Cambridge: Blackwell, 1993).
19 The quote is from Sekora, "Mr. Editor," 610. Other scholars who privilege *My Bondage* include William Andrews, "Introduction to the 1987 Edition" of Frederick Douglass, *My Bondage and My Freedom* (Chicago: University of Illinois Press, 1987), xi–xxviii; David Leverenz, *Manhood and the American Renaissance* (Ithaca: Cornell University Press, 1989), 108–34; and Sundquist, *To Wake the Nations*, 88–90.

REFLECTION

As William Andrews has shown, prefatory documents often mediate the meanings of slave narratives when white sponsors announce, authorize, and predict the claims of the slave-speaker.[20] This is certainly true of Douglass's *Narrative*, though less so in *My Bondage and My Freedom*, for Douglass retains more authorial control over his second autobiography as he uses his introductory materials to foreground a metaphysical plot. Taking up a traditional abolitionist project, *My Bondage and My Freedom* aspires to prove the intellectual equality of blacks, which Douglass does, not simply by performing his literary and oratorical skills but also by constructing a sophisticated argument grounded in a theory of the mind.

On the title page of *My Bondage and My Freedom* is a quotation from Coleridge insisting upon the fundamental difference between a "PERSON" and a "THING." That Coleridge sometimes made this Kantian distinction without reference to chattel bondage might cause a politically minded reader to question Douglass's epigraph. Though Coleridge supported British abolitionism, he was not a primary figure in the cause, nor was he by the end of his life a friend to radical reform. The distinction between persons and property was a basic antislavery principle, and Douglass could have placed his autobiography within a strict abolitionist canon by quoting Wilberforce, Equiano, David Walker, or Stowe on the difference between humans and things. Instead, from the very start of his book, Douglass tempts the reader's philosophical eye. Coleridge said before his death in 1834, "I am a poor poet in England, but I am a great philosopher in America," a statement that proved increasingly true with the rise of New England transcendentalism.[21]

Scholars have not been slow to note transcendental aspects of Douglass's thought, even if only limited evidence supports a sustained relationship. Possibly echoing Emersonian titles, James McCune Smith's glowing introduction to *My Bondage and My Freedom* applauds the book's "self-relying" spirit and calls Douglass a "Representative American man"

---

20 William Andrews, *To Tell a Free Story: The First Century of Afro-American Autobiography, 1760–1865* (Urbana: University of Illinois Press, 1988).

21 For Coleridge on persons and things, see among others citations: *The Collected Works of Samuel Taylor Coleridge: Aids to Reflection, Vol. 9*, ed. John Beer (Princeton: Princeton University Press, 1993), 115; and *The Collected Works of Samuel Taylor Coleridge: Shorter Works and Fragments, Vol. 11: 1* (Princeton: Princeton University Press, 1995), 405. The wealth of work on Coleridge and slavery is discussed in Lee's *Slavery and the Romantic Imagination*, 47–65. Coleridge's quote is from Beer's introduction to *Aids to Reflection*, cxxviii.

(129, 132). Douglass did cross paths with various transcendentalists, and his newspapers occasionally reprinted selections from antislavery transcendentalist texts. Smith had definitely read Emerson by 1855, and Douglass shares transcendentalist affinities for self-cultivation and, at times, higher law.[22] Yet no one has found an explicit connection between Douglass and specific transcendentalist works, and one possible link to romantic philosophy, Douglass's correspondence with Ottilie Assing, did not begin until the later 1850s and remains more intriguing than persuasive.[23] Moreover, to grant explanatory power to potential allusions to transcendentalism is also to credit references that suggest not collaboration but resistance. Smith excuses Douglass's thought from "the charm of transcendent excellence" (105), and Douglass may have wished to distance himself from the idealism and racism of some of his peers when he condemned abolitionists who felt that the cause had "transcended" the abilities of blacks.[24] Douglass's increasingly politicized work almost requires that he ground his thinking, not in the latest form of infidelity that favored Garrisonian non-resistance, but rather in a more practical, more popular philosophy that Smith's neglected introduction presents as Scottish commonsense.

James McCune Smith is a fascinating figure in the American antislavery movement. The Cambridge-educated Crummell called Smith "the most learned Negro of his day"; and Du Bois agreed, ranking Smith (along with Crummell and Douglass) among his "Talented Tenth."[25] When Douglass in his *Life and Times* (1881; 1893) listed the "intelligent men of color" who helped him in his work, he wrote, "[F]oremost, I place the name of Doctor James McCune Smith; educated in Scotland . . . he came back to his native land with ideas of liberty which placed him in advance of most of

---

22 Scholars who discuss transcendental influences on Douglass include John Stauffer, *The Black Hearts of Men: Radical Abolitionists and the Transformation of Race* (Cambridge: Harvard University Press, 2002), esp. 38, 66; Martin, *The Mind of Frederick Douglass*, 253–64; William Andrews, "*My Bondage and My Freedom* and the American Literary Renaissance of the 1850s," in *Critical Essays on Frederick Douglass*, 133–47; and Crane, *Race, Citizenship, and Law*, 87–130.

23 Gilroy, following McFeely, relies on Assing (*The Black Atantic*, 60). Douglass, to my knowledge, makes no direct reference to Emerson prior to 1855.

24 *FDP* 3: 16.

25 Crummell quoted in David W. Blight, "In Search of Learning, Liberty, and Self Definition: James McCune Smith and the Ordeal of the Antebellum Black Intellectual," *Afro-Americans in New York Life and History* 9 (July 1985): 7. For contemporary views of Smith as an intellectual, see William C. Nell, *The Colored Patriots of the American Revolution* (1855; New York: Arno Press, 1968), 353–55; and Delany, *The Condition, Elevation, Emigration and Destiny*, 110–12. Biographical information on Smith also includes Stauffer, *The Black Hearts of Men*; and Mia Bay, *The White Image in the Black Mind: African-American Ideas about White People, 1830–1925* (New York: Oxford University Press, 2000), 58–63.

...s of African descent."[26] Between 1832 and 1837, the ...th earned three degrees from Glasgow University. He ...York as the first credentialed black physician in America, ...itted himself to political abolitionism, writing for the ... as a contributor to Douglass's papers and the short-lived ...*Magazine* (which published Frances Harper's poetry and ...any's *Blake* [1862]). In the years leading up to *My Bondage and My Freedom*, Smith worked with Douglass on abolitionist projects and served as a kind of mentor. Thus by turning to Smith for an introduction, Douglass not only selected a friend, but also a formally trained intellectual (Douglass called him a "gentleman and scholar") who as much as any black in the antebellum era advocated African-American freedom in philosophical terms.[27] Smith wrote texts on various topics relating to slavery and race, including articles that focused on the "intellectual power" of blacks. In an age that assumed affinities between metaphysics and the physical sciences, Smith discussed "common-sense" and "mental philosophy" – invoking Locke, Malebranche, Berkeley, and Hume, as well as Scottish commonsense philosophers such as Dugald Stewart, Thomas Brown, and the founder of the school, Thomas Reid.[28]

Borrowing from Locke but unwilling to extend his faculty psychology to its critical limits, commonsense thinkers (also called Scottish realists) posited an innate commonsense possessed by all humankind. As a faculty verifying daily experience, commonsense solved – or by some standards, dodged – the skeptical potential of Locke, whose atomistic empiricism made it difficult to validate one's perceptions vis-à-vis those of anyone else. Commonsense thought also assumed a stable, discernible consciousness that tried to deflect the challenge of Hume, who argued that the intellect could never know itself and, hence, that the "identity, which we ascribe to the mind of man, is only a fictitious one."[29] Against this and other skeptical claims, Scottish realists held that commonsense was a first principle of inquiry, for no demonstrable reason could be found to doubt the accuracy of primary perceptions. Rational, Protestant, and generally

pu...
IOI

---

26 Frederick Douglass, *Life and Times of Frederick Douglass* (1893), in *Frederick Douglass: Autobiographies* (New York: Library of America, 1994), 901–2.

27 Frederick Douglass, "The Claims of the Negro Ethnologically Considered," in *Douglass: Selected Speeches and Writings*, 296.

28 James McCune Smith, "Civilization: Its Dependence on Physical Circumstances," *Anglo-African Magazine* 1: 1 (Jan. 1859): 5. Smith, "Chess," *Anglo-African Magazine* 1: 9 (Sept. 1859): 278. Both reprinted in *The Anglo-African Magazine: Volume I–1859* (New York: Arno Press, 1968).

29 Hume, *A Treatise of Human Nature* (1739), 540.

progressive, commonsense thinkers were extremely influential in America before the Civil War. They provided the philosophical basis for rhetorical and literary criticism, while shaping moral philosophy courses through the popular textbooks of Francis Wayland, William Paley, and Adam Ferguson.[30]

Which is not to say that Scottish commonsense did not and does not have its detractors. In his *Prolegomena to Any Future Metaphysics* (1783), Kant called commonsense "cheaply gained wisdom" built on "public rumor" not rational argument, and John Stuart Mill's critique of William Hamilton in 1865 more directly damaged the Scottish reputation in postbellum America.[31] Some modern philosophers have also objected to the "teleological and providentialist" aspects of the Scottish position, while literary scholars, following Terence Martin, often see the school as a rearguard "philosophy of containment" that served as an obstacle or at best a "stepping stone" for the more creative, more romantic speculations of writers like Hawthorne and Emerson.[32] Recently, however, some philosophers have begun to recoup Reid and his followers – whose relations to Hume are not obtusely antagonistic, who are more logically rigorous than often supposed, and who carefully studied the paradox of proving self-evident truths.[33] Scottish realism offers an alternative to skepticism, and its reliance on untutored individual perceptions provides a helpful philosophical direction to *My Bondage and My Freedom*.

By referring twice in his introduction to Douglass's "common sense," Smith gives the reader a philosophical framework for examining Douglass's

---

30 For commonsense in America, see Bruce Kuklick's *Churchmen and Philosophers*, esp. 128–45; and Daniel Walker Howe's *Making the American Self*, esp. 47–70. The institutionalization of commonsense philosophy in American universities appears in Howe's *The Unitarian Conscience*. For Scottish realism and antebellum literature, see Terence Martin, *The Instructed Vision: Scottish Common Sense Philosophy and the Origins of American Fiction* (Bloomington: Indiana University Press, 1961).

31 Immanuel Kant, *Prolegomena to Any Future Metaphysics That Will Be Able to Come Forward as Science*, trans. Gary Hatfield (1783; Cambridge: Cambridge University Press, 1997), 67, 28. John Stuart Mill, *Examination of Sir William Hamilton's Philosophy and of the Principal Philosophical Questions Discussed in His Writings* (1865).

32 Knud Haakonssen, *Natural Law and Moral Philosophy: From Grotius to the Scottish Enlightenment* (Cambridge: Cambridge University Press, 1996), quoted 7; Derek Brookes, introduction to Reid's *An Inquiry into the Human Mind on the Principles of Common Sense*, ed. Derek Brookes (Edinburgh: Edinburgh University Press, 1997); Martin, *The Instructed Vision*, 148, 117. See also Michael Davitt Bell, *The Development of American Romance: The Sacrifice of Relation* (Chicago: The University of Chicago Press, 1980), 12–14. For why "Reid almost disappeared from the canon," see Nicholas Wolterstorff, *Thomas Reid and the Story of Epistemology* (Cambridge: Cambridge University Press, 2001) ix–xi.

33 Wolterstorff, *Thomas Reid and the Story of Epistemology*; and Philip de Bary, *Thomas Reid and Scepticism: His Reliabilist Response* (London: Routledge, 2002).

mind. Following the footsteps of Benjamin Banneker, Smith commences by insisting upon "the abstract . . . logic of human equality" (125), and he sees Douglass's eloquence as a "mental phenomenon" that belies those critics who claim that Douglass is deficient in rational power (135). Smith ascribes this aspersion to Garrison and Phillips, who wrote introductory letters to *The Narrative*. With a severity reflecting the split between Douglass and the American Antislavery Society, Smith charges the white abolitionists with racism, "[T]hese gentlemen, although proud of Frederick Douglass, failed to fathom, and bring out to the light of day, the highest qualities of his mind; the force of their own education stood in their own way: they did not delve into the mind of a colored man for capacities which the pride of race led them to believe to be restricted to their own Saxon blood" (129). The primary purpose of Smith's introduction is to show the best qualities of Douglass's mind by highlighting in his life and work "an original breadth of common sense" (126).

To this end, Smith makes a curious move, comparing *My Bondage and My Freedom* to a Scottish autobiography – Hugh Miller's *My Schools and Schoolmasters; or, The Story of My Education* (1854), a text that describes its author's rise from uneducated laborer to prominent geologist while also presenting Miller's experience as a study in mental philosophy. Miller calls his book an "educational treatise, thrown into narrative form," and his thesis is that formal training is unnecessary because "life itself is a school." Fittingly, when Miller naively encounters "the antagonist positions of the schools of Hume and Reid," he intuitively sides with Reid, the father of Scottish realism. Miller believes that all humans possess "primary sentiments and propensities," natural intellectual faculties that he identifies as "common sense." Comparing Douglass to a Scottish geologist may appear an odd rhetorical choice. But by linking *My Bondage* to *My Schools*, Smith suggests that Douglass's book is a study in mental philosophy that reveals, howsoever paradoxically, an exceptional commonsense.[34]

Smith emphasizes that despite the oppression of Douglass's childhood in bondage, young Frederick makes the "notable discovery" in "the depths of his own nature" that "liberty and right, for all men, [are] anterior to slavery and wrong" (126). Douglass himself is quick to note that his childhood was "[l]ike other slaves" (140). All slaves, then, possess the mental potential that he comes to fulfill, for – like Miller's school of hard rocks – even a "plantation education" offers important lessons (126).

---

34 Hugh Miller, *My Schools and Schoolmasters; or, The Story of My Education* (Edinburgh: Johnstone and Hunter, 1854), v, 537, 353, 390, 354–55.

For Douglass, his master's sloop and mill were "full of thoughts and ideas," so much so that a "child cannot well look at such objects without *thinking*" (161). Douglass traces the organic growth of his intellectual faculties; and though slavery threatens their "natural course" (152), Douglass insists on other lessons antecedent to the system of bondage, "[W]ith my dear old grandmother and grandfather, it was a long time before I knew myself to be *a slave*. I knew many other things before I knew that" (142). Hannah Crafts makes a similar point when describing her childhood in *The Bondwoman's Narrative* (c. 1853–61), as does William Wells Brown in *Clotel* (1853) when the white abolitionist Georgiana proclaims, "[Y]ou may place the slave where you please; you may dry up to your utmost the fountains of his feelings, the springs of his thought . . . you may put him under any process which . . . will debase and crush him as a rational being; you may do this, and *the idea that he was born to be free will survive it*."[35]

Such lines represent a general effort to vindicate the so-called African mind from charges of inferiority. As Samuel Otter and Thomas Cooley have shown, phrenology, ethnology, and other physical sciences are well-known theaters of this struggle, though less recognized is the related role played by mental philosophy, which did not rely on physical evidence such as fossils and cranial size but rather attempted to ascertain the metaphysical operations of the mind. James Cowles Prichard's *Natural History of Man* (1845), which Douglass called "marvelously . . . philosophical," helped set the stakes for the growing debate, "If now it should appear, on inquiry, that one common mind, or psychical nature, belongs to the whole human family, a very strong argument would thence arise . . . for their community of species and origin."[36] Prichard was ultimately a monogenesist, sparking rebuttals from slavery advocates, who turned to a basic racist claim stretching back through enlightenment thinkers such as Jefferson, Kant, and Hume – that the African race does not enjoy the same mental faculties as whites.[37]

As Smith suggests by repeatedly praising Douglass's "wonderful memory," among the faculties in question were those of retrospection (129). James Beattie, a disciple of Reid, held with his mentor that memory

---

35 Hannah Crafts, *The Bondwoman's Narrative*, ed. Henry Louis Gates, Jr. (New York: Warner, 2002), 5–6; William Wells Brown, *Clotel*, in *Three Classic African-American Novels*, ed. William Andrews (New York: Mentor, 1990), 200.

36 Douglass quoted in Martin, *The Mind of Frederick Douglass*, 229; James Prichard, *The Natural History of Man* (London: Hippolyte Bailliere, 1845), 487.

37 A proximate example from antebellum America is Henry Hotz's introduction to A. De Gobineau's *The Moral and Intellectual Diversity of Races* (1856; New York: Garland, 1984), 90–91.

and reflection distinguish "men" from "brutes."[38] Similarly, George Combe's influential *Constitution of Man* (1834) followed Reid, Stewart, and Brown when arguing that memory and reflection define the human mind. Combe was by no means free from racism, but his ideas were useful to Douglass. In 1846 Douglass met Combe, whom he called "the eminent mental philosopher," and he cited Combe in "The claims of the Negro Ethnologically Considered" to show that "[m]en instinctively distinguish between men and brutes. Common sense itself is scarcely needed . . . to recognize [manhood's] presence in the negro."[39] What was self-evident to Douglass, however, was not so clear to others, particularly pro-slavery thinkers who, extrapolating from Reid's claim that dogs and horses have only "the memory of brutes," argued that blacks may in fact have memory and yet lack the distinctly human faculty of self-conscious reflection.[40] Jefferson predicted such aspersions in *Notes on the State of Virginia* (1787) when he claimed that no black had ever "uttered a thought above the level of plain narration."[41] Poe also played with this possibility in *The Narrative of Arthur Gordon Pym* when the black Tsalalian chief Too-Wit cowers before his "reflected self" in a mirror, implying that he and his fellow blacks lack what Poe would later call "the higher powers of the reflective intellect." That Too-Wit may be faking his confusion to hide a malevolent plot points to lurking concerns about the question of African intelligence. What if blacks are all-too-witty humans who possess what David Walker's "Appeal" calls "reflecting minds"?[42]

Smith and Douglass, therefore, go to great lengths to vindicate Douglass's power of reflection, a goal that *My Bondage and My Freedom* pursues in two coordinated ways. At the relatively simple level of example, Douglass's life, particularly his childhood, demonstrates that his mental faculties are undeniably human and that the commonsense of his natural intellect precedes and finally rises above the near-brutalizing nurture of slavery. Just as mental philosophers studied children to discern the operations of the mind, young Frederick's life becomes a case study objectively examined by Smith. The more salient work of *My Bondage*, however, lies

---

38 James Beattie, *Elements of Moral Science* (1790; Delmar, New York: Scholars' Facsimiles and Reprints, 1976), 3.
39 Douglass quoted in Martin, *The Mind of Frederick Douglass*, 172; *FDP* 2: 502.
40 Thomas Reid, *Essays on the Powers of the Human Mind*, 3 vols. (Edinburgh: Bell and Bradfute, 1819), 1: 496.
41 Jefferson, *Notes on the State of Virginia*, 135.
42 Poe, *Poetry and Tales*, 1138, 397. David Walker, *David Walker's Appeal to the Coloured Citizens of the World*, ed. Peter Hinks (1829; University Park, Penn: Pennsylvania State University Press, 2000), 4.

in Douglass's own reflection, in his ability to show what Francis Wayland called "the mind [turned] backwards upon itself."[43] Douglass recognized the need to display reflection as early as 1848. In *A Tribute for the Negro: Being a Vindication of the Moral, Intellectual, and Religious Capabilities of the Colored Portion of Mankind* (1848), the white abolitionist Wilson Armistead argued that the "internal consciousness of mind" distinguishes humans from animals.[44] Armistead then argued for African reflection with his third-person accounts of black genius, though as his own definitions suggest, to rise above brutes is to have an internal – a first-person – knowledge of one's mind. Douglass made this selfsame point in his otherwise friendly review of Armistead, "What a commentary upon our enlightenment that we must have books to prove what is palpable even to the brute creation – to wit: the negro is a man! . . . Let us hope that the time may come when it will not be necessary for our friends to write Tributes . . . but when we shall present such incontestable evidence of our manhood, as shall seal the lips of calumny and persecution forever."[45]

Douglass commits himself to reflection and in doing so commits himself to metaphysics; for once granting the premise of Lockean empiricism and thus collapsing metaphysics into mental philosophy, our perceptions become both the tool and the object of inquiry. Reflection was the key for early modern philosophers from Descartes to Locke to Hartley, and it remained so for later thinkers such as Charles Peirce, who held that "[t]he internal sense, reflection, . . . distinguishes us from the brutes." Many of these philosophers believed that self-consciousness was entirely attainable; or in the words of Reid, "[B]y attentive reflection, a man may have a clear and certain knowledge of the operations of his own mind." Such confidence may seem quaint today in a post-Freudian, post-modern world, but even supposedly post-enlightenment romantics advocated what Wordsworth called "turning the mind in upon itself." Coleridge, too, shared this aspiration in his *Aids to Reflection* (1825), as did Emerson in "The American Scholar" (1837) when he described the antebellum era as the "the Reflective or Philosophical age."[46]

43 Francis Wayland, *The Elements of Intellectual Philosophy* (Boston: Phillips, 1855), 121.
44 Wilson Armistead, *A Tribute for the Negro: Being a Vindication of the Moral, Intellectual, and Religious Capabilities of the Coloured Portion of Mankind* (Manchester: William Irwin, 1848), 73.
45 Douglass's review reprinted in *The Non-Slaveholder* 4: 5 (May 1849), 109.
46 Thomas Reid, *Essays on the Intellectual Powers of Man*, ed. Derek Brookes (1785; Edinburgh: Edinburgh University Press, 2002), 42. Charles Peirce, "Design and Chance" (1884), in *The Essential Peirce: Selected Philosophical Writings: Vol. 1 (1867–1893)*, ed. Nathan Houser and

James McCune Smith also valued reflection; and when his introduction to *My Bondage and My Freedom* praises Douglass's "higher faculties" of "induction," it recalls how "Ferguson resorted to geometry" to discover "the deeper relation of things" (133–34). Here Smith does not allude to James Ferguson, who popularized Newton in the early-nineteenth century. He refers instead to Adam Ferguson, the commonsense philosopher, who wrote, "The mind is conscious of itself . . . in all its operations and feelings. It is conscious of the laws of thought or reason, which are termed the *metaphysical* or *geometrical axioms.*"[47] Moreover, by praising Douglass's induction, Smith follows the system of Reid, whose *Inquiry into the Human Mind on the Principles of Common Sense* (1764) set the power of the induction over and against the skepticism of Hume. Working within the Scottish realist tradition, Smith champions Douglass's capacity for reflection as he argues for African humanity in the reigning metaphysic of the day.

Yet Smith, like Armistead, can only prove so much by interpreting Douglass's intellect, just as Douglass can only prove so much by plainly narrating the facts of his life. *My Bondage and My Freedom* understands that the rarer act is in reflection, a point that Douglass explicitly made in a later speech, "Pictures and Progress" (1861):

[T]he child experiences [growth] with every new object, by means of which it is brought into a nearer and fuller acquaintance with its own subjective nature. . . . The process by which man is able to invert his own subjective consciousness, into the objective form, . . . is in truth the highest attribute of man[']s nature. All that is really peculiar to humanity – in contradistinction from all other animals proceeds from this one faculty or power. . . . The master [God] we obey in making our subjective nature objective.[48]

In the twentieth century, psychoanalysis professionalized the process of reflection, making guided self-discovery an emblem and privilege of middle- and upper-class life.[49] In the United States before the Civil

---

Christian Kloesel (Bloomington: Indiana University Press, 1992), 222. William Wordsworth, *The Prelude* (1850), in *William Wordsworth*, ed. Stephen Gill (Oxford: Oxford University Press, 1984), 407. Ralph Waldo Emerson, "The American Scholar" (1837), in *Essays and Lectures*, 67. For the widespread belief in reflection in America, see James Hoopes, *Consciousness in New England: From Puritanism and Ideas to Psychoanalysis and Semiotic* (Baltimore: The Johns Hopkins University Press, 1989).

47 Adam Ferguson, *Institutes of Moral Philosophy* (Edinburgh: Kincaid, Creech, and Bell, 1773), 47.
48 *FDP* 3: 460–61.
49 Joel Pfister, "On Conceptualizing the Cultural History of Emotional and Psychological Life in America," in *Inventing the Psychological*, 23–25.

War, the situation was different. Not only did most mental philosophers believe that the mind could be totally known, the ability to achieve reflection defined what it meant, not to be wealthy or healthy, but human. It is ridiculous that Douglass must make such painstaking efforts to distinguish himself from an animal, but the controversy over black mental capacities demanded the technical argumentation of such seemingly self-evident truths as reflection. The intellectual office that Douglass takes up is nothing less than the office of enlightenment: Establish beyond skeptical objection how human consciousness works. More than any slave narrative, and perhaps more than any black Atlantic text before *The Souls of Black Folk* (1903), *My Bondage and My Freedom* pursues self-knowledge in the logic of Western philosophy, a project that becomes increasingly vexed when reflection reaches its limits, when "making our subjective nature objective" turns out to be harder than Reid, Smith, and Douglass initially allow.

RADICAL DISENGAGEMENT

In trying to demonstrate his humanity by making his subjective consciousness objective, Douglass encounters longstanding problems of personal identity. Pointing to the flux of our senses and judgments (and using a trope of rendition and flight), Hume argued contra the common-sense school that our faculties inevitably obscure reflection, "I never can catch *myself* at any time without a perception."[50] Charles Taylor shows how this general dilemma leads modern philosophy toward a paradox in which "self-objectification" demands a "radical disengagement" of the self in that the subject must view from an exterior position the identity it seeks to apprehend.[51] *My Bondage and My Freedom* faces this challenge of subject/object dualism as Douglass strives to define his selfhood by simultaneously claiming and holding at a distance the former selves he describes. Such efforts entail diachronic shifts and unstable narrative perspectives, features inherent to any writing engaged in the act of reflection. This seems particularly true in a period that Emerson called "the age of severance, of dissociation, of freedom, of analysis, of detachment," an age in which "the mind had become aware of itself" and thus "divides and detaches bone and marrow, soul and body, yea, almost the man from

50 Hume, *Treatise of Human Nature*, 534.
51 Taylor, *Sources of the Self*, 171.

himself."⁵² Differently than New England transcendentalists, Douglass
struggles with such double consciousness; for not only must he prove his
humanity, a task not incumbent on whites, the project of reflection
pushes Douglass toward an impossibly disembodied extreme. For him,
disengaged self-knowledge conflicts with a socially grounded black identity when the objective reflection of Scottish commonsense threatens to
turn into transcendence.

The dedication to reflection is everywhere evident in *My Bondage and
My Freedom* as Douglass insistently offers his audience proof of his self-
consciousness. From chapter 1, Douglass does not simply continue a life
so intimately begun in *The Narrative*, for *My Bondage's* ethnographic
detachment and mellifluous, urbane tone immediately create a gap between the author and the young Frederick Bailey. Like William Wells
Brown's "Narrative of the Life and Escape" (1853), *My Bondage* can have
the distancing effect of a third-person narration. These qualities are
nowhere so glaring as when Douglass refers to "the boy whose life in
slavery I am now narrating" (145). They are nowhere so provoking as
when he calls his early self, "as happy as any little heathen under the palm
trees of Africa." Such disengagement, to some readers' displeasure, tends
to dull the sharp edges of Douglass's youth. Which may have been a goal
of Douglass, who was criticized for indulging emotional language and
whose second autobiography accordingly aspires to a more objective
comportment that emphasizes the measured pleasures of reflection over
the thrills of affective immediacy.

Yet such objectivity, as Taylor suggests, proves difficult to attain.
Douglass figures his detachment as a kind of excursus that becomes an
ongoing, never-ending attempt to gain distance and perspective on his
life. In a celebrated passage from *The Narrative*, Douglass writes of the
slave songs he heard as a youth, "I did not, when a slave, understand the
deep meaning of those rude and apparently incoherent songs. I was myself
within the circle; so that I neither saw nor heard as those without might
see and hear" (24). Eric Sundquist argues that when *My Bondage*
quotes this passage, Douglass "stands outside his former self" in order
to construct a "traceable metamorphosis" and a "phenomenology of self-
possession."⁵³ Douglass does recognize in *My Bondage and My Freedom*
that "the point from which a thing is viewed is of some importance," and
he definitely finds both freedom and power in his evolving self-definitions

---

52 Emerson, "Historic Notes of Life and Letters in New England," 415.
53 Sundquist, *To Wake the Nations*, 90, 92.

(148). But for all his awareness of the shifting contingencies that alter one's personal identity, Douglass tries to make his subjectivity objective by reflecting on and providing a theory for his natural, unchanging, pre-experiential self.

In subtle but important ways, Douglass does so in the idiom of mental philosophy. *The Narrative* ends its circle passage, "If any one wishes to be impressed with the soul-killing effects of slavery, let him go to Colonel Lloyd's plantation, and, on allowance-day, place himself in the deep pine woods, and there let him, in silence, analyze the sounds that shall pass through the chambers of his soul" (24). Ten years later, *My Bondage and My Freedom* smuggles two words into the sentence, "If any one wishes to be impressed with a *sense* of the soul-killing power of slavery, . . . let him, in silence, *thoughtfully* analyze the sounds that shall pass through the chambers of his soul" (185, my emphasis). These silent revisions are not over-determining, but they do suggest that reflection requires a rational process based in perception. And as if to offer a further hint, Douglass concludes a few pages later, "But, let others philosophize; it is my province here to relate and describe; only allowing myself a word or two, occasionally, to assist the reader in the proper understanding of the facts narrated" (189). Just as the ex-slave Ottobah Cugoano disavows "the sublime science of metaphysics" before launching his own metaphysical claims, Douglass denies and in doing so implies his fugitive philosophizing.[54] More than *The Narrative*, *My Bondage and My Freedom* draws a broad psychological lesson from the slave songs, "Such is the constitution of the human mind, that, when pressed to extremes, it often avails itself of the most opposite methods" (185). In line with Scottish commonsense thought, Douglass posits a universal "mind," even as he insists that social "extremes" should not be forgotten.

One paragraph before John Collins informs him who will take care of the philosophy, Douglass recalls the heady precocity of his early Garrisonian years, "For a time I was made to forget that my skin was dark and my hair crisped" (366). If only for this remarkable instance, Douglass seems to transcend his corporeal self to become, as Gregg Crane has argued, the representative of an expansive, inclusive identity.[55] Having imbibed the spiritual idealism of the American Antislavery Society, Douglass imagines

54 Ottobah Cugoano, *Thoughts and Sentiments on the Evil and Wicked Traffic of the Slavery and Commerce of the Human Species, Humbly Submitted to the Inhabitants of Great Britain, by Ottobah Cugoana, A Native of Africa* (1787), in *Pioneers of the Black Atlantic*, 116.
55 Crane, *Race, Citizenship, and Law*, 125.

a disengagement so radical that his body slips his mind. The impulse was not Douglass's alone. American transcendentalists, who largely accepted reflective self-knowledge as a goal, simultaneously resisted the more objective identities propounded by Scottish commonsense. Emerson asks in "Self-Reliance" (1841), "Why drag about this corpse of your memory?"; and in "Circles" (1844) he writes, "The one thing which we seek with insatiable desire is to forget ourselves." In *Walden* (1854), the present-minded Thoreau can aspire to a similar "*Extra vagance!*" – particularly when his transcendental flights escape the boundaries of body and time.[56] Nowhere does Douglass seem so transcendental as when he forgets the darkness of his skin to a point where at least one critic has wondered if Douglass thought himself white.[57]

However, such radical disengagement proves impossible for Douglass to bear. Unlike Emerson's disembodied eyeball and Thoreau's runaway self, Douglass's fugitive identity is much more than a motif. The open-endedness of excursive reflection may bring the freedom of unlimited self-definition, but such potential freedom and fluidity work for Douglass in troubling ways. For a black ex-slave, a more objective self-consciousness, howsoever constraining, can prove one's humanity. And even if Douglass wants to transcend his physical identity, his experience demonstrates the impracticality of such abstracted goals. After seemingly leaving his body behind, Douglass finds that his "enthusiasm had been extravagant," a realization triggered by racism within the abolitionist cause (366). When Collins famously calls Douglass's scars a "*diploma written on [his] back*," he is not alone in making Douglass unambiguously embodied and literary inscribed (365). Margaret Fuller's review of *The Narrative* could not help but objectify Douglass as a "specimen" of "the Black Race," and neither could Thoreau imagine a transcendence that retained the African body. After hearing of Douglass's mental accomplishments, Thoreau in his journal praised but punned upon his "*fair* intellect" and "colorless reputation," reinforcing Russ Castronovo's claim that there was little space for black transcendence in the antebellum era.[58]

---

56 Emerson, "Self-Reliance," 265 and "Circles," 414, in *Essays and Lectures*. Thoreau, *Walden*, 289.
57 Peter F. Walker, *Moral Choices: Memory, Desire, and Imagination in Nineteenth-Century American Abolition* (Baton Rouge: Louisiana State University Press, 1978), esp. 244–45. See also David Van Leer, "The Anxiety of Ethnicity in Douglass's *Narrative*," in *Frederick Douglass: New Literary and Historical Essays*, 118–40.
58 Margaret Fuller, review of "Narrative of the Life of Frederick Douglass, An American Slave, Written by Himself," *New York Tribune* (June 10, 1845), in *The Portable Margaret Fuller*, 379. Henry David Thoreau, "Wendell Phillips before the Concord Lyceum" (1845), *The Writings of Henry David Thoreau, Vol. IV: Cape Cod and Miscellanies* (New York: AMS Press, 1968), 313;

My Bondage and My Freedom thus exposes the hazards of radical disengagement, suggesting that some subject-positions should not and cannot be abandoned, no matter how much one hopes to gain a perspective for reflection. Douglass proclaimed in 1846 just after his manumission, "I shall be Frederick Douglass still, and once a slave still. I shall neither be made to forget nor cease to feel the wrongs of my enslaved fellow-countrymen."[59] This is not the slippery self of Hume or an extravagant, forgetful, transcendental I. Douglass owns the identity of a black ex-slave – despite the fact that this definition is constraining, despite the fact that his "choice" is to some degree governed by social forces he despises. Douglass's years in the public eye taught him among others things, "I shall never get beyond Frederick Douglass the self-educated fugitive slave."[60] An unyielding commitment to personal history? An expression of resignation? A frustrated cry? The naming of a racist ideology within which Douglass must immanently work? Douglass responds to his objectification with a range of possible tones that depending on context and performance can serve a variety of ends. In Dickinson's words, the "Circumference" of self can be both "Possessing" and "Possessed," which Douglass discovers as he simultaneously seeks to objectify and re-invent his subjectivity.[61] To further restrict Douglass's thinking does not do him justice, for his genius is both to deploy and slip his constricted identity as *My Bondage and My Freedom* delimits the efficacy of radical disengagement, marking race as the place beyond which transcendence is no longer politically viable.

Along the way, *My Bondage* confronts double consciousness in both the Emersonian and Du Boisian sense. Douglass fails to reconcile what Emerson saw as the contrast of idealism and materialism, finally privileging the material fact of race over transparent selfhood. In Du Bois's terms, Douglass struggles against "a world which yields him no true self-consciousness" as he continues to assert his humanity against unfriendly listeners.[62] In "Introduced to the Abolitionists," the objective reflection of commonsense almost becomes disembodied transcendence, as if the Scottish Enlightenment contains the seeds of its own demise, leading

Castronovo, *Necro Citizenship*, 50–61. See also Jeannine DeLombard, "Eye-Witness to Cruelty: Southern Violence and Northern Testimony in Frederick Douglass's 1845 *Narrative*," *American Literature* 73: 2 (2000): 245–75.

59 *The Life and Writings of Frederick Douglass, Vol. 1*, ed. Philip Foner (New York: International Publishers, 1950), 205.
60 Douglass quoted in McFeely, *Frederick Douglass*, 385.
61 Dickinson, "Circumference thou Bride of Awe" (*c.* 1884), *The Poems of Emily Dickinson*, 596 (poem no. 1636).
62 Du Bois, *The Souls of Black Folk*, 364.

toward an untenable romantic subjectivity that John Dewey would pejoratively call "a centre without a field."[63] Commonsense thinkers resisted this slide, reminding Humean skeptics and transcendental idealists that tables were by every best indication real and that people who avoided banging their shins proved the realist case. There are many ways to unmoor the self. In the antebellum period, reflection was one of them – for Hume, for insatiably excursive transcendentalists, and almost for Frederick Douglass who, after exploring his personal prospects of radical disengagement, returns (and is returned) to a more commonsensical, more politically grounded self.

A SOCIAL PHILOSOPHY

So far we have seen how Douglass engages the quandary of self-consciousness – how he argues for intellectual equality by displaying his reflective capacities, how such reflection momentarily leads to a disembodied subjectivity, and how the political demands upon Douglass bring him back to a more material self. It might seem like an indictment of metaphysics in total. Theoretical abstraction turns out to be culturally embedded and prejudicial, while Douglass's commitment to enlightened self-knowledge traps him within a liberal individualism as reflection, egoistically pursued, forms the basis for a concept of freedom understood as self-possession. Making oneself objective can even look like Althusserian interpellation. When Collins hails Douglass as a black ex-slave, Douglass resents but answers the call as his subjectivity constitutes and is constituted by an ideology that grants him his humanity only if he accepts a reified self. Yet as much as Douglass critiques transcendence, *My Bondage and My Freedom* does not abandon metaphysics, in part because commonsense helps Douglass temper the threat of atomism.[64]

If, as Locke argued, individual experience is the only evidence of external reality, and if the prison of our perceptions denies any intersubjective verification of the senses, then consciousness becomes so discrete as to verge on solipsism. Poe entertains this possibility to a point where delusion and reality are hard to disentangle. As seen in chapter 2,

63 John Dewey, "I Believe" (1939), in *The Later Works of John Dewey, 1925–1953, Vol. 14: 1939–1941, Essays*, ed. Jo Ann Boydston, *et. al.* (Carbondale, Ill.: Southern Illinois University Press, 1988), 92.

64 For criticisms of Douglass's individualism, see Houston J. Baker, Jr., *The Journey Back: Issues in Black Literature and Criticism* (Chicago: University of Chicago Press, 1980), 32–46; and Leverenz, *Manhood and the American Renaissance*, 108–34. Critics who emphasize Douglass's communal work include Sundquist, *To Wake the Nations*; and Rowe, *At Emerson's Tomb*, 96–123.

sentimental thinkers such as Adam Smith and the Beecher sisters answer the challenge by offering sympathy as a means for affective connection. Reid and his associates also posited an intersubjective faculty, but they relied less on moral sentiment and more on commonsense, less on the authority of emotion and more on the claim that there is no reason to doubt primary perceptions. As George Davie notes, this argument can take "a definitely linguistic form."[65] Though his followers would sometimes smudge the point, Reid did not precisely believe that language proves common sense. By definition, axioms cannot be proven, but the fact that language works in experience shows that skepticism is unnecessary. As Reid put it, "The first principles of all science are the dictates of commonsense, and lie open to all men; and every man who has considered the structure of language in a philosophical light, will find infallible proofs that those who have framed it with understanding, have the power of making distinctions." For Reid, language is a reliable, egalitarian basis for truth-claims. It also offers relief from atomism, for the common structures of language "must be owing to some common notion or sentiment of the human mind," indicating that "The Author of our being intended us to be social."[66]

However, what was for Reid self-evident is a tenuous proposition in *My Bondage and My Freedom*, which worries that slavery negates the power of words and leads to a kind of social death understood as atomism. James McCune Smith condemned chattel bondage as an alienating system that "arrests the intercourse of mind with mind" and serves to "isolate human thought."[67] When Douglass is forbidden to read, he also associates isolation with "the true philosophy of slavery," one of the many moments in *My Bondage and My Freedom* when language painfully fails (217). Remembering his siblings and his initiation into slavery, Douglass writes, "The experience through which I was passing, they had passed through before" (149). But despite these common ties, "*[S]lavery* had made us strangers," in part because "the words brothers and sister" were "robbed" of their "true meaning." Such "non-intercourse" continues on Covey's farm when Douglass again discontinues his reading and is nearly "transformed into a brute," dramatizing Reid's point that without language humans would be

---

65 George Davie, *The Scotch Metaphysics: A Century of Enlightenment in Scotland* (New York: Routledge, 2001), 91–94. See also Patrick Rysiew's "Reid and Epistemic Naturalism," *The Philosophical Quarterly* 52 (Oct. 2002), 437–56, esp. 445.
66 Reid, *Essays on the Powers of the Human Mind*, 2: 291; Reid, *Intellectual Powers*, 56, 69.
67 Smith, "Civilization: Its Dependence on Physical Circumstances," 15.

entirely solitary and "as mute as the beasts of the field" (170, 268).[68]
Douglass fears that he "shall never be able to narrate [his] mental experience," in part because Covey's farm is a world of unnatural law (269).
Reid held that "no instance will be found of a distinction made in all
languages, which has not a just foundation in nature."[69] Thus the non-
sensical language at Covey's points to the injustice of slavery when
Douglass complains, "[W]hat is the reason for [the] distinction in names,
when there is none in the things themselves?" (261).

Even Douglass's victory over Covey does not end his isolation and
linguistic anxiety. After leaving the slave-breaker, Douglass finds succor
with the "brother slaves" he teaches to read (300–1); and he commences
his career in "public speaking" by exhorting them to escape (306). But
when their plot is foiled, Douglass is imprisoned and separated from his
friends, leaving him again "entirely alone" and "solitary in the world"
(323–24). Douglass's escape from chattel bondage is an escape from such
isolation, though the self-possession of his new freedom entails another
form of alienation. In the North, Douglass enjoys "a state of independence, beyond seeking friendship or support of any man" (358), though he
also feels like a "perfect stranger" in "the midst of human brothers," even
in the midst of freeborn blacks who "cannot see things in the same light
with the slave, because he does not, and cannot, look from the same
point" (351–52). Suddenly the freedom of liberal individualism threatens
to slide into atomism as an earlier lesson in epistemology – that "the point
from which a thing is viewed is of some importance" – jeopardizes the
possibility of intersubjectivity.

This danger is especially telling in Douglass's "Letter to His Old
Master" (1848), a text included in the appendix of *My Bondage and
My Freedom*. Douglass, who would visit Thomas Auld after the Civil
War, writes to the man who held him in bondage and still retained some
sort of hold:

I am myself; you are yourself; we are two distinct persons. . . . Nature does not
make your existence depend upon me, or mine to depend upon yours. I cannot
walk upon your legs, or you upon mine. I cannot breathe for you, or you for me;
I must breathe for myself, and you for yourself. We are distinct persons, and are
each equally provided with faculties necessary to our individual existence. In
leaving you, I took nothing but what belonged to me. (414)

---

68 Reid, *Intellectual Powers*, 69.
69 Quoted in Davie, *The Scotch Metaphysicis*, 92 (essay 1, chapter 1, *Works* with notes by William
    Hamilton [Edinburgh: James Thin, 1895], 224, 362).

This emphatic, repetitive, curious passage, nearly ironic in its insistence on such seemingly self-evident truths as autonomous walking and breathing, shows Douglass fighting for his mind, for his very subjectivity, to a point where he denies shared faculties – not only with Auld, but (as we have seen) with his siblings and every born freeman.

As powerfully as any American writer, Douglass constructs what Smith calls a "majestic selfhood"; but what makes *My Bondage and My Freedom* so dialectically compelling is that Douglass recognizes extreme individualism as a political and philosophical danger (126). In England in 1848, he quoted Robert Burns, "O wad some power the giftie gie us, / To see oursels as others see us"; and in *My Bondage and My Freedom*, he continues to worry, "Men seldom see themselves as others see them" (308).[70] As discrete subjectivity threatens the prospect of accurate self-knowledge, Douglass turns to other minds, admitting that to know oneself one must to some degree rely upon the validating perceptions of others. Or as Douglass said when praising photography in "Pictures and Progress," "Men of all conditions may see themselves as others see them."[71] This possibility, however, is an anxious one for Frederick Douglass the self-educated fugitive slave whose identity fell under constant scrutiny from unsympathetic observers. Douglass has good reason to steer between atomism and social definition, between the isolated freedom of self-possession and the bondage of an invidiously circumscribed self. Douglass is torn by this dualism throughout *My Bondage and My Freedom* as his communities are shattered by chattel bondage, throwing him into lonely self-reliance, which eventually gives way to other communities that are in turn disrupted. Douglass renders in dramatic fashion what he calls the "terrible extremities of slavery" (270). And in the closest thing to a climax of the book, he envisions a synthesis of self and society in the representative orator, whose commonsense language forges a community that the speaker himself controls.

When describing his first impression of Garrison in "Introduced to the Abolitionists," Douglass presents a theory of eloquence, subjectivity, and power: "[Garrison] possessed that almost fabulous inspiration, often referred to but seldom attained, in which a public meeting is transformed, as it were, into a single individuality – the orator wielding a thousand heads and hearts at once, and by the simple majesty of his all controlling thought, converting his hearers into the express image of his own soul"

70 *FDP* 2: 120.
71 *FDP* 3: 454.

(365). As a participant in what James Warren calls the antebellum "culture of eloquence," Douglass discovers in the orator the representative man who does not so much sympathetically imagine himself in the place of others, but who subsumes his listeners by shaping their subjectivity to his own.[72] Because the speaker draws on nature and thus touches the common nature of his audience, individual listeners are "transformed" into a "single individuality" through an intersubjective eloquence wielded by the speaker's "all controlling thought."

Robert Levine has detailed Douglass's efforts to establish a representative identity; the point here is that this work has roots in Scottish commonsense.[73] Douglass's faith in the "express image" of eloquence shares with Reid the mimetic belief that "[l]anguage is the express image and picture of human thoughts."[74] Douglass also follows Reid's colleague, Hugh Blair, whose celebrated *Lectures on Rhetoric and Belles Lettres* (1776) held that the best form of speech moves men by appealing to their natural faculties and, hence, that oratory is "very nearly connected with the philosophy of the human mind."[75] Caleb Bingham's *Columbian Orator* (1797), that "rich treasure" of Douglass's youth, borrows much of its introduction from Blair's longer and more metaphysical work (225). James McCune Smith also calls oratory a "mental phenomenon" (135). Thus Reid, Blair, Bingham, Smith, and Douglass all espouse a rhetorical theory grounded in Scottish realism, as did many antebellum intellectuals, including even romantics such as Emerson and Thoreau.[76]

By supplying both a faculty for intersubjectivity and a means for swaying other minds, Scottish commonsense proved particularly amenable to Douglass's abolitionist designs. In many ways, this is not surprising. William Paley's influential textbook, *Principles of Moral and Political Philosophy* (1785), cited Adam Ferguson when arguing against the institution of slavery. Another commonsense thinker, the American Francis Wayland – whom Douglass dubbed, "The great Doctor" – took a clear

---

72 James Perrin Warren, *Culture of Eloquence: Oratory and Reform in Antebellum America* (University Park, Penn: The Pennsylvania State University, Press, 1999).
73 Levine, *Politics of Representative Identity.*
74 Reid, *Intellectual Powers*, 45.
75 Hugh Blair, *Lectures on Rhetoric and Belles Lettres* (1776; Philadelphia: T. Ellwood Zell, 1860), 94.
76 Note that Lawrence Buell discusses how the commonsense of antebellum oratory tends to restrain the individualism of American romanticism (*New England Literary Culture: From Revolution Through Renaissance* [New York: Cambridge University Press, 1986], 154). For the popularity of Blair and Bingham in America, see Kenneth Cmiel, *Democratic Eloquence: The Fight over Popular Speech in Nineteenth-Century America* (New York: William Morrow, 1990), 40–46.

antislavery stand in his *Elements of Moral Science* (1835). This otherwise popular textbook was banned by colleges in the South, inspiring a Virginian professor to cry to his impressionable charges, "I dare not give up your minds to the dominion of Wayland's Philosophy." Moreover, when Charles Dickens in 1842 called for emancipation in America, he appealed to "every human mind, imbued with the commonest of common-sense, and the commonest of common humanity," thereby voicing antislavery sentiments in the idiom of Scottish realism. The antislavery movement and commonsense philosophy both flourished between the late-eighteenth and middle-nineteenth centuries; and though this does not necessitate a causal relation, it does suggest continuities, particularly when abolitionists described their enemies as "blundering metaphysicians" and decried the peculiar institution as "an insult to commonsense."[77]

And yet Scottish realism should not be mistaken for an inherently liberating system, a point that Cugoano made as early as 1787 by linking "Scotch floggers and negro drivers" to the "brutish philosophy" of some Scottish thinkers.[78] That same year, the framers of the U.S. Constitution drew upon the Scottish Enlightenment and still managed to countenance slavery, while fifty years later chattel bondage survived in an era of commonsense philosophy. When Wayland's *Elements of Moral Science* strayed onto abolitionist ground, the South Carolinian Jasper Adams responded with *The Elements of Moral Philosophy* (1837), a book that retained Scottish commonsense but jettisoned Wayland's antislavery views. Indeed, the very year that *My Bondage* turned to Scottish realism, Henry Hotz called upon the "commonsense of mankind" to argue the rectitude of slavery.[79]

"Bartleby, the Scrivener" (1853) nicely underscores the oppressive potential of Scottish realism when Melville's not-quite-benevolent narrator appeals to Bartleby's "common sense" when he tries to convince the recalcitrant scrivener to crosscheck the accuracy of copied documents.[80] Scottish realists, like Bartleby's boss, sought to integrate atomistic identities

---

77 Paley, *The Principles of Moral and Political Philosophy*, x; Francis Wayland, *The Elements of Moral Science*, ed. Joseph Blau (1835; Cambridge: Belknap Press of Harvard University Press, 1963), xliii; Douglass, *Life and Times*, 813; William Smith, *Lectures on the Philosophy and Practice of Slavery* (Nashville: Stevenson and Evans, 1856), 29. Charles Dickens, *American Notes* (1842; Köln: Könemann, 2000), 281. "Doctrines of the Southern Democracy," *The National Era* 11 (April 23, 1857): 66. For abolitionism and the Scottish Enlightenment, see also Thomas, *Romanticism and Slave Narratives*, 19–29.
78 Cugoano, *Thoughts and Sentiments*, 178–79.
79 Hotz, introduction to Gobineau, 93.
80 Melville, "Bartleby, the Scrivener" (1853), in *The Piazza Tales and Other Prose Pieces*, 22.

within a consensual society, inventing commonsense to guarantee that everyone was on the same epistemological page. But if minds do not compare their experiences, a threat figured by Bartleby's refusal or inability to crosscheck documents, then individual minds become solipsistic and commonsense becomes merely a word for the opinion of those with the power to enforce it. The narrator of "Bartleby" uses his authority to profit from a kind of wage slavery; and when he places a folding-screen in his office so that he need not see Bartleby unless he needs his labor, the supposed intersubjectivity of Scottish realism is revealed as an asymmetrical convenience. Considered in this way, Scottish commonsense actually hindered the abolitionist movement, for enemies and even sympathetic friends believed that if anyone lacked commonsense it was the ultra abolitionists themselves.

Tempting as it may be, it is tricky to generalize about the cultural work of the Enlightenment, even when inquiry is limited to a specific era, philosophy, and issue. In historical practice, Scottish realism was put to both anti- and pro-slavery ends; and though metaphysicians of the commonsense school took pride in the social utility of their thought, they offered few intellectual mechanisms for mediating conflicting political views. In the barely united states of America, this was a huge liability; for as the slavery debate became increasingly punctuated by various voices repeating more loudly their divergent and supposedly commonsense truths, the nation hardly supported the notion of a shared subjectivity. Antebellum Americans and later historians have certainly blamed fanatic idealists for the breakdown of the slavery dialogue. As David Blight has shown, this strategy helped the country repress divisive issues of slavery and race.[81] More indicative, however, of the failure of ideas in America before the Civil War is the fact that the slavery crisis frustrated the country's most popular, most normative metaphysic, which could not maintain a philosophical premise no more radical than this: that people see the world in similar ways and can come to some sort of agreement. Douglass does find in Scottish commonsense a theory of eloquence, personal identity, and reformist intersubjectivity. Nonetheless, for all his metaphysical work, he experienced the insufficiency of reason when his philosophy could not enact the ostensibly self-evident claims of commonsense.

81 Capper, "A Little Beyond," 18–20; David Blight, *Race and Reunion: The Civil War in American Memory* (Cambridge: Belknap Press of Harvard University Press, 2001).

FIRE AND LIGHT

Whether battling mobs for control of the podium, throwing off the yoke of Garrisonian suppression, filibustering black abolitionist meetings, or writing three autobiographies (the last of which he reissued in expanded form), Douglass insists on having his say. One might even add, *and then some.* An interpretive challenge of *My Bondage and My Freedom* is that Douglass's dedication to speech overrides his urge for concluding totality, particularly when the book presses beyond what a likeable teacher might assign in a week. That said, the appendix to *My Bondage and My Freedom* deserves somewhat more than passing attention, not only because the selected speeches are themselves remarkable performances, but because they show Douglass's stubborn commitment to the unfinished promise of Scottish commonsense. Frustrated by the impossible task of proving self-evident truth, the appendix to *My Bondage and My Freedom* takes up the difficult question of what an abolitionist orator should do when common moral faculties fail.

Taken together, Douglass's speeches tell the story of a crisis of philosophical faith. In "The Nature of Slavery" (1850), Douglass invokes a popular abolitionist trope, "Conscience is, to the individual soul, and to society, what the law of gravitation is to the universe" (421). Douglass predicts that the end of slavery is as sure as the fall of Newton's apple, a claim that figures abolition as a scientific principle in what Douglass would later call "the moral Chemistry of the universe."[82] But what happens when apples do not drop? When the law of conscience falters? Or as Douglass worries (as does Stowe) in the "Inhumanity of Slavery" (1850), what does one do when chattel bondage appears to "deaden the moral sense" (427)? Though there is a technical difference between Francis Hutcheson's moral sense and the commonsense of Reid, the concepts are compatible and easily conflated insofar as they treat morals as an extension of mental philosophy.[83] In both systems, humans have the power to recognize moral truths, even if bad habits and faulty institutions temporarily blind their faculties. Thus if what Smith calls the "unnatural

---

82 *FDP* 3: 479.
83 In brief, Hutcheson (as well as Shaftesbury and the ethically oriented work of Hume) describes moral sense as a faculty that determines moral questions after – and, thus, as a function of – perception. Reid objects, however, because such perceptions are not "necessary truths" and as such are subject to change and interpretation. Reid precludes this mutability with his notion of commonsense, which guarantees the accuracy of perception prior to moral decision-making. See J. B. Schneewind, *The Invention of Autonomy: A History of Modern Moral Philosophy* (Cambridge: Cambridge University Press, 1998), 395–403.

thing slavery" is indeed the sum of all villainies, then it should not survive, let alone flourish, in a Scottish commonsense universe (134). The problem is that with the Fugitive Slave Law and the looming expansion of the slavery empire, Douglass and other abolitionists became impatient for the fulfillment of first principles.

Douglass's bitterness famously erupts in "What to the Slave is the Fourth of July?" (1852), a speech that exemplifies and critiques the limitations of moral reasoning. In startling prose that Douglass labels his "severest language," "What to the Slave?" indulges a tone that flies in the face of those who tell Douglass to "argue more, and denounce less" (432). Douglass responds:

> I submit, where all is plain there is nothing to be argued. What point in the anti-slavery creed would you have me argue? On what branch of the subject do the people of this country need light? Must I undertake to prove that the slave is a man? . . . Would you have me argue that man is entitled to liberty? that he is the rightful owner of his own body? . . . Must I argue the wrongfulness of slavery? . . . Is it to be settled by the rules of logic and argumentation, as a matter beset with great difficulty, involving a doubtful application of the principle of justice, hard to be understood? How should I look today in the presence of Americans, dividing and subdividing a discourse? (432–33)

Such strident speech seemingly lifts outrage over logic. Yet even as Douglass scorns to defend what appears to him self-evident, he simultaneously pursues, as Charles Mills shows, a sustained discursive strategy.[84] Is the slave "a man?" Does he possess "equal manhood?" Might not he then be "entitled to liberty?" Is this even "a question for republicans?" What, indeed, remains to be argued?

Hardly a treatise to be sure, but as Stowe showed in *Uncle Tom's Cabin* and as Garrison knew early on, the most effective abolitionist rhetoric tended to assert moral principles that, for abolitionists at least, required no rational support. First appearing in the 1840s and reprinted in 1852, Garrison's "Harsh Language – Retarding the Cause" is a likely influence on "What to the Slave is the Fourth of July?" Garrison marvels, "Argue, indeed! What is the proposition to be discussed? It is this: whether all men are created free and equal, and have an inalienable right to liberty! I am urged to argue this with a people, who declare it to be a self-evident truth!"[85] Like Douglass, Garrison understands the limits of argumentation as he stubbornly holds that self-evident truths are precisely that. This

84 Mills, "Whose Fourth of July?"
85 Garrison, "Harsh Language," 127.

is why Garrison often passes by logic and proceeds directly to indictments of bad faith, "[W]e know, you know, the slaveholder knows, the slave knows, and everybody in this country, in heaven and hell knows that we are right." Moreover, "There are certain moral propositions which need no argument of proof."[86] No wonder that anti-abolitionist thinkers such as Albert Bledsoe lamented, "[I]t is to be regretted – deeply regretted – that the doctrine of liberty has so often been, . . . for the most part, a theme for passionate declamation, rather than of severe analysis or of protracted and patient investigation."[87]

The problem for both Stowe and Douglass was that chattel bondage had long been subjected to rigorous inquiry only to reveal that moral absolutes could not be logically demonstrated. This may come as no surprise to an age attuned to contingency. But for the vast majority of antebellum thinkers troubled by even the whiff of moral relativism, the slavery impasse often resulted in a rededication to absolute claims. By now the limits of this position should be clear. One might allow Reid's point against Hume that humans in fact possess consciousness; personal identity is a compelling idea to the point of Cartesian self-evidence. That slavery should be abolished, however, proved to be less obvious; for despite exposure to philosophically grounded (if relatively mild) antislavery views, many a reader of Wayland and Paley had yet to hear the commonsense whistle and board the abolitionist train. What then is a reformer like Douglass to do? What can he do after repeatedly failing to invoke a single individuality from his hostile and indifferent countrymen who, in flagrant disregard of supposedly obvious truths, do not fall finally under the sway of abolitionist law?

Even as Douglass becomes more comfortable countenancing violent resistance, and even as political stances hardened in both North and South, his response to the inadequacy of commonsense is not a rejection of natural law, but rather a very literary commitment to more pressing and more moving words. "[I]t is not light that is needed, but fire," Douglass writes in "What to the Slave is the Fourth of July?" as he agitates in a mode that is only rhetorically incendiary (434). Douglass's cry that the time for argument has passed contains its own formidable argument insofar as the failure of logic supports the self-evidence of his

---

86 Garrison quoted in Ottilie Assing, "An Antislavery Meeting" (1854), in *Radical Passion: Ottilie Assing's Reports from America and Letters to Frederick Douglass*, ed. and trans. Christoph Lohmann (New York: Peter Lang, 1999), 36; William Lloyd Garrison, "War Essentially Wrong," in *Selections from the Writings and Speeches*, 89.
87 Albert Taylor Bledsoe, *An Essay on Liberty and Slavery* (Philadelphia: J. B. Lippincott, 1856), 10.

position. "What to the Slave is the Fourth of July?" addresses the crisis of moral authority by carefully curtailing discursive inquiry and asserting the truth of what Hugh Miller called "that commonsense . . . which reasons but does not argue."[88] Thus even when Douglass appears to deny the explanatory power of logic, he works within a Scottish tradition that held that first principles cannot be demonstrated and that has been labeled with the tense but telling term of rational intuitionist philosophy.

The difference is that Douglass deploys a language that most common-sense thinkers could not abide. By burning off the dross of debate with the fire of his words, he ignores Blair's imperative that the speaker "must always preserve regard to what the public ear will bear," a circumspection of little reformist use during a national crisis in which the opinion of a misguided multitude threatened to define commonsense.[89] Douglass, Garrison, Phillips, Delany, Theodore Parker, Theodore Weld, Sojourner Truth, and the Grimké sisters all had to defend their language from charges of inflammatory rhetoric lodged, not only by their opponents, but by more diffident antislavery figures. In a fractious debate that often centered on the proper forms and usages of argument, "What to the Slave is the Fourth of July?" remains a radical performance. Yet almost as if to remind his audience of the various voices at his disposal, and not to conclude on as polemic a note as many anthologies wish, *My Bondage and My Freedom* proceeds with familiar and even inveterate excursus as the question of closure is left to the final impression of Douglass's words.

My Bondage and My Freedom ends with the "The Anti-Slavery Movement" (1855), a speech reinforcing Douglass's status as a fugitive, willful philosopher. Though Delany had recently ridiculed the "chattering" of "moral theorists," Douglass begins by linking abolitionism to "the proper study of man through all time" (445).[90] Phillips indulged a similar impulse in the "Philosophy of the Abolitionist Movement" (1853), as did Thoreau in "Slavery in Massachusetts" (1854) and Emerson in "American Slavery" (1855). In what seems an effort to supersede his one-time ally Phillips,

---

88 Miller, *My Schools and Schoolmasters*, 354–5. Miller's formulation draws from Reid's basic point, "[W]hen we attempt to prove by direct argument, what is really self-evident, the reasoning will always be inconclusive; for it will either take for granted the thing proved, or something not more evident" (*Essays on the Powers of the Human Mind*, 3: 441).

89 Blair, *Rhetoric*, 290. See also Peabody's complaint of Douglass, "His associates at the North have been among those who are apt to mistake violence and extravagance of expression and denunciation for eloquence . . . To him they have doubtless been true and faithful friends, and he naturally adopts their style of speech. But it is a mistaken one, if the speaker wishes to sway the judgment of his hearers and accomplish any practical end" ("Narratives of Fugitives Slaves," 75).

90 Delany, *The Condition, Elevation, Emigration and Destiny*, 15.

Douglass states his own metaphysical goal, "We might, for instance, proceed to inquire not only into the philosophy of the antislavery movement, but into the philosophy of the law, in obedience to which that movement started into existence" (446). For Douglass, the antislavery cause points to a more primary cause, "that law or power" which "disposes the minds of men to this or that particular object – now for peace, and now for war – now for freedom, and now for slavery." Though Douglass made juridical arguments against slavery, here he focuses on higher law. He presents the slavery crisis as a subject for mental philosophy, as a phenomenon that exemplifies the "law" that governs "the minds of men." "The Anti-Slavery Movement" in this way aspires to grand metaphysical heights, though at some point the Delany-like reader might object to Douglass's rarefied flight.

Perhaps Douglass should attack chattel bondage by all means, including philosophy. Perhaps such work might vindicate the intellectual capacities of blacks. Yet just as some critics doubt the efficacy of transcendental antislavery efforts, and just as philosophy (in the words of Charles Mills) still faces the charge that it is "really a sham" mystifying "real problems," one might worry that by choosing metaphysical light over rhetorical fire "The Anti-Slavery Movement" forgets that slavery remains first and foremost a physical fact.[91] Douglass might be defended on the grounds that philosophy has real political consequences, that despite attempts to define abolitionism in strictly material terms, the point still stands that some reformers were driven by abstract ideals.[92] One might also exonerate Douglass's thinking with the countercharge that barring him from philosophical inquiry reenacts the racism of Collins. Douglass, however, is perfectly capable of defending his metaphysics himself, which "The Anti-slavery Movement" does in the manner of a fugitive philosopher.

After calling the abolitionist cause an "open book, in which are the records of time and eternity" (445), Douglass abruptly appears to renounce his philosophical work:

[B]ut this profound question I leave to the abolitionists of the superior class to answer. The speculations which must precede such answer, would afford, perhaps, about the same satisfaction as the learned theories which have rained down upon the world, from time to time, as to the origin of evil. I shall, therefore, avoid water in which I cannot swim, and deal with anti-slavery as a fact. (446)

91 Charles Mills, *Blackness Visible*, 4.
92 *The Antislavery Debate: Capitalism and Abolitionism as a Problem in Historical Interpretation*, ed. Thomas Bender (Berkeley: University of California Press, 1992).

Here "superior class" should be read with a smirk. So, too, should Douglass's seeming disregard for "learned theories" of evil. And by the time Douglass makes the claim that he cannot swim in philosophical waters, a reader might wonder with a repetition that suggests an authorial design: Is Douglass unwilling, unable, or prohibited from entering such deep discourse? Is he really content to say again, "But, let others philosophize"?

Such disclaimers seem to me a kind of practical joke in that Douglass simultaneously accepts and decries the impositions placed on his speech. After noting that the antislavery cause is a veritable book of higher law, Douglass decides for ambiguous reasons and with some measure of irony not to read it, even though he announces the philosophy of abolitionism as the very topic of his text. This profound subject is, *of course*, left for superior thinkers as Douglass proceeds to what he presents as his more modest appointment – to summon the "one individual man" whose office is "to exemplify, and to illustrate, and to ingraft principles upon the living and practical understanding of all men" (447). This representative man of eloquence, suspiciously resembling Douglass himself, appeals to the commonsense of his listeners, for "[i]n whatever else men may differ, they are alike in the apprehension of their natural and personal rights" (448). For Douglass, all humans are born knowing freedom. All share the same perceptive "apprehension" (an important term for Reid).[93] And it is "the grand secret" of abolitionism's force that "each of its principles is easily rendered appreciable to the faculty of reason in man." With this emphasis on natural law and universal rational capacities, and by implying that to render a truth appreciable is not precisely to argue, Douglass's representative man touches a common faculty that is not dead but rather in need of eloquent awakening.

Even further, and despite his stated disdain for learned theories of evil, Douglass explains the mysterious iniquity of the anti-abolitionist: "Contemplating himself, he sees truth with absolute clearness and distinctness. He only blunders when asked to lose sight of himself" – to turn, as it were, from atomistic reflection to intersubjective ethics, and to negotiate the historically treacherous path from metaphysics to morals. Unlike the later Stowe, Douglass does not see this failure as an absence of moral faculties, a point he makes in the body of *My Bondage and My Freedom* when he watches his master (and possible father) whip his cousin Hester.

93 In brief, Reid uses "apprehension" to denote an idea that one has specifically and directly in mind (as opposed to a "concept," which can refer to an abstract belief).

Douglass reflects, "I did not, at that time, understand the philosophy of his treatment of my cousin. . . . Was he dead to all sense of humanity? No. I think I now understand it. This treatment is a part of the system, rather than a part of the man" (174). Despite the impediment of chattel bondage and the temporary paralysis of moral faculties, despite the rendition of fugitive slaves and the bloody fighting in Kansas, *My Bondage and My Freedom* yet believes in the victory of commonsense and the power of the eloquent man to bring moral recognition to pass.

In retrospect, Douglass was too optimistic. As the pragmatists would come to assert, metaphysics must always be *a priori*, capable of confirming only those truths that individuals already believe. The Civil War testifies to the teleological and political weaknesses of the commonsense system, which Douglass seems to suspect as early as "What to the Slave is the Fourth of July?" One might wish that *My Bondage and My Freedom* end with this thunderous speech, that with America headed for war Douglass conclude with an urgent fire of prophetic militancy and not a patient philosophical light encircling even his enemies. The last word, however, of *My Bondage and My Freedom* remains "The Anti-slavery Movement," a speech that returns to Scottish commonsense and represents Douglass's faith in his era's philosophy. Though *My Bondage* explores transcendental subjectivity and moves toward partisan resistance, when Douglass's excursive dialectical intellect must find a way to stop itself, it ends by affirming the natural ability of all humankind to perceive and pursue absolute moral truths within a rational, intersubjective, and (as Gregg Crane emphasizes) a consensually governed community.[94]

In the course of Douglass's long life, events would challenge such views. The Civil War came, reconstruction failed, and natural law gave way to Darwinism, evincing the slogan of one Union regiment, "No argument but the mouth of the cannon!"[95] The War made Douglass a more partisan, less forgiving thinker.[96] His increasing commitment to expediency and growing frustration with inclusive rhetoric suggest that he loses some conviction in the reformist capacities of rational debate. Douglass's work during and after the War, including his *Life and Times*, tends to emphasize practical, institutional gains, thus tracing through the later-nineteenth century the ebb of metaphysics in America. It is hard to blame Douglass for backing away from the philosophy of *My Bondage and*

---

94 Crane, *Race, Citizenship, and Law*, 114.
95 Undated recruiting poster for New York's "Fighting Zoaves" regiment (The Gettysburg National Battlefield Museum, Gettysburg, Penn.).
96 Blight, *Frederick Douglass's Civil War*.

My Freedom. The War did not rouse common faculties, and the supposed consensus of reunion was achieved at the expense of African-Americans. For all the talk of providential victory and binding up the nation's wounds, the country that Douglass imagined reborn in righteous agreement was not to be found. Testifying to Douglass's philosophical convictions is that he still believed in commonsense in 1855, even if his redoubled metaphysical efforts betray the suspicion that he might be wrong.

CODA

In the early 1830s, the black abolitionist Maria Stewart asked her African-American audience, "Where can we find among ourselves the man of science, or a philosopher?" The impetus of her challenge was clear, "Prove to the world that you are neither ourang-outangs, or a species of mere animals, but that you possess the same powers of intellect as the proud-boasting American."[97] Stewart's correlation of humanity and intelligence typifies enlightenment thinking, which largely defined "universal" equality and its attendant natural and political rights over and against less rational beings such as apes and, in many minds, blacks. Stewart hoped to vindicate African intelligence with a mastery of (among other things) philosophy; and better than any black antebellum thinker, Douglass answered the call. In *My Bondage and My Freedom*, Douglass resists but largely assumes a subjectivity based on the Lockean, liberal premise that the self is primary, rationally knowable, and metaphysically fixed. Over the course of *My Bondage and My Freedom*, Douglass complicates this position. He certainly chastises those who dwell on his body and not his mind, who speak the brotherly words of universality but whisper in racialist dualisms. Douglass also explores the paradox of reflection and the problem of moral authority, both of which expose fundamental instabilities within the empire of reason. Yet Douglass still finds in Scottish commonsense a politically useful philosophy. Despite his objections to learned disquisitions, and despite his use of a special root from the "genuine African" Sandy, little suggests that Douglass sees racism as inherent to Western rationalism, nor does he, for all his attention to the inescapable materiality of color, advocate an alternative epistemology based on essentialist concepts of race (280).

97 Maria Stewart, "Religion and the Pure Principles of Morality, The Sure Foundation on Which We Must Build" (1831) and "An Address Delivered at the African Masonic Hall" (1833), in *America's First Black Woman Political Writer: Essays and Speeches,* ed. Marilyn Richardson (Bloomington: Indiana University Press, 1987), 57, 40.

What Douglass does is strenuously oppose the oppressive application of philosophy. He seems to know (in Goldberg's words) that race is "integral to articulating the common sense of modernity's self-under-standing"; but even his most strident attacks on the practical failures of philosophy place him within an enlightenment strain of self-critical lament over what Tocqueville wistfully called America's "ideal but always fugitive perfection."[98] In *My Bondage and My Freedom*, the project of enlightenment remains scandalously unfinished; and so when Douglass calls to end its deferment, he does not despair of universalist thought, a commitment that Wilson J. Moses and Ross Posnock find in subsequent black intellectuals.[99] Douglass's balancing ultimately leans in the direction of assimilation. Still, it is not entirely unlike that of his occasional antagonist Delany, who formulated essentialist concepts of race and "*reasonably* reason[ed]" against "the white man's . . . 'book knowledge,'" while still hoping to redeem the egalitarian promise of what he called the "enlightened age of the world."[100] Douglass's dedication to Scottish commonsense sets him within the dominant metaphysic of his age, except for – or as is emphasized here, *because of* – the fact that he was a black who suffered from his nation's failure to honor the better imperatives of its intellectual heritage. For Douglass, metaphysics is extravagant only when it forgets about physical conditions, when it neglects the relation of theory and experience and aspires instead to an ideal purity at the expense of political facts. Thus Douglass is a critic of enlightenment in at least two senses of the term: He is critical of its unrealized potential, and his critique is a feature of enlightenment thought.

The extent of Douglass's philosophical salience will probably remain open to a measure of conjecture – if only because discourse must do some of the work more precisely performed by source study, if only because as (Kwame Anthony Appiah suggests) the label of philosophy is always hard to affix.[101] Considering, however, the racist proscriptions under which Douglass labored, it seems fitting to notice the word or two that he provides for our proper understanding. This is particularly true because

98 David Goldberg, "Racial Classification and Public Policy," in *A Companion to African–American Philosophy*, 255; Tocqueville, *Democracy in America*, 1: 420.

99 Wilson J. Moses, *The Golden Age of Black Nationalism, 1850–1925* (New York: Oxford University Press, 1978); Ross Posnock, *Color and Culture: Black Writers and the Making of the Modern Intellectual* (Cambridge: Harvard University Press, 1998).

100 Martin Delany, "Official Report of the Niger Valley Exploring Party" (1859), in *Martin R. Delany: A Reader*, 348; Delany, "Political Destiny of the Colored Race," 265.

101 Anthony Appiah, *In My Father's House: Africa in the Philosophy of Culture* (New York: Oxford University Press, 1992), 88–89.

commonsense is both a scholarly and vernacular concept that, for Reid, "puts the Philosopher and the peasant upon a level."[102] Reid's statement indicates egalitarian intent but assumes that peasants are not philosophers, pointing to both the liberating and prejudicial potential of the Scottish Enlightenment. Reid's claim also demonstrates a main tension in commonsense thought, which is simultaneously committed to formal metaphysics and suspicious of its sophistic power, simultaneously dedicated to abstract reasoning and its need to be tempered by experience.

Considered in this light, the appeal and shortcoming of the Scottish position is that it curtails epistemological problems on which metaphysics can founder. Subject–object dualism, intersubjectivity, the impossibility of proving absolute moral truths – these quandaries bedeviled nineteenth-century philosophers and today survive in variant forms. Positing a self-evident faculty whose explanatory power depends on the fact that it cannot by definition be argued, the commonsense answer to debilitating skepticism may not always pass logical muster, particularly if it is taken to be the diluted version taught to antebellum students who were expected to become, not Humean doubters or ever-excursive romantics, but rather productive Protestant citizens ready to take part in the world. It should be no surprise that formal education was this early a grease to the wheels of conformity and that the complacent and even authoritarian tendencies of Scottish commonsense made it an attractive way of thinking in antebellum America. Moral philosophers of the eighteenth and nineteenth centuries happily depended on God and convention, while for many the task of reconciling metaphysics and daily experience was not best served by erecting a wall between philosophy and lived life. Scottish commonsense could be complacent, but it also influenced more innovative thinkers of the nineteenth century, who are typically taken to better prefigure more modern subjectivities. As discussed in chapter 1, Coleridge helped to bring Kant's thought to the English-speaking world, but his *Lecture on the Slave Trade* (1795) appeals to "common sense" when condemning chattel bondage.[103] In their experimental moods, New England transcendentalists resist the empiricism of Dugald Stewart and Reid; but when the dialectic of double consciousness makes its material demands – in Emerson's antislavery works, in Fuller's writings on reform, and for Thoreau on Ktaadn – moral law, moral sentiment, and commonsense

---

102 Reid, *Intellectual Powers*, 193.
103 Samuel Taylor Coleridge, "Lecture on the Slave-Trade" (1795), in *The Collected Works of Samuel Taylor Coleridge: Lectures 1795 on Politics and Religion*, vol. 1, ed. Lewis Patton and Peter Mann (Princeton: Princeton University Press, 1971), 251.

come to stabilize radical subjectivity as even transcendentalists learn to treat some occasions and criteria as if they were real.

The same is true of some classical pragmatists, who slighted but did not entirely banish metaphysics from their midst. Charles Peirce associated "commonsense" with "that bad logical quality to which the epithet *metaphysical* is commonly applied." At the same time, he argued in "The Fixation of Belief" (1877):

There are real things, whose characters are entirely independent of our opinions about them; those realities affect our senses, according to regular laws, and, though our sensations are as different as our relations to the objects, yet, by taking advantage of the laws of perception, we can ascertain by reasoning how things really are, and any man, if he have sufficient experience and reason enough about it, will be led to the one true conclusion.[104]

Peirce's "laws of perception" – or for that matter, William James's "common sense stage" – should not be mistaken for Scottish realism, which remains too *a priori* and abstract.[105] Pragmatism and commonsense deal differently with the limits of metaphysics. But when confronting irreducible paradoxes of enlightenment thought, both hold that some philosophical problems are so intractable that practical experiences should point to and govern our relations with the world. Peirce and James sometimes speak highly of the empirical tendencies of Scottish realism. Peirce even sounds particularly similar to Douglass in a claim from 1872, "What brutes and other men do and suffer would be quite unintelligible to us, if we had not a standard within ourselves with which to measure others." Like Douglass, Peirce sought this standard through the work of reflection, "Common sense, which usually hits the nail on the head, has long ago held [the] looking-glass up to thought."[106]

The point here is not to undo distinctions between Scottish realism, transcendentalism, and pragmatism, nor is it to lift Douglass's philosophical status by hitching his wagon to the star of Peirce. It is to suggest that Douglass's attention to the social consequences of Scottish commonsense is not only a feature of his political program but also a way for him to think through some of philosophy's most serious questions. Perry Miller pointed out long ago that antebellum Americans faced problems of subjectivity "with no reference whatsoever to Emerson's *Nature* or to

104 Charles Peirce, "The Fixation of Belief" (1877), in *Writings of Charles S. Peirce, Vol. 3, 1872–1878*, ed. Christian Kloesel (Bloomington: Indiana University Press, 1986), 246, 254.
105 William James, "The Essence of Humanism" (1905), in *William James: Writings, 1902–1910*, 893.
106 Peirce, "Third Lecture" (1872), *Writings of Charles S. Peirce* 3: 10.

any Transcendental wrestling with duality."[107] True enough, for Scottish commonsense recognized the shortcomings of reason so much so that Bruce Kuklick calls the tradition "a half-way house on the road to disbelief."[108] As both a bulwark and a crack in the Enlightenment, commonsense understood quite well the implications of radical subjectivity; and in later figures such as William Hamilton and James Ferrier (whose *Institutes of Metaphysics* [1854] first used "epistemology" in English), it attempted to reconcile Scottish realism with the innovations of Kant.[109] Commonsense thinkers, like Douglass in *My Bondage and My Freedom*, are torn between objectivity and subjectivity, between material practice and ideal theory, between what Kant called "the fetters of experience" and what Wayland called the "suicidal" skepticism of Hume.[110]

This dilemma remains for subsequent thinkers further down the road of disbelief. Trained by William James, Du Bois and Alain Locke retain a commitment to universal law even as they know that race matters. Douglass's ambivalence toward excursive selfhood also anticipates some of the doubts expressed by later thinkers on postmodernism and race.[111] Douglass's response to the slavery crisis can even point toward recent moral philosophers who steer between the troubling extremes of essentialism and anti-foundationalism. Charles Taylor and Martha Nussbaum possess something of the commonsense urge to salvage from the wreckage of reason an intersubjective moral authority made available in literary texts. Likewise, James Livingston advocates what he calls a "moral personality" that moves beyond possessive selfhood without slipping into relativism.[112] Making subjectivity objective is a crucial part of what Douglass takes his literary and cultural work to be. That this work remained and remains unfinished is difficult to gainsay; but whereas Poe exploited the conflict between his politics and philosophy, and while Stowe sought a systematic coherence that she never found, Douglass is willing to use metaphysics as one intellectual tool among many so long as it furthers his practical goals of emancipation and equality.

107 Perry Miller, *The Life of the Mind in America: From the Revolution to the Civil War* (New York: Harcourt, Brace & World, 1965), 318.
108 Kuklick, *Churchmen and Philosophers*, 124.
109 *OED*.
110 Kant, *Prolegomena*, 116; Wayland, *Elements of Intellectual Philosophy*, 98.
111 See, for instance, bell hooks, *Yearning: Race, Gender, and Cultural Politics* (Boston: South End Press, 1990), 23–31; and Gilroy, *The Black Atlantic*, esp. 41–46.
112 Taylor, *Sources of the Self*, especially his concept of "strong evaluation" (3–24); Nussbaum, *Upheavals of Thought*, particularly her focus on compassion (297–454). Livingston, *Pragmatism and the Political Economy of Cultural Revolution*, 215.

CHAPTER 4

Melville and the state of war

Given a sufficient sense of purpose, it is possible to make all philosophy political – to embed even transcendental abstractions in temporal conditions, to evaluate the merits of theoretical speculation according to practical consequences, and to locate all intellectual efforts against a political horizon. Conversely, all politics can be made philosophical insofar as every ideological position implies an epistemology, and subjectivity describes both a way of knowing and a way of living in the world. Poe's metaphysics of slavery and race, Stowe's search for sentimental authority, Douglass's deployment of Scottish commonsense for emancipatory ends – all try to reconcile philosophy and politics, metaphysical theory and social practice, even if such reconciliation proves impossible to attain.

That said, the writings treated thus far are not exactly political philosophy, at least not as the subject was typically pursued in the antebellum United States. Though disciplinary boundaries were to some degree fluid, political philosophers before the Civil War focused on sovereignty, representation, contract, and natural rights, even as they discovered that such traditional concepts could not mediate the slavery crisis. Part of the problem, according to the erstwhile socialist and lapsed transcendentalist Orestes Brownson, was that Americans were not good theoreticians, "Notwithstanding the very general and even absorbing interest which the great mass of American citizens take in political matters, . . . politics as a science is / body of future readersalmost entirely unknown and unheeded among us."[1] Brownson may have been right, yet even more rigorous antebellum political theorists were stymied by the slavery crisis, exposing a fear voiced by Frederick Grimké in 1848, "Amidst the general progress which the human mind has made during the last two hundred years, there is one science which has remained nearly stationary, and that

---

1 Orestes Brownson, "Origin and Ground of Government," *The United States Magazine and Democratic Review* 13 (Aug. 1843), 129.

is the philosophy of government."[2] Brother to the famous abolitionist converts Sarah and Angelina, the pro-slavery Grimké was not alone in treating slavery as a question of political philosophy. More radical efforts included Thoreau's "Resistance to Civil Government" (1849), Calhoun's *Disquisition on Government* (1851), Delany's "Political Destiny of the Colored Race on the American Continent" (1854), and George Fitzhugh's *Sociology for the South* (1854) as well as *Cannibals All!* (1857). But as much as the slavery conflict provided an impetus to such innovative work, no political philosopher of the antebellum period was more provocative than Herman Melville.[3]

Melville is stirred by the possibilities of transgression, and critics trace his career with the question: How does he speak the unspeakable? What one means by unspeakable makes a difference, for God, culture, and language systems all potentially bowstring one's speech, and Melville seems to have quarreled with each as blasphemer, deviant, and proto-deconstructionist. Melville also speaks unspeakable political theory, albeit circumspectly. From the start of his career, he ran afoul of some readers with *Typee's* (1846) criticism of Protestant missionaries. He then flirted time and again with taboo, enduring chastising review upon review, until he became a clandestine writer whose work turned increasingly private and bitter before collapsing into obscure ambiguities, masquerades, and eventual silence. Various versions of this fall are supported by the facts of Melville's life. Melville depended on the book-buying public, though he was seldom frank with his readers. His cultural relativism and philosophical skepticism often set him beyond "civilized" standards and brought him much personal and professional grief. It follows that Melville's social views are rightly regarded as subversive. His careful rebellions are shrouded with irony, hidden in allegory, and to a debatable extent, refracted through narrators who, despite some resemblance, are in the end not quite their author. Such is the case with Melville's short fiction, most notably "Benito Cereno" (1855), though at least two caveats bear heavily on the story's critique of the slavery crisis.[4]

---

2 Frederick Grimké, *The Nature and Tendency of Free Institutions*, ed. John William Ward (1848; Cambridge: Belknap Press of Harvard University Press, 1968), 66.

3 The question of Melville's political philosophy has only been occasionally addressed. Two sustained efforts are Catharine H. Zuckert, *Natural Right and the American Imagination: Political Philosophy in Novel Form* (Savage, Maryland: Rowman and Littlefield, 1990), 99–129; and Julian Markels, *Melville and the Politics of Identity: From King Lear to Moby Dick* (Chicago: University of Illinois Press, 1993). For Melville's classical philosophical sources, see Merton M. Sealts, Jr., *Pursuing Melville: 1940–1980* (Madison: University of Wisconsin Press, 1982), 23–30, 250–336.

4 Accounts of Melville's political subversion, particularly regarding slavery and race, include Marvin Fisher, *Going Under: Melville's Short Fiction and the American 1850s* (Baton Rouge:

The first is that Melville's magazine fiction (1853–56) is not the run-out of a tragic career. Melville did not abandon America after *Moby-Dick's* (1851) lukewarm reception, nor did the author who expurgated *Typee* descend step-by-step, rebuke-by-rebuke to the self-destructive, labyrinthine quietism of *Pierre* (1852) and *The Confidence-Man* (1856). There remains a tendency to utterly alienate the later Melville from his culture – to forget, for instance, that *Moby-Dick* was not always misunderstood, to elide some evidence that even *Pierre* was at one time intended to profit and please, to read the end of *The Confidence-Man* as only a parting, sarcastic shot, to neglect *Israel Potter* (1855) and *Battle-Pieces* (1866) as meditations on the meaning of America. Why is Melville remembered as a brooding isolato and not a garrulous, broad-chested sailor? Is it assumed that he died a miserable wreck to gratify some desire for disaster? Melville's short fiction is not optimistic, nor is it finally intended for a casual reader. But it also recalls Ralph Ellison's claim from 1953, "Whatever else [Melville's] works were 'about' they also managed to be about democracy."[5]

Which introduces a second caveat: The cultural work of subversive politics is tricky to ascribe. Here subversive implies not only opposition to prevailing ideologies but also a cunning use of narrative that, by eluding the superficial skimmer of pages, resists the public spirit of politics. The more successfully subversive a text, the less political it becomes until at some degree of difficulty covert radicalism quietly slides into solipsistic despair. The political theory of "Benito Cereno" exists on this slippery slope, somewhere between the story's subtle commentary and its unknowable silences, between Melville's penetrating social criticism and his desire to puncture the political. To read "Benito Cereno" is thus to heed potential ironies and subtexts, for subversive politics are semiprivate insofar as they must fool a dominant culture while still speaking the unspeakable to someone. Like some other Melville texts, "Benito Cereno" is "about" the viability of truthful speech. More specifically, it explores the tenuous possibilities of enlightened public discussion in a time when the slavery crisis threatened the foundations of American democracy. For Melville, the failing debate over slavery revealed serious flaws in American

Louisiana State University Press, 1977); Carolyn Karcher, *Shadow over the Promised Land: Slavery, Race, and Violence in Melville's America* (Baton Rouge: Louisiana State University Press, 1980); Michael Paul Rogin, *Subversive Genealogy: The Politics and Art of Herman Melville* (New York: Knopf, 1979); Morrison, "Unspeakable Things Unspoken"; and Sundquist, *To Wake the Nations*, 135–82.

5 Ralph Ellison, "Twentieth-Century Fiction and the Black Mask of Humanity" (1953), in *Shadow and Act* (New York: Vintage, 1964), 40–41.

republicanism and its public sphere, suggesting that the political theories of Machiavelli and Hobbes might best explain the perilous state of a nation headed for war. In this way, "Benito Cereno" offers a wicked account of political philosophy as Melville struggles, despite himself, to speak some kind of democratic hope.

ALMOST A SHIP-OF-STATE

No Melville text invites political analysis more than "Benito Cereno." The story traces the slow discovery and violent suppression of a slave revolt as a Yankee captain, Amasa Delano, helps the Spaniard Benito Cereno recapture his slave-ship, the *San Dominick*. The drama of the story is driven by the fact that the slave-leader Babo has slyly concealed his revolt, forcing Cereno to act in front of Delano as if he were still in charge of the ship. Melville's story surely invokes issues of slavery and race. Yet no Melville text, not even *Moby-Dick*, has so thoroughly confounded its critics. After reconstructing multifarious contexts and identifying manifold allusions, interpretations of the last half-century arrive at different ends. Melville is a racist or a proto-multiculturalist. He is progressive but bedeviled by conservative fears. He ultimately advises a political tack or leaves the reader adrift.[6] Compelling scholarship has winnowed these arguments to the point where it is more or less clear that Melville is an astute observer of the American slavery debate, but his commentary on antebellum politics may not render his own stance, nor are the interests of "Benito Cereno" limited to slavery and race.

To readers of Melville, this may not be surprising; for his mysteries so often conceal new mysteries, just as "Benito Cereno" appears to climax when Cereno escapes the *San Dominick's* trap by leaping into Delano's whaleboat. Here Babo shows his daggered hand as the *San Dominick* erupts in open revolt. Here the "past, present, and future seemed one" – so much so that Melville's careful foreshadowing makes good (if not perfect) sense, so much so that critics, at the story's request, tend to

---

6 See, for instance, Sidney Kaplan, "Herman Melville and the American National Sin: The Meaning of 'Benito Cereno,'" *Journal of Negro History* 41 (Oct. 1956), 311–38 and *Journal of Negro History* 42 (Jan. 1957), 11–37 ("racist"); John Bryant, "The Persistence of Melville: Representative Writer for a Multicultural Age," in *Melville's Evermoving Dawn: Centennial Essays*, ed. John Bryant and Robert Milder (Kent, Ohio: Kent State University Press, 1997), 3–30 ("proto-multiculturalist"); Sundquist, *To Wake the Nations*, 135–82 ("progressive"); Karcher, *Shadow over the Promised Land* ("conservative fears"); Jean Fagan Yellin, "Black Masks: Melville's 'Benito Cereno,'" *American Quarterly* 22 (fall 1970): 678–89 ("political tack"); Rogin, *Subversive Genealogy*, 208–24, and Nelson, *The Word in Black and White*, 109–30 ("adrift").

privilege this "flash of revelation."[7] The scene, after all, explains so much with fulgurous, tableau-like efficiency. Delano's foot "ground the prostrate negro." His left hand "clutched the half-reclined Don Benito." His "right arm pressed for added speed on the after oar, his eye bent forward, encouraging his men" (99). Victim, attacker, rescuer, and plot seem suddenly revealed, even as Melville's emphatic prose conceals a crucial irony. This is not Emanuel Leutze's painting, *Washington Crossing the Delaware* (1851), in which a stable and self-possessed freedom fighter poses at the prow of his ship. Melville has already made ample reference to the past of New World bondage, and the scene in the whaleboat can stand for a nation presently struggling with slavery. As Delano rows from the stern, he turns his back on the *San Dominick's* past, fearfully, awkwardly, and even ridiculously propelling his panicked ship-of-state into a future he can hardly discern.

It really is a striking paragraph – so good, in fact, that the next twenty pages can seem an over-lengthy denouement. Melville leaves Delano's shifty perspective for an ornate description of the ship's recapture, followed by a dozen pages of detailed depositions, followed in turn by the last few pages that, despite returning to the three main characters and a familiar narrative voice, by now seems decidedly overdue if not, as the story itself admits, somewhat "irregularly given" (114). George William Curtis, who read the manuscript for *Putnam's*, tended to agree: "It is a great pity [Melville] did not work it up as a connected tale," for the "dreary documents at the end" make the plot "a little spun out," enough to precipitate the cry, "Oh! dear, why can't Americans write good stories."[8] As rash as this may sound in retrospect, Curtis is not simply wrongheaded. With just a few editorial touches, the narrative might conclude with the defeat of the revolt – no shifting perspectives or intrusive depositions, no repetitions or chronological leaps, mysteries explained, conflicts resolved, everything over except the interpreting and the rights to a dynamite screenplay.

Yet interpretation will take its time. Some undergraduates can be made to confess that they first saw Delano as the hero of the story. It is also easy to mistake him for Melville, so intimate is the narrative with the good captain's mind. After noting that Melville is not Delano, however,

---

7 Herman Melville, "Benito Cereno" (1855), in *The Piazza Tales and Other Prose Pieces*, 98, 99. Hereafter cited in the text.

8 Curtis to J. H. Dix, 19 April 1855 and 31 July 1855 in Jay Leyda, *The Melville Log: A Documentary Life of Herman Melville, 1819–1891, Vol. II* (New York: Hardcourt, Brace, and Co., 1951), 500–1, 504.

subtexts rise toward the surface. The politically minded will find relevant contexts – French revolution, the Fugitive Slave Law, the slave rebellions of the *Amistad* and Santo Domingo. There are racial, regional, and national types, as well as references to the American slavery crisis as it stood in the mid-1850s. Melville can even be made to predict a kind of civil war; and more than Poe's stories of phenomenological racism, he seems to anticipate *The Black Image in the White Mind* (1971). But if political clues are by no means wanting, "Benito Cereno" continues to mystify, especially if the supposed climax in the whaleboat steals attention from the story's rightful end.

This climax is no tableau. As if to contrast the frantic cries and contorted poses in the whaleboat scene, Delano speaks easily with Don Benito after the revolt is put down. Like the reader, and perhaps even Melville, Delano is doggedly seeking some closure, trying to convince his moribund friend that "the past is passed. . . . Forget it" (116). "You are saved," Delano insists, "what has cast such a shadow upon you?" "The negro," Cereno famously answers, and "[t]here was no more conversation that day." One paragraph later, Melville reveals the fate of his final player, "As for the black, . . . he uttered no sound" and, with an aspect that seemed to say, "since I cannot do deeds, I will not speak words," he meets "his voiceless end." This silence speaks volumes, but the message can range from despair and confusion to racist erasure to more sensitive thoughts about the meaning of silence and the politics of open-ended narration.[9] Melville's conclusion also points to the failure of public speech, for the *San Dominick* is a society dominated by a problem it will not or cannot name, as an allegory of antebellum America where debate over slavery was often pre-empted, suppressed, or misunderstood.

Douglass charged in 1853 that a main goal of the "Slavery Party" was the "suppression of all anti-slavery discussion," and abolitionists often traced their movement in terms of the struggle for speech – from Garrison's *Liberator*, to Theodore Weld's Lane Seminary, to Elijah Lovejoy's murder and the Gag rule, to more personal moments of speech and suppression at variously contested public sites.[10] Melville seems keenly aware of this emphasis on the discursive battles of the slavery crisis. John Quincy Adams tried the *Amistad* case during the heart of his Gag rule fight.

9 The best discussions of silence in the text include Sundquist, *To Wake the Nations*, 135–82; and James Kavanagh, "That Hive of Subtlety: 'Benito Cereno' and the Liberal Hero," in *Ideology and Classic American Literature*, ed. Sacvan Bercovitch and Myra Jehlen (Cambridge: Cambridge University Press, 1986), 352–83.
10 Douglass, *My Bondage and My Freedom*, 440.

The year 1799, the setting of the story, witnessed not only the slave revolution of Toussaint L'Ouverture, but also the Alien and Sedition Acts, which used the "black Jacobins" of Santo Domingo to justify domestic attacks on free speech, a reference "Benito Cereno" sharpens in its famous shaving scene by comparing Cereno to James I.[11]

Yet if the "morbidly sensitive" Cereno appears to harbor the "slumbering dominion" of a southern slave-master, fugitive slaves and abolitionists are not the only parties suppressed, nor are only anti-abolitionists to blame for the silence aboard the *San Dominick* (54). The oakum-picking blacks, after all, serve as "monitorial constables," and the reticent, stammering, slave-trading Cereno lacks the "power to tell a single word" (110). Mary Boykin Chesnut, Moncure Conway, and Poe teach a similar lesson. Speaking truly about slavery and race was peculiarly painful for southern whites, even to the point where psychological repression precluded the need for external restraint. Nonetheless, the terror aboard the *San Dominick* – Nat Turner's axes, Denmark Vesey's poison, and the inverted hierarchy of Santo Domingo – is no more effective at quelling expression than the horrors of a southern plantation.

Despite Babo's mastery, discipline fails as Delano stumbles on clue after clue, until it becomes evident that the good captain's dullness is not simply a function of his racism, that his convenient misreadings keep him "light of heart" as he pursues quite commercial "ulterior plans" (95). Surely Delano's "benevolent interest" (54) is not Samuel Hopkins's disinterested benevolence (as advertised in the divine's antislavery writings collected in 1854). At the same time, despite his Yankee caginess, Delano betrays the exact sort of blindness that pro-slavery advocates were quick to condemn in their blithe antislavery foes. As a self-aggrandizing "charitable man" so fond of blacks that he wants to buy Babo, Delano indulges, abolitionist-like, in the kind of ignorance that Poe ascribed to slave liberators like Baron Metzengerstein (72). The captain also betrays the sort of hypocrisy that anti-abolitionist critics found in Stowe and that Douglass condemned in his Garrisonian allies. Most forcefully, Delano so woefully misinterprets the political crisis he presumes to solve that his faith in providence and man's good nature brings him unwittingly right to the verge of deadly, incendiary words. Thus with a maddening evenhandedness, Melville satirizes abolitionists and fire-eaters alike. He seems

11 See, for instance, Jedidiah Morse, "The Present Dangers and Consequent Duties of the Citizens" (1799), in *The Fear of Conspiracy: Images of Un-American Subversion from the Revolution to the Present*, ed. David Brion Davis (Ithaca: Cornell University Press, 1971), 47.

even to echo the more moderate pleas of Daniel Webster, Henry Clay, and other compromising men, who held that what the nation needed most was decorous discussion in reason's clear light.

But what happens when speech does become "free" for Cereno, Delano, and (to some extent) Babo? What happens when the charade comes to a close and the three principle characters show their true colors in the whaleboat tableau? Surprisingly, dialogue does not ensue. Delano mistakes Cereno for a pirate, and Babo struggles silently, while Cereno emerges from his "speechless faint" "half-choked" and croaking "husky words, incoherent to all but the Portuguese" (99). Even later aboard Delano's *Bachelor's Delight* and conversing with an ostensible "fraternal unreserve," there remains a singular lack of commerce as the victors rehash their experience (114). "See, yon bright sun has forgotten it all, and the blue sea, and the blue sky; these have turned over new leaves," a forward-facing and vaguely transcendental Amasa Delano gushes (116). "Because they have no memory," Cereno replies, unable to shake his all-too-reflective, all-too-human mood. "You are saved," Delano urges, putting a providential Puritan spin on their fortunate escape. "The negro" is Cereno's only answer, for his slavery-dominated view of the world has no place for northern conceptions of grace. These men are speaking different discourses, even as they share the same tongue. And when the Yankee Delano earlier wonders, "How unlike we are made!" (61), he voices the secessionist sentiments of Calhoun, "[I]t is difficult to see how two peoples so different . . . can exist together in a common Union." Emerson expressed a similar pessimism in the wake of the Fugitive Slave Law when after claiming that the "Union" is "a real thing," in part because it shares "one language," he lamented, "[T]here are really two nations, the north and the south."[12]

By 1855, Cavaliers and Yankees preferred different dictionaries, used different textbooks, and often drew on different intellectual traditions,[13] while the slavery dialogue had reached a stage where there was precious little left to be said – where the most compelling topic of discussion was at what point endlessly repeated arguments must finally give way to war, where the "great debate" over American slavery would not include a southerner, and where the subsequent signs on the road to disunion were

12 John C. Calhoun to Thomas G. Clemson, 10 March 1850, *Correspondence of John C. Calhoun*, ed. J. Franklin Jameson (Washington, D. C.: American Historical Society, 1900), 784. Emerson, "Address to the Citizens of Concord," 67.

13 Cmiel, *Democratic Eloquence*, 87; Edmund Wright, *An Empire for Liberty: From Washington To Lincoln* (Cambridge: Blackwell, 1995), 471–84; Simpson, *Mind and the American Civil War*.

not orations, compromises, and sentimental novels, but violent acts in bleeding Kansas, the Senate, and Harper's Ferry. In "Benito Cereno," Melville predicts that language will not solve sectional conflict, that whether mistranslated, ignored, or suppressed, words will eventually end in deeds, the dark prophecy of Babo's demise. More than most of his peers, Melville implicates both the North and South in what Clay called the "state of eternal non-intercourse."[14] Melville also notes the plight of blacks when Babo illustrates Douglass's charge, "[Y]ou [white Americans] shut our mouths, and then ask why we don't speak," an accusation also brought by the slave rebel George Green of *Clotel*, "As I cannot speak as I should wish, I will say nothing."[15] Perhaps "Benito Cereno" even anticipates an older revisionist version of the War that "blames," not the ethics or economics of slavery, but the failure of two alien political cultures to talk over differences peaceably, a view often preferred by "Lost Cause" historians and one that Melville to some degree shared in the conciliatory gestures of *Battle-Pieces*. To find such meaning in "Benito Cereno" is not wrong, and yet it still misses much of the story; for when demographic types jump the *San Dominick*, political allegory fails.

If Cereno's *San Dominick* is the South and Delano's ship the North, then is the whaleboat the District of Columbia or some kind of border state? Considering the story's prairie imagery, we could be in Kansas, after all. Or more likely, when Delano thinks he sees the "silent signs of some Free-mason" (66) and Cereno claims to "know nothing" of rebellion (89), Melville might recall the conspiratorial silences pervading northern political life. In 1854, the Know-Nothings staged what Emerson called a "revolution," and their secret societies sparked "ridiculous gossip about guns, and poison, and massacre."[16] Allegory, as Melville (and Hawthorne) knows, encourages a paranoid style. The anxious critic, Delano-like, may watch a stiffened scabbard, all the while mistaking a slave rebellion for the mystery of iniquity. "Benito Cereno," like the Sperm Whale's brow, invites an allegorical eye. Locks, knots, masks, tableaus – read them if you can, dear critic, construct a towering thesis, though the more weight you ask your allegory to bear, the less stable its empire becomes.

14 Henry Clay, "Petitions for the Abolition of Slavery" (1839) in *The Life and Speeches of the Honorable Henry Clay, Vol. II,* ed. Daniel Mallory (New York: Van Amringe and Bixby, 1844), 359.

15 Frederick Douglass, "The Church and Prejudice" (1841), in *The Life and Writings of Frederick Douglass, Vol. I,* 104; Brown, *Clotel,* 263.

16 Emerson, "American Slavery" (1855), in *Emerson's Antislavery Writings,* 96; *The Boston Daily Advertiser,* August 15, 1854, quoted in John R. Mulkern, *The Know-Nothing Party in Massachusetts: The Rise and Fall of a People's Movement* (Boston: Northeastern University Press, 1990), 72.

Bannadonna of "The Bell-Tower" (1855) learns this lesson. So too, perhaps, does Ahab. And in "Benito Cereno," it happens again; for while the
story's political types allegorize misprision, they themselves are also facti-
tious. They, too, are part of the problem.

The 1850s hardly invented racial and regional stereotypes, but they were
powerful weapons in a slavery debate turned increasingly polemical. *Uncle
Tom's Cabin* both drew from and popularized a tradition of political
tropes, showing that stock characters and reiterated scenes could paint a
compelling picture of slavery, howsoever imagined that picture might be.
"Benito Cereno" dissents at this point. As both Nat Turner and Uncle
Tom, Babo belies black stereotypes. Just as the Cavalier Don Benito is
both sickly Hamlet and "bitter hard master" (94), the Yankee Delano
conflates sectional types as a pious idealist who minds the main chance.
These more or less obvious contradictions may create psychological
complexity and depth, but Melville seems more seriously committed to
subverting the elements of his allegory. There is too much allusion and
too many references to determine political analogies; and in this sense, the
story is not so much sunk in silence as inundated with discourse. Though
Melville is careful to raise the issue of slavery and free speech, his over-
abundance of political types moves beyond antebellum concerns
toward drearier and ultimately more fundamental failures of American
democracy.

NOT QUITE A PEOPLE'S HISTORY

Let us return to the start of "Benito Cereno" to examine the relation of
narrative and power in light of Curtis's complaint that Melville's story is
not a "connected tale." When the "commanding" Delano first boards the
San Dominick, he hears "in one language, and as with one voice" a
"common tale of suffering"; but being "impatient of the hubbub of
voices," he brushes past the "less conspicuous" scores and seeks whomso-
ever "commanded the ship" (49–51). This is one of Delano's flaws.
Despite an alleged "republican impartiality" (80), he trusts a "brother
captain" (52) to tell the "whole story" (54), so that when the *San Dominick*
later explodes in a "clattering hubbub" of hatchets (98), his hierarchical
mind can only suppose that Cereno is faking an abduction. The story will
show that Don Benito is in fact a "paper captain" (59) and that Delano's
ordering of the "unmanageable ship" (56), though inspired, is also a lie.
Such deception is most likely attributed to Babo who, according to the
court's opinion, served as "the helm and keel of the revolt" (112), a

description that points to the *San Dominick's* hull and its motto, "*Follow your leader*" (99).

Yet Babo should not be placed too confidently at the forefront of things, for a subtext suggests that his command is not as sure as the court (and most critics) conclude. Cereno requires constant supervision. A black youth cuts a white. Sailors lurk, cast meaningful glances, and hint to Delano in English. As dire as Cereno's situation is, Babo's can hardly be comfortable; and when Delano dispenses needful provisions with a supposed "good-natured authority," his casual "half-mirthful, half-menacing gesture" nearly sets off a second revolt. "Instantly the blacks paused" while, telegraph-like, "an unknown syllable ran . . . among the perched oakum-pickers" who, "dropping down into the crowd," "forced every white and every negro back" with gestures that, like Delano's menacing mirth, also threaten physical violence (79). The oakum-pickers and Ashantees are Babo's appointed authorities, and when at his word the most precious goods are reserved for the cabin table, it would not be surprising if some African rebels felt a little put out, perhaps even as hungry and dispossessed as the foot-soldier Israel Potter. Melville does alter his historical source to create a more masterful, more vicious Babo. But even as the story's fictional court lists crimes performed at Babo's "command" (112), there are instances where he is not in control – where simply "the negroes" commit certain acts, where "the negresses used their utmost influence," and where a suspicious reader can well imagine that a lone, diminutive slave from Senegal might struggle to convince Ashantees, ex-kings, and a "restless," "mutinous" populace that he is, in fact, the leader to follow – and to his homeland, not theirs (105–6). Which is to say that the militant Ashantees and judicious oakum-pickers keep tenuous control over white and black "pawns" (71), and that the executive "ring-leader" Babo is at least as vexed as Delano, who leaves his ship to a rumored pirate and cannot trust his crew (105).

Delano, of course, shows remarkable leadership when trying to aid the *San Dominick*. "Snatching a trumpet" and "issuing his orders" while Cereno lies incapacitated, the imperialist American is almost too glad to take control of the vessel. Suddenly, however, Babo appears "faithfully repeating his orders," playing the "part of captain of the slaves," Melville's nod toward our actual leader. And yet a wink follows this nod, for just when Babo seems truly in charge, Delano wonders, "who's at the helm" and finds yet another tableau. A sailor, described as an experienced tar, grasps the head of a "cumbrous tiller" with two "subordinate" blacks working a pulley that helps to handle the weight (92). Thus after Delano replaces Cereno, and Babo in turn takes over, Melville follows one more lead to suggest that if anyone steers the *San Dominick*, it is not any one person at all, but rather two nameless African rebels, a ragged lifelong tar, and the men and women at the rigging and ropes who come together to harness the breeze.

What does Melville hope to accomplish by subverting the command of his captains? To begin with, he implicates yet again his reader in Delano-like blindness insofar as we focus so intently on Babo that we ignore the less prominent rebels, even to the point where, as with Cereno, one singular black casts a shadow over every aspect of the text. In doing so, the reader unwittingly joins in an unjust verdict of Babo, for the white deponents have varying claims on the *San Dominick's* human cargo; and the more that Babo is held responsible, the more of his cohorts survive to be sold, a legal issue painfully apparent in the real Amasa Delano's *Narrative* (1817). The court documents borrowed by "Benito Cereno" are thus far from objective, for the "partial renumeration of the negroes" (111) brings a remuneration partial to whites as Babo's silence saves the lives, though not the liberty, of his fellow conspirators. Finally, by challenging the concept of command, not only does Melville further belie his Negro, Yankee, and Cavalier types, he suggests that, despite his fore-grounded threesome, another perspective is available – an egalitarian tale that might be called a People's History of the *San Dominick*.

When Cereno desperately jumps for the whaleboat, "[T]hree sailors, from three different and distant parts of the ship" also abandon the vessel, suggesting both the presence and the absence of simultaneous, alternative narratives (98). If there is indeed a common tale beneath Babo's dominant plot, and if Melville re-writes from the bottom up Amasa Delano's *Narrative*, then this grassroots story ought to appear when the sailors re-take the *San Dominick*, for here and here only the text's three great men are noticeably absent from events. However, the battle is like the *Serapis* fighting the *Richard* in *Israel Potter*, for Melville casts "a light almost poetic over the wild gloom of its tragic results," and "[o]bjects before perceived with difficulty, now glimmered ambiguously."[17] Earlier, and through Delano's eyes, the rebels are described as sheep, deer, dogs, leopards, crows, and bats, while white sailors, in turn, are compared to sheep, foxes, centaurs, and bears. Yet the battle is no better when the

---

17 Herman Melville, *Israel Potter* (1855), in *Herman Melville: Pierre; Israel Potter; The Piazza Tales; The Confidence-Man; Uncollected Prose; Billy Budd, Sailor* (New York: Library of America, 1984), 561, 564.

sailors become "sword-fish rushing hither and thither through shoals of black-fish," who then become in ironic mixed metaphor "wolf-like" with lolling red tongues. When the chief mate cries, "Follow your leader!" and the sailors rally into "a squad as one man," Melville may appear to be waxing poetic, his rhetoric rising with the attackers' "huzza," until the sailors ply their swords like the "carters' whips" of a slave-master and make a violent, victorious surge in which "not a word was spoken."

The recapture of the *San Dominick*, then, is not a story of democratic heroism. With the rebels compared to Dominican inquisitors, and with sailors, "one leg sideways flung," "fighting as troopers in the saddle" (102), "Benito Cereno" recalls "Areopagitica" (1644) and Milton's call for free speech:

[T]hey [Parliament] will . . . execute the most *Dominican* part of the Inquisition over us, and are already with one foot in the stirrup so active at suppressing, it would be no unequall distribution in the first place to suppresse the suppressors themselves; whom the change of their condition hath puft up, more then [sic] their late experience of harder times hath made wise.[18]

Like Parliament, the sailors of "Benito Cereno" are unimproved by their recent, hard-ridden experience. Or as Melville writes in *Mardi* (1849), despite "glorious Areopagiticas," "[H]e who hated oppressors, is become an oppressor himself."[19] Thus "Follow your leader" makes a wicked point in the *San Dominick's* bloody re-capture. Melville suggests that his sailors' view is as fallacious as the perspective of his captains, that both revolution and counter-revolution end with the violent suppression of speech, and that political divisions finally obviate any attempt to tell a true story, whether that story be "common" or "whole," and regardless of who's at the helm.

The same is true of the subsequent court documents that, though based on biased testimony, systematically pretend to an objective account of the events aboard the *San Dominick*. As Curtis worried, they may seem "a little spun out," for Melville himself seems impatient. Editing catalogs, extracting portions, and recounting the *"prolonged and perplexed naviga-tion"* (108), he appears almost to complain toward the end, *"And so the deposition goes on"* (110). By the time Melville relates *"various random disclosures referring to various periods of time"* (112), one might – Oh! dear –

---

18 John Milton, "Areopagitica" (1644), in *John Milton: Selected Prose, New and Revised Edition,* ed. C. A. Patrides (Columbia: University of Missouri Press, 1985), 246.
19 Herman Melville, *Mardi: And a Voyage Thither* (1849), in *Herman Melville: Typee, Omoo, and Mardi* (New York: Library of America, 1982), 1183.

think less well of the story as a dramatic and unified narrative, and one might not give a wilted pumpkin for the names of other rebels, any more than give a basket of fish for the rest of the gentlemen and tars. In his *Narrative's* preface, Amasa Delano feared this very response, "It may be considered . . . that I have been at times too minute in giving details in this narrative concerning officers and crew. . . . But notices of this kind are valuable to the cause of morality and humanity."[20] That the Duxbury captain is not particularly moral is an irony Melville indulges, but the elisions and inventions of "Benito Cereno" portray a much more masterful Babo while often suppressing Delano's egalitarian, if hypocritical and laborious, details. In the absence of sustained characterization, of personal history and voice, the minor players of "Benito Cereno" remain stubbornly inaccessible, not simply because they are obscured by Delano's perspective and Babo's genius, but because Melville is already too long in his trying depositions. As if aware that the biographies of great men sell better than cultural histories, Melville has his own plot concerns that preclude a more common tale.

Which does not square with Melville's reputation as a democratic writer.[21] With the exception of "Benito Cereno," every Melville maritime text includes a voice from before the mast. There may be, as in *Redburn* (1849), a tyrannical Jackson or some not-so-innocent race baiting (as can be found in the "Midnight, Forecastle" chapter of *Moby-Dick*). Nonetheless, the laboring communities of his novels are often marked by humor, camaraderie, and loving squeezes of the hand that suggest at least a guarded optimism in the possibilities of democracy. In "Benito Cereno," however, revolution brings only new oppression. Melville may challenge slavery and racism by inverting color supremacy, but class solidarity remains largely inchoate – regardless of whether Melville bemoans the tension between labor and antislavery reform, regardless of his efforts (as Brook Thomas has shown) to complicate wage and chattel bondage.[22]

20 Amasa Delano, *Narrative of Voyages and Travels in the Northern and Southern Hemispheres* (Upper Saddle River, NJ: Gregg Press, 1970), 20.
21 See, for instance, Larzar Ziff, *Literary Democracy: The Declaration of Cultural Independence in America* (New York: Viking, 1981), 260–79; Rogin, *Subversive Genealogy*; David Reynolds, *Beneath the American Renaissance: The Subversive Imagination in the Age of Emerson and Melville* (Cambridge: Harvard University Press, 1988), 135–65, 275–308; and Nancy Fredericks, *Melville's Art of Democracy* (Athens: University of Georgia Press, 1995). For challenges to this view, see Wai Chee Dimock, *Empire for Liberty: Melville and the Poetics of Individualism* (Princeton: Princeton University Press, 1989); and Dennis Berthold, "Class Acts: The Astor Place Riots and Melville's 'Two Temples,'" *American Literature* 71 (Sept. 1999), 429–61.
22 Thomas, *Cross-Examinations of Law and Literature*, 93–112.

Even more troubling than the failure of sailors and slave rebels to find common ground is the suggestion that such ground does not exist, either between or within class and racial categories. What if the "one voice" of a totalized narrative is always an authoritarian plot? What if rallying together "as one man" is always mock-heroic? Is a democratic literature even possible when the voice of the people is random and various, when it is a clamorous din of "hubbub" – and dreary hubbub, at that? The legal and political theorist Francis Lieber wrote in 1853, "[E]verything depends upon the question who are 'the people,'" for "even if we have fairly ascertained the legitimate sense of this great yet abused term, we frequently find that their voice is anything rather than the voice of God."[23] "Benito Cereno" takes Lieber's complaint to a skeptical extreme. The story is hardly Melville's first text to subvert the power of captains, but its undermining of the people is originally cynical, for the voice of the forecastle is not simply suppressed or itself potentially tyrannical. The voice of the people does not exist when it is too diverse to be represented, when the people suppress the Other people, and when impatient readers expect from their narratives more commanding and dramatic performances, even as they, like the autocratic Delano, consider themselves "republican."

SEEMING REPRESENTATION

"Benito Cereno" is ill at ease with monolithic narrative, though it is sensitive to readers like Delano and Curtis who expect a connected and totalized tale. Melville's story is multicultural in its attention to voices suppressed, and its fractured, self-referential form can loosely prefigure postmodernism. It may go too far to suggest that Melville knows what comes after the New Criticism. More surely, by 1855 few Americans could describe their political scene without dwelling on the increasingly prevalent themes of fragmentation, uncertainty, and impending apocalypse. This was especially true after Webster and Clay followed Calhoun to the grave, as bloodshed in Kansas came to anticipate a widely (if vaguely) feared war, and when the Whigs collapsed in 1854 prompting cries from northern observers that "we are to have political chaos – 'confusion worse confounded.' "[24] While the organizing conflicts of Jacksonian America

23 Francis Lieber, *On Civil Liberty and Self-Government*, ed. Theodore Woolsey (1853; Philadelphia: J. B. Lippincott, 1883), 398.
24 Washington Hunt to Hamilton Fish, August 2, 1854, quoted in William E. Gienapp, *The Origins of the Republican Party, 1852–1856* (New York: Oxford University Press, 1987), 129.

centered on tariffs and banks, the slavery question was divisive enough to sever the bonds of Calhoun's union, to dissolve Martin Van Buren's party connections, and to generate platforms so evasive and specious that Thoreau, after calling his country a "slave-ship," would compare its cacophonous political discourse to "that universal aboriginal game . . . at which the Indians cried *hub, bub!* "[25] In its leaderless, violent, fractious confusion, "Benito Cereno" is timely indeed, particularly when Melville doubts the tenability of a republic founded on a diverse and often incompatible body of political philosophy.

For the last few decades, discussions about the ideological origins of the United States have centered around the conflict between the civic virtue of classical republicanism and a liberal individualism associated with Locke. Other work, however, complicates this duality, advancing what Daniel Rogers calls a "post-structuralist reaction" that allows into play "all the messy, multitudinous possibilities of speech and discourse."[26] The plot of early national politics and its nineteenth-century legacies has become too tangled, too complicated to be organized around a stable dichotomous structure. As is so often the uncanny case, Melville antici- pates such confusion when "Benito Cereno" questions in both a political and a linguistic idiom fundamental (and related) concepts of contract and representation.

After Babo and his cohorts stage a revolution aboard the unwatchful *San Dominick*, they kill the aristocratic Aranda so they can "be sure of their liberty" (106). Cereno then arranges to "draw up a paper signed by [himself] and the sailors who could write," as well as by Babo, "for himself and all the blacks," thus ceding the ship to the rebels (108). Abolitionists often drew parallels between the American War for Independence and the struggle of slaves against tyranny, a comparison William Cooper Nell made explicit in *The Colored Patriots of the American Revolution* (1855). But if the *San Dominick's* African rebels can come to resemble the Minute Men, Babo's constitution, which helps to establish something of a three-branched regime, is from its fractious inception coercive and only dubiously representative, retaining the injustice but switching the color hierarchy of what Charles Mills describes as the "Racial Contract" of

---

25 Henry David Thoreau, "A Plea for Captain John Brown" (1859), in *Walden and Other Writings*, 694, 693.
26 Daniel T. Rogers, "Republicanism: The Career of a Concept," *The Journal of American History* 79 (June 1992), 35.

American democracy.[27] In *Clarel* (1876), Melville – like James Madison before him – compares the Constitution to a Gordian knot that some men "cut but with a sword."[28] And in "Benito Cereno," the ship's puzzling polity introduces a host of contractual problems at a time when Garrisonians burned the Constitution, southern radicals insisted on the right to break compacts, and women and African-Americans questioned the viability of virtual representation. Richard Hildreth, the abolitionist political theorist, followed Locke in calling chattel bondage "a permanent state of war" that "bears no resemblance to any thing like a social compact."[29] In "Benito Cereno," Melville goes further, subverting the authority of all political contracts with the help of Machiavelli and Hobbes.

Scholars have done much to reclaim Machiavelli and Hobbes as influential thinkers in the founding of the United States.[30] However, such a genealogy would have been distressing to many antebellum thinkers, who considered both philosophers fairly notorious – Machiavelli for brazen amorality, Hobbes for suspect piety, each for his anti-democratic tendencies and cynical views of human nature. Both men put survival and self-interest at the center of natural law, and both voiced misgivings about rational efforts to order and perfect the political world. They did advance a civic individualism that made republican theory possible, but they also called for a powerful sovereign to prevent a tyranny of the masses. Not surprisingly, Jefferson and Madison generally preferred the more catholic contracts of Locke, Rousseau, and Montesquieu, who recognized the threat of political corruption but hoped that a natural aristocracy could rationally resist the temptations of power. When such leaders did not arise under the Articles of Confederation, the framers reached what J. G. A. Pocock has called a "crisis of confidence" – one only partly allayed by placing sovereignty in "the people," and one that remained a serious concern for antebellum political theorists who, like the constitutional scholar Joseph Story, began to wonder, "Is not the *Theory* of our govt. a total failure?"[31]

27 Mills, *The Racial Contract.*
28 Herman Melville, *Clarel: A Poem and Pilgrimage in the Holy Land,* in *The Writings of Herman Melville,* Vol. *12,* 402. This pairing is suggested by Thomas Gustafson, *Representative Words: Politics, Literature, and the American Language, 1776–1865* (Cambridge: Cambridge University Press, 1992), 37, 57.
29 Hildreth, *Despotism in America,* 50, 39.
30 J. G. A. Pocock, *The Machiavellian Moment: Florentine Political Thought and the Atlantic Republican Tradition* (Princeton: Princeton University Press, 1975); Frank M. Coleman, *Hobbes and America: Exploring the Constitutional Foundations* (Toronto: University of Toronto Press, 1977).
31 Pocock, *Machiavellian Moment,* 516; Story to John McClean, 16 August 1844 (quoted in Thomas, *Cross-Examinations,* 79).

Story, Hildreth, Grimké, and other thinkers for the most part clung to the *Federalist Papers*, advocating an equitable balance of interests guaranteed by an enlightened population. Yet even the progressive Hildreth drew on the "keen-sighted Machiavel" to argue that virtue in the United States did not tend toward positions of power, while "conservative republicans" like Calhoun and Fitzhugh used Machiavelli and especially Hobbes to contradict the "great and dangerous error . . . that all men are born free and equal."[32] Even if the U.S. Constitution marked an end of classical politics, and even if the 1840s witnessed a peak of civic optimism, the cynical thought of Machiavelli and Hobbes survived in the antebellum era, particularly as the slavery crises appeared to follow the violent examples of Renaissance Florence and seventeenth-century England in the throes of civil war. Melville is aware of such unhappy precedents. *Israel Potter* describes Benjamin Franklin as a "tanned Machiavelli"; and when the novel equates "Hobbes and Franklin" as men who are at once "politicians and philosophers," Melville makes the uncomfortable point that the project of the Founding Fathers may have less than republican roots, a possibility mercilessly suggested in "Benito Cereno."[33]

In 1854, Bohn's Standard Library released a new version of Machiavelli's *The History of Florence, and of the Affairs of Italy . . . with The Prince and Various Historical Tracts.*[34] *The Prince* might serve as Babo's conduct manual, so explicit is it in describing the uses of murder, terror, and dissembling. Most poignantly, Melville's "centaur" at the tiller and the "dark satyr" on the *San Dominick's* stern recall *The Prince's* allegorical centaur and Machiavelli's infamous claim that wise men rule by both human law and vicious animal stealth (72, 49). By turning his tar into a centaur and zoomorphically describing sailors and blacks, Melville takes the "double form of man and beast" that Machiavelli reserves for his prince and applies it more liberally aboard the *San Dominick* to

---

32 Richard Hildreth, *Theory of Politics: An Inquiry into the Foundations of Governments and the Causes and Progress of the Political Revolutions* (1853; New York: Augustus M. Kelley, 1969), 46–7; Calhoun, *A Disquisition on Government*, 44. For "conservative republicanism" and pro-slavery thought, see Tise, *Pro-Slavery*, 339–61.

33 Melville, *Israel Potter*, 477.

34 Melville owned a copy of *The History of Florence* prior to 1851, and one assumes he had access to *The Prince*. See Merton Sealts, Jr., *Melville's Reading: Revised and Enlarged Edition* (Columbia: University of South Carolina Press, 1988), 92. For Machiavelli and "Benito Cereno," see John Schaar, *Legitimacy in the Modern State* (London: Transaction Books, 1981), 68–71; and John Diggins, *The Lost Soul of American Politics: Virtue, Self-Interest, and the Foundations of Liberalism* (New York: Basic Books, 1984), 281–86.

every last sovereign, duplicitous soul.[35] The very viability of American republicanism depends on a virtuous people, and so Melville's irony is brutal indeed when he describes the *San Dominick's* animal masses as the ship's "republican element" (80).

If doubt remains that "Benito Cereno" presents a Machiavellian world, *The History of Florence* describes a disinterment, a tyrant who is cannibalized, a man who murders a prince and displays his head on a stake in the piazza, and one Francesco, yet another tyrannicide, who shares the name of a *San Dominick* rebel and before being executed could not "be induced, by . . . words or deeds . . . to utter a syllable."[36] Perhaps the *San Dominick* is actually Florence, and in some senses it is. By comparing the sea to a "Venetian canal" (49), Melville tricks both his reader and Delano, for the proverbial stability of republican Venice will give way to Florentine violence. Typee or Happar? Venice or Florence? Such dualisms loom, especially in light of Carolyn Karcher's conjecture that "Benito Cereno" and "The Bell-Tower" were originally intended as a diptych.[37] Both texts allude to each other while suggesting the setting of Venice; and when read together, they smudge the difference between the Old World and the New. The ostensibly Renaissance setting of "The Bell-Tower" is modernized by the presence of pocket watches; and in spite of Delano's New World optimism, the *San Dominick* is governed by less forward-looking rules. In the end, and as in all Melville diptychs, supposed distinctions blur. The bloody government of "Benito Cereno" is as Florentine as the putative republic of "The Bell-Tower," while the agreement drawn up by Cereno and Babo is as defective as Bannadonna's tower which as a symbol of enlightenment reason founded in social oppression can stand for the U.S. Constitution fatally flawed by slavery.[38] With subtle precision, "Benito Cereno" offers the terrible truths that the people are all Machiavellian princes and that all the world's a Florence.

Reading "Benito Cereno" with *Leviathan* (1651) reinforces such radical claims, for as Dugald Stewart wrote in his popular history of philosophy, Hobbes gives "offence to the friends of liberty" by arguing that "man is a

---

35 Niccolò Machiavelli, *The History of Florence, and of the Affairs of Italy, from the Earliest Times to the Death of Lorenzo the Magnificent; Together with The Prince and Various Historical Tracts, A New Translation* (London: Henry G. Bond, 1854), 459.
36 Ibid., 362.
37 Karcher, *Shadow over the Promised Land*, 144–46. For Venice as a political symbol, see Pocock, *Machiavellian Moment*, 100–2; and Diggins, *Lost Soul of American Politics*, 180–87.
38 For antebellum analogues in "The Bell-Tower," see Fisher, *Going Under*, 95–104.

beast of prey."[39] Though Hobbes claims not to be lead "by some strange Prince," *Leviathan* follows Machiavelli in holding that the "condition of Man . . . is a condition of Warre," which proves the case aboard the *San Dominick* where violence and deception rule. The locks and keys of "Benito Cereno" recall *Leviathan's* introductory advice that in judging the "dissembling" doctrines of others we should also consider our own "designe," lest we (like the designing Delano) "decypher without a key, and be for the most part deceived."[40] Most telling is the *San Dominick's* stern piece tableau, the prophetic "dark satyr in a mask, holding his foot on the prostrate neck of a writhing figure, likewise masked" (49). In a crucial section on representation, Hobbes traces the etymology of "*Person*" to "*Face*" and, because faces can be "counterfeited on the Stage," to that "which disguiseth the face, as a Mask." In this way, the Commonwealth is composed of "Persons Artificiall," for "a *Person*, is the same that an *Actor* is," and on this basis an individual can "*Represent* himselfe, or an other," not only as a metonymic figure but on "diverse occasions, diversly." Interestingly, Hobbes uses this argument to establish the legitimacy of "Covenants." "The Actor," though inconstant, artificial, and masked, does in fact "acteth by Authority," but by an authority seeking practical order more than absolute truth, and one founded on an inseparable sovereignty, for "*a Kingdome divided in it selfe cannot stand*."[41]

Melville, however, has made up his mind to strike through practical masks, even if in doing so he seriously undermines United States republicanism. When Madison scattered his notion of sovereignty amongst an ill-defined "people," he rejected Machiavelli, Hobbes, and every republican theorist who believed that a unified concept of power was a needed defense against faction. Madison understood quite well that he walked a new and dangerous path. He wrote in *Federalist 10* that the "causes of faction" are "sown in the nature of man," while he also admitted that "[e]nlightened statesmen will not always be at the helm." Accordingly, national safety lies in a "scheme of representation" that balances interests so that any faction "will be unable to execute and mask its violence under the forms of the Constitution." The trick is that the division

39　Dugald Stewart, *Dissertation, Exhibiting a General View of the Progress of Metaphysical, Ethical, and Political Philosophy, since the Revival of Letters in Europe* (1821), in *The Works of Dugald Stewart, Vol. VI* (Cambridge: Hilliard and Brown, 1829), 81.

40　Thomas Hobbes, *Leviathan*, ed. Richard Tuck (1651; Cambridge: Cambridge University Press, 1991), 299, 91, 10.

41　Ibid., 112, 127.

of powers must steer between "the cabals of a few" and "the confusion of a multitude," a feat the *San Dominick* cannot accomplish with no sovereign presence at the helm and no common story that the populace can share. Thus the events of "Benito Cereno" are better predicted by *Federalist 37*, in which a skeptical Madison complained about the "dark and degraded pictures which display the infirmities and depravities of the human character" as revealed in its "history of factions, contentions, and disappointments."[42]

Drawing upon and continuing this history, the *San Dominick* erupts, "not in misrule, not in tumult," but "with mask torn away" in "piratical revolt" (99). The ship is not, as Delano believes, a scene of disorder and anarchy so much as a polity fractured by faction, the predicted result of a sovereign people lacking a chief representative – even if that Hobbesian Actor is both thespian and agent, even if he is a paper captain or a literal figurehead such as Aranda. The Old World court of "Benito Cereno" misses this subtlety. By beheading Babo, "whose brain, not body, had schemed and led the revolt" (116), it forgets *Leviathan's* frontispiece and Hobbes's not-wholly-monarchial claim that the head of the state is a political construction and that revolution comes from below. As Nancy Ruttenburg shows, Melville would return to this point in "Billy Budd" (1891); for the voice of the people is again inarticulate and painfully unrepresented when the "wedged mass of upturned faces" silently witnesses Billy's execution, recalling once more *Leviathan's* frontispiece in which representative government is a pyramid scheme with an imagined monarch at the top. Decapitation will not dispel the shadow of political upheaval when, as Melville quotes Hobbes in *Moby-Dick*, the "Commonwealth or State . . . is but an artificial man."[43]

In this sense, "Benito Cereno" abides by a brutal Hobbesian logic. Melville rejects the pro-slavery views of Hobbes, Calhoun, and Fitzhugh, though he does affirm Grimké's allusion of 1848, "Men throw the mantle of politics over their faces and fight each other in masks."[44] Like Grimké, Daniel Webster lamented the dangers of such factional strife, proclaiming

42 James Madison, Alexander Hamilton, and John Jay, *The Federalist Papers* (Washington: Robert B. Luce, 1976), 55–60, 230–32.

43 Herman Melville, "Billy Budd" (1891), in *Herman Melville: Pierre; Israel Potter; The Piazza Tales; The Confidence-Man; Uncollected Prose; Billy Budd, Sailor*, 1427; Melville, *Moby-Dick*, xx. Nancy Ruttenburg, *Democratic Personality: Popular Voice and the Trial of American Authorship* (Stanford: Stanford University Press, 1998), 344–78.

44 Grimké, *The Nature and Tendency of Free Institutions*, 402.

in his celebrated speech, "The Constitution and the Union," that no side held "the helm in this combat" and that "fraternal sentiments between the South and the North" were the only way to solve the grievances that "alienate [their] minds."[45] Though Melville agrees with Webster's diagnosis, he suggests that the Union will not be saved, for the terrible stasis of the slavery crisis must finally give way to violence. "Benito Cereno" is a telling attack on American republican theory. By combining Machiavelli's centaur with Hobbes's mantled actor, Babo's "play" cuts to the quick of contractual civic humanism (87). For Melville, leaders always dissemble, political representation is false, social compacts are therefore constitutionally flawed, and throwing off the mask of these republican fictions ends in factional strife that in 1799 or 1855 takes the likely form of a race war.

All of which poses a serious challenge to rational public discussion. Or as Melville wrote in 1838 in precocious exception to perfectionist optimism, "What doth it avail a man, though he possess all the knowledge of a Locke or a Newton, if he know not how to communicate that knowledge."[46] For Machiavelli, speech is essentially a means of deception and influence. Hobbes worries in *Leviathan's* chapter "Of Speech" that without language human society would revert to a *San Dominick*-like brutality with "neither Commonwealth, nor Society, nor Contract, nor Peace, no more than amongst Lyons, Bears, and Wolves." Hobbes also warns to "take heed of words; which besides the signification of what we imagine . . . have a signification also of the interests of the speaker."[47] Not precisely *différance*, but skeptical enough for the seventeenth century and quite germane to an antebellum America beset with misprision and faulty typology, commanding hegemony and clattering hubbub. Melville's critique of republican theory can constitute the local relevance of "Benito Cereno," though Melville's satyr suggests a problem that has as much to do with the human condition as with the national slavery crisis. That is, Don Benito may be right to cry that the truth is "[p]ast all speech" (81), for given the failures of linguistic and political representation, how can anyone tell an honest story?

---

45 Daniel Webster, "The Constitution and the Union" (1850), in *The Works of Daniel Webster, Vol. V*, 325, 360.

46 Quoted in Merton M. Sealts, Jr., "Historical Note," *The Piazza Tales and Other Prose Pieces*, 462.

47 Hobbes, *Leviathan*, 24. For Hobbes and language in American politics, see also Gustafson, *Representative Words*, 44–49; and David Simpson, *The Politics of American English, 1776–1850* (New York: Oxford University Press, 1986), 30–35.

As might be expected, "Benito Cereno" offers no unequivocal options. Melville does not turn from a condition of "Warre" to a pre-social state of humanity. Though Delano spies "pure tenderness and love" in the "naked nature" of a negress, he later learns that the women rebels are brutal political actors (73). Hobbes can turn to a "perfect Speech" that is the sovereignty of God.[48] But when the captains of "Benito Cereno" cheat death and thank their lucky *fortuna*, it is hard to take seriously Delano's claim that "all is owing to Providence," just as Cereno cannot praise "the Prince of Heaven" without a Machiavellian twist (115). Nor even in "Benito Cereno" do private relations escape political plots. The needy and gregarious Delano may overcome Cereno's reserve. One might even pitch a psychological thriller: Man who lost brother displaces affection on a brother captain who may have eaten a friend. "Benito Cereno" is not devoid of sentimental (even homosocial) content, but if the buddy instinct is strong in Melville, politics finally rule. At the very height of "sympathetic experience," Delano verges on the terrible truth that Cereno can never tell, and Babo convinces him "not again to broach a theme so unspeakably distressing" (61). Babo, in fact, is always under-foot – in the private meetings of Cereno and Delano, in their lengthy hand-squeeze "across the black's body" (97), even aboard the *Bachelor's Delight* when the shadow of the "negro" falls upon what should be a budding relationship. *Together we escaped a political disaster but, well, we don't talk much anymore.*

Finally, silence seems the only thing left. Babo's end can point to the fact that African Americans were not free to speak. His reticence also suggests what Delany charged in 1852, that the "colored people are not yet known, even to their most professed friends among the white Americans."[49] But rather than style Babo's "hive of subtlety" as an alien African mind (116), and in addition to mentioning that bee-hives were a symbol for conspiratorial Freemasons,[50] it should also be noted that in "Benito Cereno" no one really understands anyone and that Babo's "hive" may very well point to Bernard Mandeville's *Fable of the Bees* (1714), a cynical work of political philosophy in the tradition of Machiavelli and Hobbes. Like Mandeville, Melville places selfishness at the core of all

48 Hobbes, *Leviathan*, 287.
49 Delany, *The Condition, Elevation, Emigration and Destiny*, 10.
50 See Melville's marginalia in *Mosses from an Old Manse* (Herman Melville, *Journals*, in *The Writings of Herman Melville, Vol. 15*, ed. Howard C. Horsford and Lynn Horth [Chicago: Northwestern University Press, 1989], 607).

interactions. Private relationships do not flourish when public masks are ostensibly dropped, and language falters even at the moment it seems free of devious dissembling. As in his diptychs, Melville baits the reader when Cereno and Delano's "fraternal unreserve" appears to be "in singular contrast with [their] former withdrawments" (114); for the two captains never share an intimate understanding, and in Cereno's wordless exit, he "unconsciously gathered his mantle about him, as if it were a pall" (116).

Black or white, who ain't masked? – even if the actor is a supposed "dear friend" (114). What if the other of cultural difference is a more atomistic Not Me? Such questions can lead by various paths to a despairing and skeptical Melville who believes that the truth is past all words – whether because language always mistranslates, because the self is too total or splintered, or (more in line with the present argument and borrowing Carlyle's ironic allusion to Christ) because "[w]heresoever two or three Living men are gathered together, there is Society . . . with its cunning mechanisms."[51] If any two people constitute a state with all its dishonest implications, then the failings of political discourse subvert all human speech, be it antebellum or antediluvian, be it between leaders, followers, or friends. Such a claim stands as a dire estimation of our ability to talk truly with anyone. Benevolent laws appear to fall silent in a condition of perpetual war. As Habermas has written of the liberal public sphere in the first half of the nineteenth century, "While it penetrated more *spheres* of society, it simultaneously lost its political *function*."[52] "Benito Cereno" richly describes the expanding reach and limited grasp of a fearfully politicized language, carefully constructing a theory of government beneath the *San Dominick's* events to suggest that America's political estate is, in fact, a world of lies.

PAST, PRESENT, AND FUTURE

Which may or may not leave little to say. Perhaps politics for Melville are a mere point of entry on a more metaphysical quest, or a destination at which he never arrives, having discovered his theoretical lessons unsuited to practical use. "Benito Cereno" may be in the end a consciously constructed, unsolvable knot that – tragic, ironic, quietistic, or cruel – is Melville's best account of reality. The story is descriptive more than

---

51 Thomas Carlyle, *Sartor Resartus: The Life and Opinions of Herr Teufelsdröckh*, ed. Kerry McSweeney and Peter Sabor (1833; Oxford: Oxford University Press, 1987), 179.
52 Habermas, *The Structural Transformation of the Public Sphere*, 140.

prescriptive, more critical than actively engaged. It knows the slavery debate but defies its categories, for terms like "racist," "abolitionist," "apologist," and "democrat" do not sufficiently define Melville's thought. "Benito Cereno" in this sense betrays an indeterminate politics of deconstruction, though it seems to me a keener pleasure to view Melville's mistrust of representation, not through the kaleidoscope of postmodern theory but rather through the historically available lenses of Machiavelli and Hobbes that focus less on unknowability and more on the uses and abuses of power in an ambiguous world. Either way – that is, whether one's skepticism tends toward the old-fashioned or new – the question remains whether "Benito Cereno" performs any cultural work.

By most standards, the story does not do much in terms of antebellum politics. Though *Putnam's* under Frederick Law Olmsted took an increasingly antislavery stand, no evidence suggests that the ranks of any crusade swelled as a result of "Benito Cereno." Nonetheless, some scholars discover in the story potential for social reform. Eric Sundquist argues that the threat of revolt survives beyond Babo's demise, and others note that the story resists readerly racism by exposing Delano's ignorance.[53] Such arguments rely to varying degrees on the possible responses of readers, which makes sense, for to judge the work of a text is also to consider its audience. Thus having traced Melville's subversive critique, the question becomes: To whom does it speak?

By 1855, Melville struggled to sneak the unspeakable past anyone. *Typee* may have driven him underground, but it also marked him for intensified scrutiny, both because a debate erupted over the novel's authenticity and because a handful of reviewers, including Hawthorne, recognized a lurking "laxity of principle."[54] In the words of Hershel Parker, Melville had become "the first American literary sex symbol."[55] *Omoo* (1847) received a psychosexual review more invasive than "Hawthorne and his Mosses" (1850), and *Redburn* revealed more of Melville's life than its author may have wished. By the time *Pierre's* incivilities arrive, antebellum America was not much mistaken in the dark-eyed sailor Herman Melville. He thus becomes an intriguing paradox, a famously subversive writer – one closely monitored by pious reviewers (whose ire may have initially boosted

53 Sundquist, *To Wake the Nations*, 180–82; Yellin, "Black Masks."
54 Nathaniel Hawthorne, review of *Typee*, *Salem Advertiser*, 25 March 1846, *The Melville Log, Vol. II*, 206.
55 Hershel Parker, *Herman Melville: A Biography, Vol. I, 1819–1851* (Baltimore: Johns Hopkins University Press, 1996), xii.

his sales), and one who even after *Pierre* had if nothing else economic motives for courting an American readership. "Benito Cereno" is shaped to some degree by audience anxiety. So much of the story revolves around what one is forbidden to say. Who knows but that in these trying years of declining sales and poor reviews, Melville created in Cereno (or Babo) the figure of a suppressed author who, seemingly destined for misunderstanding, slides into wordless oblivion.[56] Without being able to tell his whole story. And with nary a word from Hawthorne.

Melville can indeed appear to be a writer out of joint with his time. Just as Emerson discerned in *Sartor Resartus* (1833) Carlyle's "despair of finding a contemporary audience," the fascinating obliquities of "Benito Cereno" point to Melville's own insecurities.[57] Given his recidivist history of transgression and his doubts about American democracy, it would be no surprise if Melville gave up on reaching a sympathetic antebellum audience without also drawing unwelcome attention to his unpopular political views. Readers of the day may have been better equipped than modern academics to decipher Melville's story. For them, discourse was all around, not something reconstructed from archives. Be that as it may, reviews of *The Piazza Tales* (1856) did not expose Melville's story. The *New York Daily Tribune* worried "not a little" over Melville's "perversity," but even the touchy *Southern Literary Messenger* and the abolitionist William Ellery Channing did not mention Melville's critique of democracy or his allusions to the slavery debate.[58] It is doubtful that such controversial subjects simply failed to interest reviewers; and once noting that early Melville scholarship also neglects the politics of "Benito Cereno," the tale's subversion appears to "work" – at least insofar as Melville escaped the censure of contemporary readers, at least insofar as his radical thoughts survive to this later date. The story reaches and seems intended to reach an audience beyond Melville's time, for when pressing political problems become tangled in stubborn metaphysical knots, Melville does not fall into skeptical silence. He defers instead to the future.

---

56 Stephen Railton, *Authorship and Audience: Literary Performance in the American Renaissance* (Princeton: Princeton University Press, 1991), 192–95.
57 *Correspondence of Carlyle and Emerson, Vol. I*, ed. Charles Eliot Norton (Boston: James Osgood, 1883), 13.
58 The review of *The Southern Literary Messenger* appears in Leyda, *The Melville Log, Vol. II*, 516. Channing placed Melville's stories in "other worlds beyond this tame and everyday place we live in" (quoted in Hershel Parker, *Herman Melville: A Biography, Vol. 2, 1851–1891* [Baltimore: The Johns Hopkins University Press, 2002], 284).

This tendency is evident as early as *Mardi's* satire of antebellum politics. In its "Vivenza" chapters, *Mardi* subverts the providential hubris of the United States when a mysterious scroll belies "the grand error" of a "universal and permanent Republic," complaining that in the states of Vivenza "the lessons of history are, almost discarded."[59] The scroll offers a cyclical theory of history that denies American exceptionalism, a theory portrayed in Thomas Cole's *Course of Empire* (1836), which Melville viewed in 1847. The scroll continues its Whiggish pronouncements against the promises of manifest destiny until suddenly Young America rises, "Time, but Time only, may enable you to cross the equator; and give you the Arctic Circles for your boundaries." *Mardi* thus simultaneously rejects and predicts a coming American empire, while the source of the scroll is additionally confusing, for the monarchical King Media and the progressive Babbalanja each accuse the other of authorship. The narrator Taji rejects both claims, concluding, "[T]his question must be left to the commentators on Mardi, some four or five centuries hence," a deferral that recalls Melville's response to the confused reviews of his novel: "Time, which is the solver of all riddles, will solve 'Mardi,'" he predicted.[60] In the same way that Pocock's republicans worried about the stability of democracies working within time, Melville holds that only Time will tell, that the meanings of America and its literature are reserved for future readers, a claim that in *Mardi* is mainly expository (a mode marring much of the book). In "Benito Cereno," however, Melville's appeal is dramatic, for when faced with national insecurity and the failure of enlightened discussion, he reaches toward a future audience in careful narrative practice.

Before reader-response became a school, and before heteroglossia entered the argot, scholars recognized in "Benito Cereno" a dialogic relationship with its audience. The story anticipates potential reactions. It is sensitive to the psychology of otherness.[61] It is proleptic, satiric, self-deconstructing, preternaturally self-referential. Which displeases some readers, who feel usurped or disappointed by a lack of political commitment. Yet despite all the charges of quietism and evasion, a wonderful irony remains – that a story about the failure of speech from so supposedly alienated an author remains remarkably engaging for students

59 Melville, *Mardi*, 1180–81. All subsequent quotations from *Mardi* are from pages 1180–87.
60 Herman Melville to Lemuel Shaw, 23 April 1849, in Leyda, *Log, Vol. I*, 300.
61 Arnold Rampersad, "Shadow and Veil: Melville and Modern Black Consciousness," in *Melville's Evermoving Dawn*, 162–80.

and teachers, for minds on both sides of the veil, and for scholars who feel, revelation-like, as if the past, present, and future are one:

Melville's interest [in "Benito Cereno"] is in a vast section of the modern world, the backwards peoples, and today, from the continents of Asia and Africa, their doings fill the front pages of our newspapers. (C. L. R. James, 1953)

"Benito Cereno" is truly a story whose time has come, whose currency will not soon pass, and whose present readers must be encouraged to use their own knowledge and experience in undoing the knot that Melville's contemporaries were less equipped to handle. (Marvin Fisher, 1977)

It took the urban rebellions of 1964–68, the Vietnam War, and the subsequent economic and moral decay of America during the period of its apparent global triumph to create an audience capable of comprehending the deadly message of 'Benito Cereno.'[62] (H. Bruce Franklin, 1997)

Subversive politics include and exclude, and Melville apparently speaks to *us* at the expense of an earlier *them*. From a privileged *now*, we can descry, with some condescension, a less enlightened *then*.

Perhaps there comes some "aha!" moment with every interpretive leap as skeptical theories of language and knowledge give way to intimations of intelligibility and (one almost whispers it) *truth*. For many readers of "Benito Cereno," the sense of now is uncanny. Only at this moment can the story be known. Only now is Time right. And not simply because of a scholarly discovery, but because human history is ripe. That this now occurs decades apart is a measure of "Benito Cereno's" ability to, as it were, pre-construct itself in the eyes of a future reader – to reflect on its narrative in the same way Melville recalls Florence, England, and Santo Domingo, and to extrapolate the gap of historical difference while at the same time speaking beyond it. The "strange history" of "Benito Cereno" invites diachronic reading (78); and when the foolish Delano suggests that Cereno simply drop the burdens of the past, Cereno and Melville insist on the tragic, abiding presence of memory. Like a dreamy Whitman in *Leaves of Grass* (1855), Melville endeavors "To think of time. . . . to think through the retrospection, / To think of today . . and the ages continued henceforward."[63] Or as Melville writes in "Hawthorne

---

62 C. L. R. James, *Mariners, Renegades and Castaways: The Story of Herman Melville and the World We Live In* (New York: Allison and Busby, 1953), 119; Fisher, *Going Under*, 117; H. Bruce Franklin, "Slavery and Empire: Melville's 'Benito Cereno,'" in *Melville's Evermoving Dawn*, 158.

63 Walt Whitman, "To Think of Time" (1855), in *Walt Whitman: Complete Poetry and Collected Prose*, 100. Ellipses are Whitman's.

and His Mosses," to master the "great Art of Telling the Truth" is to be able to say, "I am Posterity speaking by proxy," "even though it be covertly, and by snatches."[64]

Unlike Whitman, Melville's trans-historicism is never vatic or even confident. Melville knows that history is hard to read right and, hence, that the future is difficult to imagine. The elusiveness of history also makes it difficult to work purposefully toward political ends. Francis Wayland wrote in 1855, "Without a knowledge of what has been . . . [one] can form no decision in regard to the present," a bromide of political thought now and before the Civil War.[65] The antebellum public sphere brimmed with historical learning, encouraging efforts of impressive and sometimes laughable sweep, as if a road could not be patched without the blessings of Thucydides. Yet Melville remains, like Henry Adams, an accomplished student of history who cannot make sense of its lessons. In "Poor Man's Pudding and Rich Man's Crumbs" (1854), Melville intentionally makes the mistake of dating Waterloo in 1814, frustrating Wayland's rational premise that "no one can doubt that the battle of Waterloo was fought on the 18th of June, 1815."[66] By suggesting, as he does in *Israel Potter*, that history is always "retouched," Melville questions the authority of those who too blithely, too surely draw on the lessons of history, subverting politics as it was conceived and practiced in the antebellum United States.[67]

For Melville, historical logic cannot chart a prudent and willful course. To think otherwise risks the "crazy conceit" of Ishmael steering the *Pequod*, for Ishmael's hermeneutic is too easily "inverted" when he misperceives his agency, when he supposes that he somehow leads from the prow when he actually trails with the tiller, an error that almost causes him to capsize the ship-of-state. Aboard the *San Dominick*, agency is similarly uncertain. The tiller is at the command of multiple captains, in the hands of a factionalized crew, and manipulated by a complex system

---

64 Herman Melville, "Hawthorne and his Mosses," in *Herman Melville: Pierre; Israel Potter; The Piazza Tales; The Confidence-Man; Uncollected Prose; Billy Budd, Sailor*, 1160, 1170.
65 Wayland, *The Elements of Moral Science*, 254.
66 Wayland, *The Elements of Intellectual Philosophy*, 319. Note that Melville's story antedates Wayland's book, though Wayland refers to W. H. Maxwell's *Life of Field-Marshal His Grace the Duke of Wellington, Vol. III*: "The time when the battle [Waterloo] began has been stated with a marked contrariety" (479). That historians were, in Maxwell's words, "bewildered" by this uncertainty supports Melville's implication in both "Poor Man's Pudding" and "Benito Cereno" that history is never entirely recoverable and official accounts are not always trustworthy.
67 Melville, *Israel Potter*, 425.

of pulleys, ropes, and *fortuna*-like wind. Again one thinks of *Moby-Dick*, specifically "the Loom of Time," in which "chance, free will, and necessity" combine to determine the course of events.[68] Delano, however, does not recognize that his authority in only nominal. He is too quick to forget about history, exemplifying John Quincy Adams's complaint that "Democracy . . . is swallowed up in the present and thinks of nothing but itself."[69] Yet even more serious students of history are not for Melville reliable guides, for if nothing else history teaches a lesson that undermines its predictive power: The past performances of human civilizations do not guarantee future results.

Once again, only Time will tell in Melville's unfinished America. Unlike so many self-assured politicians and reformers, Melville does not invoke coming generations to advocate present designs. Rather, he sees inscrutable puzzles and defers to future commentators. This is an urge in *Mardi*, *Moby-Dick*, and "Benito Cereno"; and when facing the task of reconstruction in post-Civil War America, *Battle-Pieces* advises Northern forbearance with the forward-looking hope, "Posterity, sympathizing with our convictions, but removed from our passions, may perhaps go further here." Constantly reminding a confident nation that destiny is never manifest, Melville points to the contingent and unpredictable course of history – in the unfinished capitol dome that looms over "Lee in the Capital" (1866), in the familiar but alien presence of the past that is everywhere in *Clarel*, and in the moral of the historical poem "Timoleon" (1891), "Men's moods, as frames, must yield to years, / And turns the world in fickle ways."[70] For better or worse, Melville's stubborn commitment to a historically haunted yet open-ended America tends to make his position on current events stubbornly non-committal. This can be seen as a failure to take up the moral duties of the day. But because Melville lacked immediate relevance, he is less inclined to wear the mask of self-interest. Despite – or more accurately, *because* – of his skeptical depiction of political discourse, "Benito Cereno" helps us to talk about how we talk about politics.

Silence, then, does not end the story. Melville's distrust of the political present and his profound epistemological concerns compel him

---

68 Melville, *Moby-Dick*, 424, 1022.
69 Adams, quoted in Jack Rakove, *Original Meanings: Politics and Ideas in the Making of the Constitution* (New York: Knopf, 1996), 366.
70 Herman Melville, *Battle-Pieces, and Aspects of the War* (New York: Da Capo Press, 1995), 261; Herman Melville, "Timoleon," in *The Works of Herman Melville: Poems, Vol. xvi* (New York: Russell and Russell, 1963), 252.

to imagine a future discussion in which, hopefully, speech is more profitably practiced and some truths are not beyond words. Melville is hardly the only author to consider a later-day audience. Indeed, the act of writing presupposes some measure of diachrony. "Benito Cereno" is exemplary, however, in that its remarkable interlocutory energies are so much focused on *us*. Melville counts on a careful reader with the tenuous ability and obstinate need to reclaim meaning from silence. When readers hear it, they may be surprised by speech to the point of feeling chosen. But to think that this *now* is ours alone is to repeat Delano's mistake, for the past, present, and future are not one but are in constant, dynamic interaction. In this way, Melville's hermeneutics lean more toward the new than old, more toward a differentially interpreted past than a stable, univocal history.

Such hermeneutics have done much mischief to the prospects of representation, and yet Melville stubbornly rises to the challenge of speech. Though Melville found no common story for 1855, as a writer at work he managed to imagine a receptive community for his words. In this he responds, but does not quite answer, to failures of rational deliberation that obviate honest communication and truthful storytelling while casting the shadow of philosophical uncertainty on the possibilities of democracy. Melville's future is hopeful insofar as he willfully suspends his disbelief. His skepticism is not finally despair, nor is his patience quietism; and though most readers wish it otherwise, "Benito Cereno" takes no partisan stand in the antebellum slavery conflict. At a time when no one could solve slavery's knot without recourse to the sword, and when many voices were crying apocalypse and foretelling the end of the American experiment, envisioning a body of future readers required a little hope, if not a drop of Whitman's optimism and ecstatic disregard for the scores and hundreds of years that might come between him and his audience.

By demanding both a political commitment and one that matches modern convictions, some readers neglect Melville's point that historical lessons are under constant construction. To demand firmer answers is to try to bring closure to a willfully open-ended tale. Notoriously, Melville did not vote. Regrettably, perhaps, "Benito Cereno" is not ultimately interested in local practices, even so iniquitous a practice as slavery, which Melville knew to be wrong. But if even a present-minded democracy can strive for a better tomorrow, Melville's appeal to a future readership fulfills a kind of cultural duty, though that duty remains largely literary in its attention to language and form and severely constrained by the suppressive realities of antebellum America. George William Curtis liked

"Benito Cereno" just enough to recommend publication, and his final complaint of the once great Melville was that he "does everything too hurriedly now."[71] Perhaps it was Curtis who was too much hurried. And by seeking a harder and faster politics, we too rush Melville's tale, for one province of literature and those who would read it is to seek and imagine an honest speech – in the antebellum then, in the present now, and in the on-going talk over Melville.

71 Curtis to Dix, April 20, 1855 in Leyda, *Log, Vol. II*, 501. Melville may have gotten the last word by lampooning Curtis (and not Thoreau) in *The Confidence-Man's* Mark Winsome (Hans-Joachim Lang and Benjamin Lease, "Melville and 'The Practical Disciple': George William Curtis in *The Confidence Man*," *Amerikanstudien/American Studies* 26 [1981]: 181–91).

CHAPTER 5

Toward a transcendental politics: Emerson's second thoughts

In their writings on the slavery crisis, Poe, Stowe, Douglass, and Melville treat topics that are recognizably philosophical – the constitution of reality, the foundations of moral authority, the operations of the mind, representation and language. Still, addressing philosophical topics and drawing on available philosophical concepts may not be the same thing as doing philosophy, at least insofar as the authors in question do not employ the rigorous logical methods of formal philosophical analysis and ultimately seem most interested in applying, not inventing or discovering, philosophical ideas. Emerson is similarly improvisational and opportunistic, but he has more cachet in philosophical circles. Though Emerson was seldom a systematic student, he read widely and intensely in philosophy, and though for most professional philosophers he remains on the margins of the field, he directly influenced Nietzsche and the pragmatists and has been the subject of powerful work by Stanley Cavell and Cornel West. As Lawrence Buell has recently suggested, whether we call Emerson a philosopher or not may have more to do with definitions of philosophy than with Emerson's lifelong, if somewhat idiosyncratic, dedication to epistemology and ethics.[1] Such dedication, along with his growing participation in the abolitionist movement, might rightly make Emerson the star of a book about the conjunction of slavery and philosophy in antebellum American literature.

Yet the intersections of philosophy and the literature of slavery cannot be centripetally structured around a single writer, for even as canonical a thinker as Emerson is in many ways an anomalous figure in this book. Of the principal authors treated here, Emerson is the only wealthy white male and the only author to finish college. He is also the lone figure of New England transcendentalism, and the only writer who was considered a philosopher by many of his peers. Emerson is not always a representative

1 Buell, *Emerson*, 199–241.

man nor are his writings necessarily climactic. His pride of place in this book, if going last is such, stems from other reasons. More than Melville, Douglass, Stowe, and Poe, Emerson's commitment to philosophy and slavery spans the antebellum era, from writings of the 1830s to texts written during the Civil War. Emerson's reactions to the slavery crisis are similarly expansive, for as much as any antebellum author his thinking on slavery is dialectical, indicating the various potentials of philosophy under pressure from political forces.

Mary Moody Emerson wrote of her nephew in 1833, "A reformer! Who on earth with his genius is less able to cope with opposition? Who with his good sense [has] less *force* of mind – and while it invents new universes is lost in the surrounding halo of his own imajanation."[2] Emerson's transcendentalism can indeed seem unsuited for the earthly work of reform. Throughout his career, he struggled to reconcile his philosophy and politics, and no single issue exposed this tension more than the slavery crisis. Like so many white abolitionists, Emerson's racism did not preclude vigorous antislavery convictions, nor did his attentions to fate keep him from advocating political freedoms.[3] Yet even after adding his voice more forthrightly to the abolitionist cause, Emerson retained a stubborn aversion to the partisan work that seemingly detracted from his transcendental investigations, the vocation Emerson once called "my post which has none to guard it but me."[4] Making sense of such dissonance is a difficult and potentially tendentious task, for faced with the inconsistency, breadth, and sheer bulk of his writings, one fears that only sampling error can invent a coherent Emerson, that no account of his literary output and no amount of attention to rhetorical occasion can explain away Aunt Mary's sense that Emerson's philosophy and his social activism do not get along.

There are at least two ways to argue that Emerson's vision is irreconcilably split, the first of which originates from materialist and often multicultural perspectives. John Carlos Rowe comes not to praise but rather to bury Emerson, whom Rowe depicts as the architect of a transcendental philosophy "at fundamental odds with the social reforms regarding

---

2 Mary Moody Emerson to Charles Chauncy Emerson, January 8, 1833, *The Selected Letters of Mary Moody Emerson*, ed. Nancy Craig Simmons (Athens: The University of Georgia Press, 1993), 330.
3 Gougeon offers a comprehensive account of Emerson's abolitionist work in *Virtue's Hero*. Booklength studies also include von Frank, *The Trials of Anthony Burns*; and Patterson, *From Emerson to King*.
4 Ralph Waldo Emerson, *The Journals and Miscellaneous Notebooks of Ralph Waldo Emerson*, ed. William H. Gilman et al., 16 vols. (Cambridge: Harvard University Press, 1960–82), 13: 80. Hereafter cited in the text as "JMN."

slavery and women's rights." Russ Castronovo also finds an "antimaterialist polemic" in Emerson, while Timothy Powell more generally charges that "Transcendentalism strives, by definition, to rise above the ceaseless flux of history."[5] Antebellum detractors of New England transcendentalism also objected to its supposed impracticality, and pro-slavery thinkers often linked transcendentalism with pie-in-the-sky abolitionists who propounded a dangerously "new-fangled and ethereal code of morals."[6] The problem with such views is that transcendentalism is notoriously tricky to define; and one of Emerson's most explicit attempts in "The Transcendentalist" describes its ethos as "Idealism as it stands in 1842," an account that does not disregard the demands of temporality but seeks instead to mediate the claims of theory and real-world practice. This effort can be and has been condemned on political grounds, though to do so convincingly is to consider the dialectic of double consciousness and not too quickly conjure an image of Emerson as an utterly abstracted thinker. That is, what Emerson writes in "Circles" should not be discounted: "There are degrees in idealism," some of which are "practical."[7]

A second way to assert the incompatibility of Emerson's philosophical and political work is to marginalize the later pursuit as a kind of moonlighting. The political philosopher George Kateb sees Emerson's abolitionism as a "deviation" from Emerson's primary impulse toward self-reliant theorizing and not institutional action.[8] Emerson himself could give this impression, though there is ample evidence to the contrary. As Len Gougeon has shown, the first biographies of Emerson decidedly downplay his antislavery activism, a tendency shared by Cold War critics and one that persisted well into the multicultural age. Even West and Sacvan Bercovitch, who carefully read Emerson in cultural contexts, maintain that he "never really gave serious thought to social reorganization."[9] The rub is to see what "serious" means, for if Emerson never mounts a systematic critique of liberal capitalism, he nonetheless wrote quite a bit on reform, advocating positions that are variously radical, utopian, anarchic, and even potentially terrorist. Emerson's

5 Rowe, *At Emerson's Tomb*, 21; Castronovo, *Necro Citizenship*, 6; Powell, *Ruthless Democracy*, 79.
6 Hammond, "Letter to an English Abolitionist," 175–76.
7 Ralph Waldo Emerson, *Ralph Waldo Emerson: Essays and Lectures* (New York: Library of America, 1983), 407. Subsequent references to this work will be by page number only.
8 George Kateb, *Emerson and Self-Reliance: New Edition* (New York: Rowman and Littlefield, 2002), 178.
9 Gougeon, *Virtue's Hero*; Sacvan Bercovitch, *The Rites of Assent: Transformations in the Symbolic Construction of America* (New York: Routledge, 1993), 325; West emphasizes Emerson's "minimal" resistance to dominant political structures (*The American Evasion of Philosophy*, 23).

writings on reform may lack the philosophical intensity and concentrated lyricism of his most celebrated essays. He may very well be at his best when dancing in the footsteps of Plato, Montaigne, Kant, Goethe, and Coleridge, while indulging an extraordinarily intricate, whimsical, and original expository style. When Emerson marches with the abolitionist Thomas Clarkson and joins the chorus of the American Antislavery Society, the performances can be a bit disappointing, like watching Michael Jordan play baseball. Except that Emerson was participating in the most serious public issue of his day. Except that he works remarkably hard to synthesize politics and transcendental idealism. And except that the slavery controversy is not simply an opportunity for the application of his philosophy but also a fundamental issue in his writings and worldview. Albert von Frank has demonstrated that Emerson's abolitionism and transcendentalism are not easily disentangled.[10] In fact, his hopes for societal regeneration are premised on his philosophical idealism, which was itself provoked and shaped by political concerns such as slavery.

A main purpose of this chapter is to show how densely slavery is woven into Emerson's thought. To his neo-platonic sensibilities – and under the aegis of transcendental unity – beauty, truth, and goodness should all eventually harmonize. The aesthetic pleasures of well-turned words do not exist for Emerson in a separate world; rather they should accompany or at least cohere with moral authority, epistemological confidence, and political justice. In theory, the imperative is startlingly clear: The transcendentalist must see, act, and write well as the world moves toward perfection. In doing so, and here Emerson can be maddeningly opaque, the transcendentalist somehow discovers himself as an agent of social change. For Emerson, at least early in his career, such change is enacted through the power of words and through a process of inspiration and intellection in which an eloquent hero forges consensus not by participating in politics as such but by rising above partisan argument. The problem is that Emerson's experience often belies this conviction as the slavery conflict forces him to face what he once called "the absence of any appearance of reconciliation between the theory and practice of life" (JMN 9:65). This was particularly true and particularly painful in Emerson's America where "the genius of the country is more splendid in its promise, and more slight in its performance" (577). Some manifestation of this disappointment appears in a range of Emerson's works as the

---

10 Albert von Frank, "Mrs. Brackett's Verdict: Transcendental Antislavery Work," in *Transient and Permanent*, 385–407.

slavery crisis continually frustrates his vision of an all-encompassing (and almost always male) man who heralds a transcendental politics.[11]

Emerson's conflicted abolitionism can be traced through four figurations of this hero – the patient, eloquent man of "The Times" (1841–42), who forbears from polemic politics; Odysseus, who appears in "Experience" (1844) to predict the victory of practical genius; Daniel Webster, a fallen hero and unrepresentative man, whose Fugitive Slave Law forces Emerson to rethink the power of words; and finally Thoreau, whom Emerson eulogizes with admiration and censure as he compares his own political tacks to the straighter path of his one-time disciple as if announcing the death – or is it the promise? – of a heroic though unfulfilled eloquence. What is especially poignant in all of these writings is how Emerson manages to keep his faith in the real-world agency of art, even as the facts of chattel bondage compel him to qualify his beliefs, making him both an exemplar and critic of the Emersonian self.

THE ACTOR, THE STUDENT, AND THE ELOQUENT MAN

Before his first major antislavery address, "Emancipation in the British West Indies" (1844) and before the 1850 Fugitive Slave Law forced him into active abolitionism, Emerson voiced antislavery sentiments with varying degrees of dedication. An 1821 college essay condemns the "plague spot of slavery."[12] An 1837 address denounces defenders of chattel bondage for crimes against free speech. Emerson's journals from the 1820s and 30s also attack the national sin and tend to sympathize with progressive reform, not conservative Whiggery. At the same time, Emerson also derides abolitionists as an "odious set" rife with egoistic fanatics and "the worst of bores and canters" (JMN 9:120). Well into the 1840s and beyond, Emerson balked at what he saw as abolitionist monomania, preferring instead to treat chattel bondage as a topic "throwing great light on ethics into the general mind."[13] Such are the abstracted tendencies of "Politics" (1837), "Reforms" (1840), and "Man the Reformer" (1841),

---

11 Accounts of the heroic in Emerson, neither of which focus on slavery, include Mark Patterson, *Authority, Autonomy, and Representation in American Literature, 1776–1865* (Princeton: Princeton University Press, 1988), 137–88; and Ronald Bosco, "The 'Somewhat Spheral and Infinite' in Every Man: Emerson's Theory of Biography," in *Emersonian Circles: Essays in Honor of Joel Myerson*, ed. Wesley Mott and Robert Burkholder (Rochester: University of Rochester Press, 1997), 67–103.
12 Quoted in Gougeon, *Virtue's Hero*, 31.
13 Ralph Waldo Emerson, *The Early Lectures of Ralph Waldo Emerson, 1836–1838*, ed. Stephen Whicher, Robert Spiller, and Wallace Williams, 3 vols. (Cambridge: Belknap Press of Harvard University Press, 1959–72), 3: 257.

though Emerson's most sustained early efforts to confront the challenge of politics appear in "The Times" (1841–1842), a lecture series he gave after declining to join Brook Farm. Of the eight talks that make up "The Times," Emerson published the three most political in *Nature; Addresses, and Lectures* (1849) – "Lecture on the Times" (1841), "The Conservative" (1841), and "The Transcendentalist" (1842), all of which stand as fair examples of Emerson's quarrel with organized reform and establish some basic arguments and terms of his heroic eloquence.

"Lecture on the Times" explores the role of the thinker in society and in the cosmos. Beginning with a customary dualism that privileges ideals, Emerson posits universal truths, "The Times are the masquerade of the eternities" (153). This masquerade is not impenetrable as in some of Emerson's more skeptical works, nor does the gap between idealism and materialism appear to be unbridgeable. For Emerson, the "attention of the philosopher" brings light to "practical questions," including questions battled over by the forces of "Conservatism" and "Reform." What follows, however, does not much resemble a political discussion. Just as "The American Scholar" (1837) praises the universal "One Man," "Lecture on the Times" calls upon the "personal ascendency" of the "eloquent man," "There is no interest or institution so poor and withered, but if a new strong man could be born into it, he would immediately redeem and replace it" (155). Such hero worship comes from Emerson's faith, not just in the individual, but also in the progress of the times toward the fulfillment of what he calls "spiritual law" (156). Because this teleology might lead to complacency, Emerson reminds his audience (as well as his own reportorial self), "But we are not permitted to stand as spectators of the pageant which the times exhibit: we are parties also, and have a responsibility which is not to be declined" (157). These are not the words of an escapist intellectual. They may even sound civic-minded when Emerson invokes the "foundations of nations" and a "new and better order of things."

In typical Emersonian fashion, however, "Lecture on the Times" diverges from its path. Seemingly headed for political statement, Emerson eschews a prescriptive posture, creating instead a sub-distinction within the dualism of Conservatism and Reform by splitting reformers into "two classes, the actors, and the students" (158). Actors are the "leaders of the crusades against War, Negro slavery, Intemperance, Government based on force, Usages of trade, Court and Custom-house Oaths, and so on to the agitators on the system of Education and the laws of Property." This lengthy list with its deflating "and so on" can indicate Emerson's limited interest in specific social causes. It also suggests his distaste for the work of such fellow transcendentalists as Bronson Alcott, George Ripley, and Theodore Parker, all of whom encouraged Emerson to join in various reformist crusades. That Emerson does not name their names is not the result of politeness. Turning his defensiveness into aggression, he charges that the "bigotry" of active reformers "drive[s] all neutrals to take sides" (158). He accuses them of settling for "the Better" instead of aiming (presumably) for the Good (159). Moreover, the "theory" of actors is noble, but their "practice is less beautiful," for they "affirm the inward life, . . . but use outward and vulgar means," which Emerson associates with "material force," institutional "tactics," and an indecorous, partisan "clamor" that is "a buzz in the ear" (162).

Emerson prefers a more studious posture to the grandstanding pose of such actors, proclaiming that the "Reform of Reforms must be accomplished without means." Indeed, "We do not want actions but men" and until then "must consent to inaction" (163). All this can sound like various forms of capitulation – a "rite of assent," "corporate submission," or "barbarous idealism."[14] In this instance, Emerson is not a pragmatist or a Nietzschean superman, nor does he seem the likely subject of a book titled *Virtue's Hero*.[15] Modern readers, along with Delany and Douglass, may allow Emerson's cynical point about the hypocrisy of many abolitionists, "[The] denouncing philanthropist is himself a slaveholder in every word and look" (164). But when Emerson claims, "[I]f I am just, then is there no slavery, let the laws say what they will" – and when he marvels, "[H]ow trivial seem the contests of the abolitionist, whilst he aims merely at the circumstance of the slave" – Emerson's dedication to self-reliant individualism and disregard for material conditions threaten to belie his stated commitment to civic responsibility.

None of which is lost on Emerson, who in "Lecture on the Times" turns from actors to students with a tone of chagrin. Lamenting the "torment of Unbelief" that keeps the thoughtful student out of politics, Emerson questions the very viability of philosophy, "Can there be too

---

14 Bercovitch, *Rites of Assent*; Christopher Newfield, *The Emerson Effect: Individualism and Submission in America* (Chicago: The University of Chicago Press, 1996); Sharon Cameron, "The Way of Life by Abandonment: Emerson's Impersonal," *Critical Inquiry* 25 (Fall 1998): 24.
15 David Robinson, *Emerson and the Conduct of Life: Pragmatism and Ethical Purposes in the Later Works* (Cambridge: Cambridge University Press, 1993). Robinson presents a pragmatic Emerson who is amendable to social reform. For a less political, but still pragmatic Emerson, see Jonathan Levin, *The Poetics of Transition: Emerson, Pragmatism, and American Literary Modernism* (Durham: Duke University Press, 1999); and Richard Poirier, *Poetry and Pragmatism* (Cambridge: Harvard University Press, 1992), 3–75.

much intellect?" (165). No, he decides; but admitting the gap between practical work and philosophy, he complains that the "genius of the day does not incline to a deed, but to a beholding," for "criticism . . . ends in thought, without causing a new method of life." This moment of crisis lies at the crux of Emerson's double consciousness. Like Delany, who criticized the "exhausted moralizing" and "quaint theory" of Garrisonian abolitionists, and like Garrison himself who also feared that the movement was "melting away into abstractions," Emerson cannot help but voice a practical concern.[16] Does too much intellection disable activism? How can the thinker verging on skepticism inhabit and change the world?

"Lecture on the Times" ultimately answers, "[H]ave a little patience" – a recommendation that reflects not only Emerson's discomfort with the clamor and buzz of reform but also his faith that consensus can be reached in a decorous public sphere (166). In this Emerson concurs with William E. Channing's mildly abolitionist *Slavery* (1835), a text that concludes, "Let the free States be firm, but also patient, forbearing, and calm." Like Catharine Beecher's *An Essay on Slavery* (1837), which chides the impatient Grimké sisters, Channing calls for rhetorical restraint, lamenting the "fierce, bitter, exasperating" language of abolitionists such as Garrison.[17] Garrison was accustomed to such censure, even from such antislavery supporters as Lydia Maria Child and Margaret Fuller (who compared him to a man so used to screaming to deaf audiences that he could no longer speak in a normal tone).[18] Garrison responded with "Harsh Language – Retarding the Cause," proclaiming without apology, "I am accused of using hard language. I admit the charge. I have not been able to find a soft word to describe villany [sic]."[19] In the most vivid abolitionist literature, the South becomes a brothel, a hell, a torture chamber, and a monolithic monster. Slavery is the sum of all villainies and a harbinger of the apocalypse. Such rhetoric divided the antislavery movement as much as any ideological question; and Emerson generally preferred a more temperate language to that of the abolitionist "roarers."[20] He could even

---

16 Delany, *The Condition, Elevation, Emigration and Destiny of the Colored People*, 158; William Lloyd Garrison, *The Liberator* (October 11, 1839): 1.

17 Channing, "Slavery," 157, 134.

18 See, for instance, Child's *An Appeal in Favor of that Class of Americans Called Africans* (1833): "Mr. Garrison is a disinterested, intelligent, and remarkably pure-minded man, whose only fault is that he cannot be moderate (*Against Slavery*, 173); Fuller, review of "Narrative of the Life of Frederick Douglass," 380.

19 Garrison, "Harsh Language – Retarding the Cause," 121.

20 Ralph Waldo Emerson, *Emerson in His Journals*, ed. Joel Porte (Cambridge: Belknap University Press of Harvard University Press, 1982), 267.

prefer no words at all, "A silent fight without warcry [sic] or triumphant brag . . . is the new abolition of New England" (JMN 9:128). Thus when choosing between vociferous actors and impotent but decorous students, Emerson in "Lecture on the Times" admits a guilty pleasure, "I own, I like the speculators best" (166), a preference for theory that Kateb places at the center of Emerson's liberalism. Then as he so often does when faced with present failures, Emerson promises "new modes of thinking, which shall recompose society" (167), "recompose" implying both *reform* and also *regain composure.*

Readers looking for a plan, however, will be disappointed. Perhaps with Emerson optative eloquence is the opiate of the masses. This seems the case when flowing language washes away political worries, for "Lecture on the Times" ends as it began – with transcendental idealism. "The Time is the child of the Eternity," Emerson writes. The "generation of appearances rests on a reality" (168). Emerson then praises the student's perception with a hint of the stridency of active reform, "For that reality let us stand: that let us serve, and for that speak. Only as far as *that* shines through them, are these times or any times worth consideration" (169). For Emerson, however, thinking comes first. Or as he announced in 1840, claiming a prerogative granted by Locke and echoing the language of Wordsworth, "I shall persist in wearing this robe . . . of inaction, this wise passiveness until my hour comes when I can see how to act with truth as well as to refuse."[21] In this way, the rigorous student procrastinates pressing political duties, even if Emerson can (for now) repress the skeptical suspicion that correct perception is a life-long task that may never reach things-in-themselves. This is why Emerson must insist on the penetrable masquerade of the times. Only with faith in the subject's true sight can Emerson predict a new world.

The final sentence of "Lecture on the Times" ends with this great hope, imagining that humans will witness the arrival of "disguised and discredited angels" (170). These agents of change are never explained, except that they are "the highest compliment man ever receives from heaven," a boon that more than anything else sounds like revelation. Thus after rejecting the clamor and buzz of antebellum reform, Emerson offers a passive patience less in the logic of political prescription and more in the

---

21 Emerson, *Early Lectures*, 3:266. Locke writes, "Liberty, it is plain, consists in a power to do, or not to do; to do, or forbear doing, as *we will*" (*An Essay Concerning Human Understanding*, 2 vols. [Oxford: Clarendon Press, 1894], 1: 352). As we shall see, Emerson borrows this Lockean language more explicitly in "The Transcendentalist." In "Expostulation and Reply" (1798), Wordsworth defends his romantic dreams by appealing to a student-like "wise passiveness."

spirit of epiphany. Along the way, insult and chagrin give way to prophetic speech, a rhetorical victory anticipated by Emerson in a letter to his brother William regarding "The Times":

I have a dream sometimes of an eloquence . . . that drawing its resources from neither politics nor commerce but from thought, from the moral and intellectual life and duties of each man, shall startle and melt and exhalt the ear that heareth, as never the orators of the caucus or the parliament or the forum can.[22]

Perhaps, as Anita Haya Patterson suggests, Martin Luther King Jr. shared a similar dream.[23] Note, too, that Emerson's ideal eloquence exists beyond the traditional venues of civil government. After resisting the noisome strategies of partisan, active reform, "Lecture on the Times" expresses a faith in the vision of the heroic speaker, a figure who may or may not be Emerson. Only the future will tell.

Originally the first talk of the series but placed after "Lecture on the Times" in *Nature; Addresses, and Lectures*, "The Conservative" further pursues the plot of prospective heroic reform. Despite its title, and though sometimes thought to balance "Man the Reformer," the lecture in itself is sufficiently dialectical to represent both "the party of Conservatism and that of Innovation" (173). In some senses, "The Conservative" is less challenging than "Lecture on the Times." The latter's distinction between actors and students is finer and, for Emerson, more personally vexing than the difference between stasis and innovation. A main point of "The Conservative," however, is that such dichotomies are false, "[I]t may be safely affirmed of these two metaphysical antagonists [Conservatism and Reform], that each is a good half, but an impossible whole. Each exposes the abuses of the other, but in a true society, in a true man, both must combine" (175). The force of "The Conservative" does not lie in its fine distinctions. The greater the distance between "antagonists," the more powerful their eventual synthesis and the larger the capacity of the "true man" who subsumes conflicting halves.

Modeling this process of reconciliation, and displaying a novelist's ear for dialogue, Emerson stages a debate between a paternal voice of stasis and a youthful proponent of change, bringing ideological questions "home to the private heart" (187). As with Stowe, the drama on the surface is mainly a domestic affair. The lecture's interlocutors often sound

22 Ralph Waldo Emerson to William Emerson, October 17, 1841, *The Letters of Ralph Waldo Emerson, 1836–1841*, ed. Ralph Rusk and Eleanor Tilton, 10 vols. (New York: Columbia University Press, 1939–1995), 2: 460.
23 Patterson, *From Emerson to King*.

like parent and child as familiar contempt threatens to sabotage moments of understanding. "Young man," the Conservative complains, "Your opposition is feather-brained and overfine" (179). To which the Reformer responds by calling the Conservative's world, "a universe in slippers and flannels, with bib and papspoon, swallowing pills and herb-tea" (185). Remembering that Emerson describes his Conservative as "affluent and openhanded" (184), one almost imagines a dinner scene with a college student home for the holidays – *Dad, you're a sellout and lack self-reliance; can I borrow the keys to the car?* For a time, "The Conservative" gives the advantage to its titular character, as if the difference between Emerson and his reformist followers is that he cannot shake a cultural conservatism he learned before Federalism's fall.[24] Before concluding, however, that political strife is really a generation gap, "The Conservative" figures reconciliation not so much as a happy family but within a single man.

When Emerson ends what is an entertaining and even emotionally nuanced dialogue, he invokes the "man of courage" who transcends "the fury of faction" (187). Stasis and change may tend respectively toward old age and youth, but the coming hero can realize a synthesis and herald an "ideal republic" (177). The final rhetorical flight of "The Conservative" announces in ecstatic first person, "I am primarily engaged to myself to be a public servant of all the gods, to demonstrate to all men that there is intelligence and good will at the heart of things" (188). Committed to the project of self-culture, Emerson strives for heroism, even as his confidence wavers with the regret, "I allow myself in derelictions, and become idle and dissolute" (189). As is so often the case with Emerson, dull moods threaten self-reliance as high expectations prove to be both inspiring and disabling. Nonetheless, Emerson manages to end with the optimistic – though suddenly less personal – pledge, "The boldness of the hope men entertain transcends all former experience . . . . It predicts that amidst a planet peopled with conservatives, one Reformer may yet be born." In this instance, Emerson revises his terminology to suggest that in pregnant, unrealized times even activists are "conservatives," a conflation that anticipates the one true Reformer, whose arrival is assured by our "boldness

---

24 For the politics of Emerson's peers, see Barbara Packer, *The Transcendentalists*, in *The Cambridge History of American Literature, Vol. 2: 1820–1865*, ed. Sacvan Bercovitch (Cambridge: Cambridge University Press, 1995), 459–94, 548–604; and Anne C. Rose, *Transcendentalism as a Social Movement, 1830–1850* (New Haven: Yale University Press, 1981). For Emerson and Federalism, see Mary Kupiec Cayton, *Emerson's Emergence: Self and Society in the Transformation of New England, 1800–1845* (Chapel Hill: University of North Carolina Press, 1989), 3–32.

of hope." In Emerson's final formulation, if we can imagine him, he will come, for inspired subjectivity is itself the hero that resides within all men.

Fair enough, except that "The Transcendentalist" struggles to see clearly when, by dwelling on the personal hardships and seeming failures of studently patience, Emerson's speech becomes as much a confession as a manifesto. Though the essay, in Buell's words, is somewhat "cavalier" in its philosophical terminology, it offers a related series of dualisms and potential reconciliations.[25] One dialectic of the day is "Materialism" versus "Idealism" as "double consciousness" is initially formulated as an epistemological condition (205). At the same time, Emerson writes of the idealist as he appears in 1842, "From this transfer of the world into the consciousness, this beholding of all things in the mind, follow easily his whole ethics. It is simpler to be self-dependent" (195). In moving from subjectivity to ethics, Emerson follows the leads of Coleridge and Kant.[26] But when he discusses self-trust in terms of antebellum politics, the bridge between ideal theory and material practice threatens to collapse.

Among its various dualistic forms, double consciousness is a dialectical conflict between the "infinitude and paradise" of eternity and the "buzz and din" of active reform (206). As in "Lecture on the Times," Emerson shows an aversion to activism, so much so that he excludes many friends and associates from his philosophical club when he writes that transcendentalists are "not good members of society" and "do not willingly share in the public charities, in the public religious rites, in the enterprises of education, of missions foreign or domestic, in the abolition of the slave-trade, or in the temperance society" (202–3). But while Emerson dismisses reformist causes, he confronts the counter-complaint that patient idealists are in truth "paralyzed, and can never do anything for humanity." The weight of this charge is indicated by the fact that it comes, not from a parental conservative, but from the entire "world." "What will you do?" the world asks (204). "We will wait," the transcendentalist answers. "How long?" the dubious world persists. "Until the Universe rises up and calls us to work." To which the world responds with a merciless charge that Emerson hints at in "The Conservative," "But whilst you wait, you grow old and useless" – a point that sends Emerson reeling.

Earlier in "The Transcendentalist," Emerson writes that the "idealist can never go backward to be a materialist," but he also worries that such dedicated seekers never fulfill their potential (193). "So many promising

---

25 Buell, *Emerson*, 206.
26 Gustaaf Van Cromphout, *Emerson's Ethics* (Columbia: University of Missouri Press, 1999), 127–29.

youths, and never a finished man!" Emerson laments, building to what sounds like a sad folk song, "Where are the old idealists?" (201). Apparently they cannot go backward but neither can they go on; for although "The Conservative" predicts a synthesis of old age and youth, "The Transcendentalist" fears that they are irreconcilable and "stand in wild contrast" (205). The universe may merrily move toward perfection in a progressive, millennial plot, but the aging idealist does not. And Emerson has no greater fear than that he and the universe are out of joint, that he will patiently "perish of rest and rust" (204) and become a (pun intended) "[g]rave senior" (207), a member of that class that "Self-Reliance" (1841) dubs "seniors very unnecessary" (261).

Emerson's dedication to a youthful comportment helps to explain his lifelong penchant for younger, inspiring colleagues. It also suggests why he spends so much time defending his patient politics, not only from such actor-friends but also from his own misgivings. Emerson has seen how traumatic it is when idealism falters in the world. "The Conservative" may even have Emerson's friend, the depressive reformer Alcott, in mind when it says of activists, "Whatever they attempt in [their] direction, fails, and reacts suicidally on the actor" (177). "The Transcendentalist," however, weighs instead the personal cost of a studently politics that leads less heroically, perhaps even in flannels, to a rusty and obsolete grave. In "The Transcendentalist," it is the "old guardians" who run the risk of "suicide" (207). Not yet taking consolation in the wisdom that "Terminus" (1867) brings, Emerson fears that political postponement is a slow dying of the visionary light, that at the end of the day there is little distinction between paralysis and patience. "The Transcendentalist" thus wonders, "Cannot we screw our courage to patience and truth, and without complaint, or even with good-humor, await our turn of action in the Infinite Counsels?" (204-5). The question is not entirely rhetorical. What if the wild contrast of double consciousness is finally irreconcilable? What if Emerson's optative dialectic is finally a negative one forever dividing the struggling subject and precluding political rebirth?

Whereas "Lecture on the Times" confidently discerns eternity in political moments, and whereas "The Conservative" optimistically lingers over the one true man, "The Transcendentalist" worries that theory and practice "really show very little relation to each other, never meet and measure each other." For this reason, the idealist may never succeed in efforts of worldly reform, even if Emerson rebounds with a diction that he himself is growing to suspect, "Patience, then, is for us, is it not? Patience, and still patience" (206) – a locution suggesting doubts that reappear when Emerson descends to uncharacteristic supplication, "[W]ill you not tolerate one or two solitary voices in the land?" (208). "The Transcendentalist" does recover a glimmer of hope when it predicts that the world will tread "the path which the hero travels alone." But Emerson, perhaps also resisting the personal advances of Fuller, concludes with the less-than-stirring promise that a "fuller union" will only occur in "other, perhaps higher endowed and happier mixed clay than ours" (209).

In his still influential transcendentalist anthology, Perry Miller describes "The Transcendentalist" as a synthesis of and an escape from "The Conservative" and "Lecture on the Times."[27] The talk, however, also marks a devolution of Emerson's utopian hopes that can no longer maintain the optimism of the two earlier works. "The Transcendentalist" is a conflicted text that faces up to powerful fears – so powerful that present political inadequacy slides toward personal failure and suicide, so powerful that Emerson's eloquent swells do not dispel what the lecture calls "frightful skepticism" (204). The final balance, of course, depends on one's sense of Emerson's tone and emphasis, for it is hard to tell deep-seated despair from jeremiad-like motivational lament. Emerson himself may not be sure of the difference, though "The Transcendentalist" does escalate the quarrel with politics found in "The Conservative" and "Lecture on the Times." Patient reform in "The Transcendentalist" survives only with the lurking doubt that waiting is a losing game for the aging idealist who by admission and by deed aspires to public eloquence. By this route, "The Transcendentalist" brings politics home to Emerson's private heart. Retaining an uneasy faith in the coming heroic reformer, the moody prophet of individualism takes his political waking slow.

THE GODLIKE ODYSSEUS

A number of texts from 1844 can play a part in the narrative of Emerson's reluctant, uneven move from political abstention toward activism. A journal entry from 1844 cries, "Let our community rise en masse," though Emerson does not abandon his commitment to individual power, "[O]r let the private man put off the citizen, and awake the hero" (JMN 9:161). For Linck Johnson, "New England Reformers" (1844) represents Emerson's continuing doubts about politics.[28] Like many of Emerson's earlier works,

27 Perry Miller, *The Transcendentalists: An Anthology* (Cambridge: Harvard University Press, 1950), 471.
28 Linck Johnson, "Reforming the Reformers: Emerson, Thoreau, and the Sunday Lectures at Amory Hall, Boston," *Emerson Society Quarterly* 37 (winter 1991), 235–89.

the talk resists organized reform and embraces the "sufficiency of the private man" (592). But whereas the earlier "Man the Reformer" excuses "extreme and speculative" views (136), "New England Reformers" satirically warns of single-minded movements which hold that something as mundane as yeast lies at the root of all evil. For Emerson, such monomaniacal focus lacks universal faith, and "New England Reformers" calls instead on the "man of great heart and mind" (602). This familiar figure also appears in the essay "Politics" (1844) as the "wise man" who reconciles the "strife of ferocious parties" (567, 565). Published in *Essays: Second Series* (1844), "Politics" was a widely available work; and both *The Blithedale Romance* (1852) and *Walden* (1854) appropriate some of Emerson's tropes, even if the essay has not been a main fixture in recent accounts of Emerson and reform.[29]

More crucial for many modern scholars is "Emancipation in the British West Indies," an 1844 address that marks Emerson's enlistment in the antislavery cause and denounces in no uncertain terms the brutal facts of chattel bondage. These are significant developments, yet Emerson's speech is hardly a retraction of his previous views. "Emancipation in the British West Indies".[30] discusses abolitionism as the "fortification" of an "ethical abstraction". Condescendingly, Emerson praises the movement for "making dull men eloquent," while he also instructs his antislavery audience (as well as his fellow-speaker Douglass), "Let us withhold every reproachful, and, if we can, every indignant remark" (AW 8). Emerson even plays a subtle and somewhat specious game of I-told-you-so. Admitting, apologetically it seems, his erstwhile "weakness" on the slavery question, he then presents a curious account of political causality, "[B]y speech and by silence; by doing and by omitting to do, [emancipation] goes forward." This language echoes "The Transcendentalist" and its praise for student reformers, who work "by silence, as well as by speech, not only by what they did, but by what they forbore to do" (209). In this way, "Emancipation in the British West Indies" continues to espouse reform without means as Emerson insists that his patient politics

---

29 In *Walden*, Thoreau concurs with Emerson's statement: "We think our civilization near its meridian, but we are yet only at the cock-crowing and the morning star" (568). Hawthorne, in a less friendly allusion, complicates the final line of "Politics" which claims that society can be organized "as well as a knot of friends, or a pair of lovers" (571). *The Blithedale Romance* points out, however, that there is a dangerous and not always clear difference between the "knot" of communal friendship and the bond of sexual love.

30 Critics emphasizing the importance of "Emancipation in the British West Indies" include Gougeon, *Virtue's Hero*, 75–85; and Robinson, *Emerson and the Conduct of Life*, 81–82. Emerson, *Emerson's Antislavery Writings*, 7. Hereafter cited in the text as "AW."

successfully work toward justice. More active reformers did not object in 1844. At a time when abolitionists lacked influential friends, Emerson's talk was welcome support, even if it was less an adjustment of his views and more an occasion to read historical evidence into his cosmology, "There is a blessed necessity by which the interest of men is always driving them to the right" (AW 33). Pointing less to American bondage and more toward foreign liberty, "Emancipation in the British West Indies" takes heart that good things happen in the world. Evil, loss, despondency, the failure of society to move toward the Good – these contingencies are more formidable challenges for Emerson that find their most profound expression in another text from 1844.

Major readers of Emerson – including Stephen Whicher, Barbara Packer, Sharon Cameron, Stanley Cavell, Richard Poirier, and Lawrence Buell – take "Experience" to be a crucial and even singularly momentous text in Emerson's career.[31] The essay, however, is not generally read into the story of Emerson's hesitant abolitionism, which makes it a useful place to examine the importance of slavery in Emerson's thought. Clearly "Emancipation in the British West Indies" and the Fugitive Slave Law addresses are about slavery. Clearly it takes a determined reading to make chattel bondage a main topic in, say, *Nature* (1836), "Intellect" (1841), or "The Over-Soul" (1841). But how might slavery figure in "Experience," as comprehensive an Emerson essay as there is and one that suggests in subtle ways the relationship of Emerson's transcendentalism and his temporal life?

"Experience" does not lend itself to summary or redaction, even if "the lords of life" give belated and approximate structure to Emerson's compilation of themes – "Illusion, Temperament, Succession, Surface, Surprise, Reality, Subjectiveness" (490–91). The essay shifts between depressed, practical, and optative moods, while turning back upon itself to revisit earlier claims. One effect of this stream of self-consciousness is the potential conflation of philosophy and politics, particularly when Emerson asks himself, "[W]hy not realize your world?" (492). In "Experience," Emerson's idealism struggles as true perception ebbs and flows against grief, inconstancy, solipsism, and the tempting relief of the

31 Stephen Whicher, *Freedom and Fate: An Inner Life of Ralph Waldo Emerson* (Philadelphia: University of Pennsylvania Press, 1953), 109–22; Barbara Packer, *Emerson's Fall: A New Interpretation of the Major Essays* (New York: Continuum, 1982), esp. 151–55; Sharon Cameron, "Representing Grief: Emerson's 'Experience,'" *Representations* 15 (summer 1986): 15–41; Stanley Cavell, *This New Yet Unapproachable America: Lectures after Emerson after Wittgenstein* (Albuquerque: Living Batch Press, 1989), 77–118; Poirier, *Poetry and Pragmatism*, 47–75; Buell, *Emerson*, 124–35.

"mid-world" (481). Emerson names his conditions for victory over these various "skepticisms": "[T]he new philosophy must take them in, and make affirmations outside of them," a goal requiring a redeemed subjectivity ultimately possessed by the hero who can realize his ideals (487). Such heroic individualism is, of course, a staple of literary romanticism in general and transcendentalism in particular. The point here is that "Experience" imagines this great man as both a philosopher and reformer.

"Experience" begins by bemoaning the dreamy, alien state of the self in which the transparent eyeball of *Nature* has lost its visionary power, "Of what use is genius, if the organ is too convex or too concave, and cannot find a focal distance within the actual horizon of human life?" (474). Genius, then, must make sense in and of experience, particularly an experience recently marred by the death of Emerson's five-year-old son and by the failure of reformers who "never acquit [their] debt" and "die young." Part of the problem is that illusion occludes the vision of the subject-hero. Emerson doubts if he can recognize the all-encompassing "new individual," so much so that he makes the startling admission, "There is no adaptation or universal applicability in men" (477). Rather, one "needs the whole society, to give the symmetry we seek," a claim that may appear amenable to a more communitarian, less romantically liberal politics, except that reliance on social institutions is not for Emerson an enjoyable thing. He compares party promises to a western road that turns into a "squirrel-track" and runs "up a tree" (478). Chiding the organizers of Brook Farm, who barely stayed solvent, not by farming but by reluctantly taking in students, Emerson notes that "Education-Farm" has failed to achieve its original promise of grounding labor in the soil. The same is even true of reformers more studious than active, "Our young people have thought and written much on labor and reform, and for all that they have written, neither the world nor themselves have got on a step." Like "Benito Cereno," "Experience" suffers what it calls the "vertigo of shows and politics" (479), though Emerson's angst comes not from Hobbes but from Hume and Kant, who pressed the possibilities of radical subjectivity to potentially skeptical extremes.[32] More than Melville and Poe, and like Douglass and Stowe, Emerson is uncomfortable with his unbelief; and so the deeper that "Experience" sinks in despair, the more it fights for hope.

---

32 For Hume, see Robinson, *Emerson and the Conduct of Life*, 19–29; Evelyn Barish, *Emerson: The Roots of Prophecy* (Princeton: Princeton University Press, 1989), 99–115; and John Michael, *Emerson and Skepticism: The Cipher of the World* (Baltimore: Johns Hopkins University Press, 1988), 36–57. For Kant, see David Van Leer, *Emerson's Epistemology: The Argument of the Essays* (New York: Cambridge University Press, 1986).

For a few famous paragraphs, Emerson advocates the civil life of surface, "Let us treat men and women well: treat them as if they were real." Let us, too, "do broad justice where we are, . . . accepting our actual companions and circumstances." As if to preempt political critiques of transcendental disengagement, Emerson privileges communal justice over solipsistic doubt and utopian fantasy, momentarily assuming a *we* so that we can all get along. The idealist, however, cannot go backwards to be a materialist, for human experience is too richly complex for the logical laws of the mid-world. This is why Emerson's oft-quoted line, "[T]he true art of life is to skate well," is not the simple concession to material reality that it is sometimes taken to be (478). When resisting the mechanical universe posited by David Hartley, Coleridge described in *Biographia Literaria* a "water-insect on the surface of rivulets" that "*wins* its way up against the stream by alternate pulses of active and passive motion, now resisting the current, and now yielding to it in order to gather strength . . . . This is no unapt emblem of the mind's self-experience in the act of thinking."[33] The skating that Coleridge and Emerson describe leads toward the victory of transcendentalism. To skate well is not to travel in circles but rather fitfully to move upstream toward the origins of truth. In this sense, the chill that "Experience" feels brings both a paralyzing, icebound depression *and* an opportunity for movement and growth, progress that "Experience" begins to achieve when it skims over – and past – surface.

By proclaiming, "Life is a series of surprises," Emerson opens himself to a universe, seeking reality in "flashes of light" and in "sudden discoveries of . . . beauty and repose" (483–84). He worries, however, that such seeming truths are merely a "flux of moods" (485–86). Thus again the threat of skepticism looms, and it is not until Emerson remembers *Nature* that he recalls how to realize his world. He writes, "People forget that it is the eye which makes the horizon, and the rounding mind's eye which makes this or that man a type or representative of humanity" (487). This "great man" is not a figure external to the self; he evinces the creative power of the mind to synthesize spherical, absolute truths (489). If we perceive the hero, he is come, not so much to save society, but rather to demonstrate the reliability and primacy of the self. In doing so, the representative man potentially brings on solipsism when "every object fall[s] successively into the subject itself." Earlier in "Experience," this prison of the perceptions sent Emerson running for the mid-world. Later, he continues to worry that life is only a "solitary performance." The difference now is that he has learned to accept

33 Coleridge, *Biographia Literaria*, 1: 124.

his subjectivity and the partiality it entails, "It is a main lesson of wisdom to know your own [facts] from another's. I have learned that I cannot dispose other people's facts" (490). Once granting that this limitation is a "constitutional necessity" of the mind – and taking Emerson's pun that his inability to "dispose" of other people's experiences means that he can neither use them nor entirely discard them – solipsistic anxiety finally gives way to a naturalized if tenuous "self-trust." This conclusion of sorts represents Emerson's redemption of a self-reliant subjectivity that is independent of and yet connected to other subjectivities. In the terms that Emerson uses in "Experience," this subjectivity retains a spherical autonomy but touches others at points. The inability to get nearer to them is both a burden and boon. If "Experience" had exclusively epistemological worries, the essay might end here. But whether Emerson suffers, accepts, or celebrates his negotiation of self and other, he knows and to some degree has internalized potential political accusations.

Immediately after reclaiming his transcendental subjectivity, "Experience" moves unrepentantly toward the problem of social duty, as if this – and not the dangers of theoretical skepticism – pose a final challenge. Insisting that he cannot dispose of other people's facts, Emerson compares the "sympathetic person" to a swimmer surrounded by "drowning men" who would drag the swimmer down and on whom "[c]harity would be wasted." Using this trope of drowning (originally from Cicero and one that Thoreau would later adopt),[34] "Experience" verges on hard-hearted selfishness to the point where a reader might prefer the uncertain, grief-stricken Emerson, who at least laments that he cannot lament for those he cannot touch. Parker, Whitman, Fuller, and Julian Hawthorne agreed that there was something cold and ungenerous in Emerson's idealism.[35] Emerson, however, is in no rush to assure his readers of his compassion, nor does he consider self-reliance to be only a philosophical state. "In this our talking America," he writes, announcing the political case, "we are ruined by our good nature and listening to all sides," a rejection of sentimental benevolence, civic humanism, and political discussion.

34 In *De Officiis*, III, Cicero imagines a case where a wise man is drowning while a fool holds a plank from their sinking ship. Thoreau asserts in "Civil Disobedience" that one may not wrest a plank from a drowning man even to save oneself (See *Transcendentalism: A Reader*, ed. Meyerson, 550, 565). Emerson's version of this problem is more troubling insofar as there is no plank with which to save another. There is only a self-reliant swimmer who can only save himself.

35 For Parker and Whitman, see Eduardo Cadava, *Emerson and the Climates of History* (Stanford: Stanford University Press, 1997), 141. Julian Hawthorne says of Emerson, "[T]here was a chill at the bottom of his charity" (*The Memoirs of Julian Hawthorne*, ed. Edith Garrigues Hawthorne [New York: MacMillan, 1938], 97). For Fuller, see her 1844 review of *Essays: Second Series*.

The fierce individualism of this position becomes particularly troubling when Emerson describes a John Flaxman drawing of a scene from *The Eumenides* in which the abject Orestes begs Apollo to save him from the Furies. "The face of the god," Emerson writes, "expresses a shade of regret and compassion, but calm with the conviction of the irreconcilableness of the two spheres. He is born into other politics, into the eternal and beautiful." As in "The Transcendentalist," synthesis seems impossible, mainly because Emerson's poet-god is detached from the human sphere – more detached than the Apollo of Aeschylus's *Eumenides*, who at least takes a grudging but active role in defending the mortal Orestes. Apollo's intellectual control certainly stands in contrast to the atavistic vengeance of the Furies. But Emerson's account emphasizes the gap between ideal god and material man, whose heaven-ordained, inconsolable suffering Emerson all but ignores (in the same way he resisted the reformist importunities of that other Orestes, Mr. Brownson).[36] Focusing instead on the "other politics" of "the eternal and the beautiful," Emerson attends and even aspires to the bearing of Apollo, the god with whom he identifies in "Threnody" (1846) when again he mourns the loss of his son.[37]

That Emerson imagines himself as a god of poetry is provoking but not entirely surprising. Throughout his career and most emphatically in the 1830s and 1840s, Emerson tends to see himself as a poet more than a reformer. "Experience" continues to both interrogate and defend this claim, admitting that the calling of Apollo may be socially irresponsible in specific political ways. With the kneeling Orestes begging at the feet of the elevated Apollo, Flaxman's drawing resembles an archetypal abolitionist image in which the prostrate African slave supplicates the superior white, who either offers philanthropic relief or responds with disdain, even violence.[38] Apollo's compassionate detachment, however, walks a middle road, which Emerson – unlike abolitionist polemics and perhaps to our political chagrin – exculpates by denying the connection between poetry and social duty. Apollo simply "cannot enter" into the "turmoils of the earth." He remains a vaguely regretful idealist "surcharged with his divine destiny." Apollo thus figures Emerson's urge to transcend the

36 See, for instance, Brownson's "Emerson" (1839).
37 Poirier points out that "Threnody" calls Waldo "The hyacinthine boy," a reference to Apollo's beloved boy, Hyacinthus, whom the god mistakenly killed (*Poetry and Pragmatism*, 60).
38 As Kirk Savage shows, this image persists in the post-bellum period (*Standing soldiers, Kneeling Slaves: Race, War, and Monuments in Nineteenth-Century America* [Princeton: Princeton University Press, 1997]).

messy work of reform, suggesting that to be godlike is to be free of entanglements such as abolitionism. Having unapologetically implied that such freedom is literally inhumane, Emerson in "Experience" leaves the challenge of politics behind and proceeds to his final comments.

Pointing toward a conclusion, the lords of life roughly summarize the essay, while Emerson offers what can sound like disclaimers free from self-accusation, "I gossip for my hour concerning the eternal politics . . . . I know that the world I converse with in the city and in the farms, is not the world I *think*. I observe that difference, and shall observe it. One day, I shall know the value and law of this discrepance" (491–92). Emerson has learned to live with double consciousness, but he still looks forward to a better "one day." "Patience and patience, we shall win at the last" is the promise that survives from "The Times." What also survives is Emerson's desire to go out on a high note; for if the penultimate paragraph of "Experience" speaks in a more or less measured voice, Emerson finishes with a thrilling burst of familiar eloquence that predicts the end of the discrepance between his ideal and material worlds. After the despondency of the opening sections, after the recurrent masquerade of illusion, after the insufficiency of surface, after learning – drowning men notwithstanding – to accept a stubborn self-reliance more lonely than inspired, the concluding sentence of "Experience" imagines a message voiced by "solitude," "Never mind the ridicule, never mind the defeat: up again, old heart! – it seems to say, – there is victory yet for all justice; and the true romance which the world exists to realize, will be the transformation of genius into practical power." What "practical power" means for Emerson is not easily pinned down. His essay "Power" (1860) does not limit power to the political realm and indeed suggests a kind of agency beyond political definition. At the same time, Emerson does not disregard the nation-moving potential of power, nor does he at the end of "Experience" disregard political applications. In fact, when Emerson comes to predict the realization of ideals in the world, he does not identify with the "other politics" of a disengaged divine; for when he writes, "up again, old heart!" he invokes a figure less like Apollo and more like another Greek – the human but godlike, honey-tongued Odysseus, who stands as a model for heroic reform and for the transformation of genius.

When Homer's Odysseus returns to Ithaca, he watches in the guise of a beggar as the reckless suitors defile his house and insult the unrecognized king. There is much pleasure in our knowledge that the villains are messing with the wrong individual, for Odysseus has come to redeem, not just his country, house, and family, but his faith that the gods, though biased and flaky, serve justice in the end. First Odysseus must overcome illusion and impatience, endure the jibes of fortune and men, and wait for the gods to send him a sign before he wreaks his revenge. Thus at the beginning of Book XX, Odysseus struggles to sustain his hope, crying more or less in the face of adversity, *Up again, old heart!* Allusion can be a tricky business when requiring the task of the translator, particularly considering that Emerson rendered passages from Homer with disputed degrees of skill. Robert Fagles's recent version of the *Odyssey* translates the line, "Bear up, old heart!" and there is more to suggest that Emerson has the King of Ithaca on his mind.[39]

The transcendentalists loved Greek myth in general and Odysseus in particular, so much so that Fuller and Thoreau both named Odysseus as an intellectual forerunner.[40] "Experience" itself recommends Homer as one of five authors who ought to be read; and Emerson reread the *Odyssey* in 1842 while composing the essay. "Experience" generally draws from Odyssean tropes of sea, sleep, and illusion, while also adopting the redemptive figure of the disguised and discredited king. In the essay, Emerson waits for "my lord, . . . in what disguise soever he shall appear. I know he is in the neighborhood hidden among vagabonds" (475). Many romantics and romancers favored this trope, more Odyssean than Christological, a fact implied in *Representative Men* (1850), "Every novel is a debtor to Homer" (620). In this way, Odysseus realizes life as a "true romance"; and he shows that humans are already kings, although they and their fellows do not always know it. In this context, the puzzling poem of "Experience" may make a kind of sense. The "Little man" who seems in danger of being stepped on by the "lords of life" is not unlike the pawn Odysseus embroiled in larger Olympian plots (469). Happily, Emerson's harried man is befriended by a personified "nature," who maternally assures him that he is one of the deified race. Odysseus, too, receives whispered encouragement as Athena takes him in hand; and in the pantheistic rough and tumble of Homer's Greek cosmology, he shows himself to be quite godlike, though not exactly a god. Like Carlyle's *Heroes, Hero-Worship, and the Heroic in History* (1841), "Experience" turns

39 For Emerson's familiarity with Greek, see Robert Loewenberg "Emerson or Inference: Could Emerson Read Greek?", *English Language Notes* 18: 1 (Sept. 1980): 27–30. *The Odyssey*, trans. Robert Fagles (New York: Viking, 1996), 411. Other translations include *The Odyssey*, trans. Richard Lattimore (New York: Harper and Rowe, 1965), 298 ("Bear up, my heart!"). Emerson also owned Greek and Latin versions of the *Odyssey*.

40 Fuller to W. H. Channing [?], August 1842, *The Letters of Margaret Fuller*, 3: 80; *The Writings of Henry D. Thoreau: Journal, Vol. 2: 1842–1848*, ed. Robert Sattelmeyer (Princeton: Princeton University Press, 1984), 156.

to ancient myth to conflate great men and deities. Fallen but with immortal souls, humankind is a god in ruins.

"Experience" is not, of course, a strict rewriting of *The Odyssey*. Emerson is no King of Ithaca in sexual prowess and warlike skill, and he would no doubt object to Odysseus's dishonesty, cunning, and political machinations. More personally, no amount of worldly travel will bring Emerson back to Waldo, and no amount of suffering will bring about a father–son reunion on earth. Yet Emerson's longing for the impossible may make the myth of Odysseus that much more appealing. Fantasy may even be a necessary step in the project of social reform, particularly for a thinker like Emerson who tends to conceive of his life and times in literary terms. Early in "Experience," Emerson writes of the king disguised as a vagabond, "I carry the keys of my castle in my hand, ready to throw them at the feet of my lord" (475). By the end, however, Emerson writes that the "key" is "my own" (490); and he takes over the role of king by adopting Odysseus's rallying cry, "[U]p again, old heart!" In "The Times" and beyond, Emerson does not usually cast himself as the coming reformer. Rowe notes in admonishing Emerson's politics that Emerson more often compares his doubts to the hesitant failures of Hamlet.[41] The Prince of Denmark is a suitable figure for an overly intellectual, epistemologically paralyzed, and even cowardly skeptic whose patient reflection is a kind of deferral that leads to a bloody catastrophe.

At the conclusion of "Experience," however, Emerson is not Prince Hamlet, or at least is not meant to be. He figures his patience as the wise forbearance of Odysseus who, after yet again lifting up his heart, witnesses the thunderclap of Zeus, throws off his beggarly rags, and with Apollo directing his arrows sets aright his world. Odysseus even regains the youth that "The Times" associates with active reform, for Athena has aged him as part of his disguise, only to return his natural form when the moment of crisis arrives, making him less the Ulysses of Tennyson and more the great man of Homer and recalling the opening verse of "The Poet" (1844): "Olympian bards . . . find us young, / And always keep us so" (446). In "Experience," Emerson does not in the end cast off his robe of inaction, though "Emancipation in the British West Indies" in some ways fulfills his prediction. "Experience" stops on the very threshold of Odysseus's metamorphosis that heralds an onslaught more daring and grisly than the climax of an action movie. That "Experience" never crosses the threshold is one indication of Emerson's doubts about the value of political reform.

41 Rowe, *At Emerson's Tomb*, 17–41.

Yet he also recognizes the appeal of practical power. On the verge of heroism, Emerson waits for a flash of light from the gods. His message remains one of studently patience but his posture is that of an actor.

What to make of Emerson's identification with Odysseus is no simple thing. Though Emerson, like Thoreau and Jones Very, saw Odysseus as a figure based in history and thus a plausible model for a real world politics, it is not hard to read Emerson's narrative of empowerment as a postponement of social responsibility, perhaps even a delusion of grandeur (a position recently taken by Jay Grossman in his account of the politics of "Experience").[42] More specifically, Adorno and Horkheimer see Odysseus as a "prototype of the bourgeois individual" representing an effort to enlist myth in the service of enlightenment instrumentalism.[43] Emerson is certainly an heir to the legacy of democratic liberalism. But if "Experience's" faith in the conquering hero points to a nostalgic and mystifying failure to resist a domineering modernity, Odysseus also offers Emerson an answer to the problem of realizing his world.

Recalling Emerson's simultaneous affinity for neo-platonic and romantic philosophy, "Experience" follows allegorical readings by Plotinus and Schelling that interpret Odysseus as a figure of idealism brought into the world.[44] Along these lines, Martha Nussbaum sees Odysseus as a figure of humanism, who is tempted by the transcendence of the gods but finally accepts his earthly duties. By tempering Apollo's immortal detachment with the godlike but human Odysseus, "Experience" aspires to a way of living that Nussbaum calls "transcending by *descent*," an ethic that seeks to enact guiding truths by accepting moral imperatives.[45] *Representative Men* will praise Odysseus as a "working king" (735); and "Experience" discovers in Odysseus a kind of philosopher-king, a personal, political, and philosophical hero who protects his son, saves his family and country,

42 Grossman, *Reconstituting the American Renaissance,* 197–205.
43 Horkheimer and Adorno, *Dialectic of Enlightenment,* 43.
44 See M. H. Abrams, *Natural Supernaturalism: Tradition and Revolution in Romantic Literature* (New York: Norton, 1971), 147–49, 222–25. In brief, Plotinus sees Odysseus as a figure who instructs us to deny the "pleasant spectacles" of Circe and Calypso and, instead, "stir up and assume a purer eye within" (Thomas Taylor, *Concerning the Beautiful; or, A Paraphrase Translation from the Greek of Plotinus* in *Thomas Taylor the Platonist,* ed. Kathleen Raine and George Mills Harper [Princeton: Princeton University Press, 1969], 156–57). Schelling, in his *System of Transcendental Idealism,* describes Odysseus's saga as a return of the ideal spirit to the human, historical realm; and in *Ages of the World* (1811), Schelling invokes a Homeric poet who bridges the gap between "the world of thought and the world of reality" (quoted in Abrams, 31). Emerson more explicitly discusses Odysseus as a figure of synthesis in "Powers of the Mind" (1858), in *The Later Lectures of Ralph Waldo Emerson, 1843–1871, Vol. 2: 1855–1871,* ed. Ronald Bosco and Joel Myerson (Athens: The University of Georgia Press, 2001), 2: 76.
45 Nussbaum, *Love's Knowledge,* 377–91.

redeems a self-trusting subjectivity, and finally retires into private life (not unlike another favorite of the antebellum era, the farmer-statesman Cincinnatus). Odysseus thus plays a number of roles attractive to Emerson and even manages in his synthetic capacity to strike a deal with destiny.

In "The Times" and beyond, Emerson's thoughts on reform obscure political causality insofar as Emerson says almost nothing specific about how he will remake his world. "Experience" is particularly vague about the agency of social change, in part because Emerson often defers to the power of "constitutional necessity," also described at various points as "great Fortune," "divine destiny," and "beautiful limits." Whicher overstated the case by using "Experience" to announce Emerson's phase of fatalism; and Christopher Newfield probably goes too far in making submission the main message of Emersonian thought. But even if Emerson throughout his career advances both freedom and determinism in complicated and not always coherent ways, it is only more reason to view his politics in these conflicted terms. Indeed, some of Emerson's best readers have found the question of fate impossible to ignore when making sense of Emerson's politics in general and his responses to slavery in particular.[46]

Here the waters become quite choppy. No matter how friendly and subsuming the universal mind or over-soul, a power greater than the self cannot help but curtail, or at least mediate, the autonomy of self-reliance. Moreover, as we have seen in Melville and as Emerson suggests in "Lecture on the Times," belief in fate can dissipate political energies, whether one sees the workings of necessity as a revealed or undisclosed telos. Emerson writes of Calvinists in "Fate" (1860), "Wise men feel that there is something which cannot be talked or voted away" (944); and his view of race as a fated aspect of character can suggest a kind of resignation in the face of racial inequality. That said, Bercovitch finds in Emerson and his Puritan predecessors a sense of providence that actually spurs civil efforts and constructs profoundly politicized selves.[47] Nor did Abraham Lincoln's deep-seated belief in a godly design keep him from playing an

46 Whicher, *Freedom and Fate*, 109–22; Julie Ellison corrects Whicher in *Emerson's Romantic Style* (Princeton: Princeton University Press, 1984), 5. Newfield, *The Emerson Effect*. For fate and politics in Emerson, see Phyllis Cole, "Emerson, England, and Fate," in *Emerson: Prophecy, Metamorphosis, and Influence*, ed. David Levin (New York: Columbia University Press, 1975); West, *The American Evasion of Philosophy*, esp. 28–35; Robinson, *Emerson and the Conduct of Life* (which sees "Experience" as a key text in Emerson's attempt to reconcile fate and social reform); Lawrence Buell, "Emerson's Fate," in *Emersonian Circles: Essays in Honor of Joel Myerson*, ed. Wesley Mott and Robert Burkholder (Rochester: University of Rochester Press, 1997), 11–28; and Cavell's reply to Packer, "Emerson's Constitutional Amending: Reading 'Fate, in *Emerson's Transcendental Etudes*, 192–214.'"
47 Bercovitch, *The Puritan Origins of the American Self*, 157–86.

active role in the dispensation of American slavery. How Emerson's activism relates with his determinism is not consistent across his career. But when "Experience" in 1844 broaches the paradox of political duty and irredeemable suffering in America, it does not recall Cotton Mather's hagiography or a racist ethnographic taxonomy, nor does it turn to discussions of necessity from Jonathan Edwards or Kant. Instead, Emerson remembers Flaxman's scene alluding to Orestes's successful appeal for relief from the fate-ordained Furies, and one that eventually gives way to the *Odyssey* and its marginally free hero.[48]

"Experience" thus balances fate and free will, less in the logic of covenant theology, cranial capacity, or modern philosophy and more in the slippery context of *moira* – the shifting, demanding, and irregularly prophesized will of Homer's gods, who themselves appear at times to be bound by their own divine destinies. Despite many references in the *Odyssey* to an iron-wired fate, Zeus marvels in Book I, "Perverse Mankind! whose Wills created free, / Charge all their woes on absolute Decree," a view of agency that leaves some space for individual heroism and one that Bernard Williams finds particularly congenial to philosophy in the modern era.[49] Like the Greek tragedians, Homer does not treat fate with systematic rigor. He teaches instead a conduct of life for humans living as best they can among the unpredictable wills of the gods, who – in Emerson's case – do not live on Olympus but stand more for the shifting moods of the self. Or as Emerson writes in "Experience" as he, too, leaves off systematic analysis, "Life itself is a mixture of power and form" (478), a claim also expressed in "Fate" when Emerson finds a "just balance" between what he calls the "mixed instrumentalities" of "power and circumstance" (944, 946, 949). "Fate" builds altars to the Beautiful Necessity. "Experience" is less adoring when it recommends keeping freedom and fate in their proper "proportion" (481).

What this means for the politics of "Experience" is that the hero must endure the unavoidable trials and setbacks that his *moira* has in store. The hero, however, must also attend to signs that mark his opportunity for action. He must wait with patience and watch with care to play his destined and yet willful part in the universe. In this sense, "Experience" is no less prospective than the lectures from "The Times." It shows the depths of Emerson's faith in forbearing heroic reform, even in an essay

---

48 While the Furies are not the Fates, Emerson conflates them in his 1847 poem "Fate" (Ralph Waldo Emerson, *Collected Poems and Translations* [New York: Library of America, 1994], 25).

49 *The Odyssey, Vol. 1*, trans. Pope, 13. Bernard Williams, *Shame and Necessity* (Berkeley: University of California Press, 1993), 21–49.

most often associated with skepticism, Waldo, and fate. It may be tempting to divorce Apollo's "other politics" from the turmoil of mortals and from reformers' "manipular attempts to realize the world of thought" (492). As Poirier warns, we should not reduce Emerson's essay to "local and blinkered historicist readings."[50] And yet for Emerson practical power means, among other things, politics. If Odysseus is any indication, and much suggests that he is, "Experience" imagines Emerson on the verge of actively realizing his world. Soon enough, the essay predicts, a political battle will be joined. That the arrows would fly over chattel bondage was not immediately apparent in 1844, though Flaxman's drawing and Emerson's references to slavery and freedom suggest that "Experience" hears and defers the call to abolitionism. Though by no means as explicit as "Emancipation in the British West Indies," "Experience" can be taken to be part of the long foreground of Emerson's activism. Six years later, Webster's Compromise would become a sign that called forth Emerson's most political commitments. Only then does he join the antislavery fray, reservations and all.

THE COMPLEMENTAL MAN

One obstacle to understanding Emerson is that he sometimes becomes an author-function. This is particularly true when his name is made synonymous with a liberal, self-possessive identity that feels entitled to personal rights but refuses social duties while at the same time claiming sole authority in matters of politics, morals, and epistemology. Emerson certainly places the individual at the center of his thought, and clearly he is ill at ease with communal projects of reform. Yet Emerson is extremely sensitive and often responsive to political summons; and though his Emersonian self at times aspires to a totalized autonomy, it remains across the course of his career in a state of unsettled duress. "The Times" excuses the transcendentalist from the pressing demands of an impatient world. "Experience" finds in the eloquent hero temporary relief from a host of doubts. Such self-defenses are so carefully wrought as to constitute self-criticisms, particularly when Emerson questions the power of the representative man, a worry brought to a head not by the death of his son but by a national tragedy.

Emerson's "Address to the Citizens of Concord on the Fugitive Slave Law" (1851) compares the Compromise of 1850 to "a sheet of lightning at

---

50 Poirier, *Poetry and Pragmatism*, 53.

midnight. It showed truth." (AW 55). This recalls the surprising "flashes of light" that reveal reality in "Experience." Perhaps Emerson even has Zeus's fulgurous signal to Odysseus in mind. "Benito Cereno" will come to insinuate that in the matter of fugitive slaves a "flash of revelation" does not always undeceive. But for Emerson and many northern observers, the Fugitive Slave Law unmasked the aggression of a monolithic slave power that dominated the servile politicians and populace of the North. After the Compromise of 1850 and at the height of his political outrage, Emerson reassured himself of his region's moral worth, writing in his journal, "[T]he genius of Boston is seen in her . . . *northern* acuteness of mind, a versatile Ulysses, which is generically antislavery" (JMN 11:395).[51]

Emerson was not alone in needing the impetus of the Fugitive Slave Law to push him from the antislavery threshold into full-fledged abolitionism. Even after "Experience" and "Emancipation in the British West Indies," Emerson described reform in general and abolitionism in particular as distractions from his primary intellectual and artistic work. His "Ode to W. H. Channing" (1846) concisely expresses many of these misgivings. Again resisting the political pressures of his transcendental friends, Emerson complains of the "statesman's rant" and "politique / Which at the best is trick." Most troubling is that some of the poem's claims resemble those of slavery proponents when Emerson notes that chattel bondage is not the only form of slavery and holds that nature "exterminates / Races by stronger races," the implication being that "white faces" will supersede the "Black." As racist as this is, Emerson is far from advocating chattel bondage. For him, politique – including southern institutions – cannot stand against natural law, an order based on a providential plan with which the poet-philosopher will align. In this way, as Laura Walls has argued, Emerson thinks within an enlightenment framework, even if his sense of noetic authority is not precisely rationalistic but rather based in what he variously calls "moral sense," "moral sentiment," "intuition," and "Reason."[52] It is only by shunning the logic of politics and the statesman's faulty language that the innocently "astonished Muse finds thousands at her side." As might be expected by now, the agency of this happy coalition goes unexplored by Emerson. His "Ode," like "The Times" and "Experience," does not dabble in tactics, expressing instead a faith also apparent in an 1848 lecture from *Mind and*

---

51 "A versatile Ulysses" is the translation from Emerson's Greek provided by the editors of the journals.
52 Laura Dassow Walls, *Emerson's Life in Science: The Culture of Truth* (Ithaca: Cornell, 2003).

Manners of the Nineteenth Century: "Every truth tends to become a power. Every idea from the moment of its emergence, begins to gather material forces, and, after a little while makes itself known in the spheres of politics and commerce. It works first on thoughts, then on things; it makes feet, and afterward shoes."[53] One problem here is what Emerson means by "a little while," for after the passage of the Fugitive Slave Law, his patience wears increasingly thin.

"Address to the Citizens of Concord" retains some familiar reservations about abolitionism. Decrying the Fugitive Slave Law only somewhat ironically as a "personal inconvenience," Emerson sets inviolable selfhood and regional pride before the welfare of slaves (AW 53). He also condemns the "canting, fanaticism, sedition, and 'one idea'" of reformers, while tending toward his usual ideal abstractions, "The crisis is interesting as it shows the self-protecting nature of the world" (AW 56,57). Following Thoreau's "Resistance to Civil Government" (1849), which itself follows "The American Scholar," Emerson eventually ends his speech with an appeal to the righteous "one man" (AW 72). But before he does, the "Address" expresses what is for Emerson an unprecedented sense of urgency insofar as the Fugitive Slave Law "has forced us all into politics, and made it a paramount duty to seek what it is often a duty to shun" (AW 53).

There are a number of reasons why the Fugitive Slave Law was for Emerson what he described as a "new experience." A decade earlier, "Self-Reliance" mocked the "incredible tenderness for black folk a thousand miles off" (262). In 1851, however, slavery stalked the streets of Boston, not only threatening the freedom of fugitive slaves but the civil rights of all. Here was a likely chance to demonstrate one of Emerson's favorite premises, that immoral material statutes cannot stand before higher law. "Address to the Citizens of Concord" calls "negro slavery" the "greatest calamity in the universe," a claim that the early Emerson would have considered monomaniacal (AW 57). But what if some abolitionists were right? What if the soul of the nation was at stake in a struggle of good against evil? – a possibility that seemed increasingly likely as violence exploded over the rendition of the fugitive slave Thomas Sims. The Compromise of 1850 and the civil strife that followed convinced Stowe that a "mighty influence is abroad, surging and heaving the world, as with an earthquake."[54] In a similar vein, Theodore Parker described the

---

53 Emerson, "The Relation of Intellect to Natural Science" (1848), in *The Later Lectures of Ralph Waldo Emerson*, 1:169.
54 Stowe, *Uncle Tom's Cabin*, 476.

Fugitive Slave Law as a deluge that "rained forty days and forty nights, and brought a flood of slavery over this whole land."[55] Emerson, too, was profoundly disturbed, though his rhetoric avoids apocalyptic imagery. "Address to the Citizens of Concord" laments (and uses as motivation) the fear that some transcendental tenets are wrong – that subjectivity is too discrete to make men "sharers of a certain experience," that there is no solid reality "independent of appearances," that ecstatic "angels" will not sing even in "the best hours," and that there is no ideal "counterbalance" to material force (AW 58). These uncertainties are precisely those that Emerson confronted in "Experience." The difference now is that the slavery crisis is explicitly the occasion for concern as Emerson more than ever before questions the uses and abuses of eloquence by focusing on a very real figure.

Like many abolitionist texts, "Address to the Citizens of Concord" blames the Compromise of 1850 on "Mr. Webster's treachery" (AW 54). But whereas John Greenleaf Whittier called Webster a "fallen angel," Emerson eschews Miltonic typology in favor of diminutive insult.[56] He likens Webster's arguments to "the spray of a child's squirt against a granite wall," extraordinary rhetoric for a writer who bemoaned the excesses of partisan language, demonstrating that there is no invective like that of a former admirer's scorn (AW 60). Early in his career, Emerson committed himself to the prospects of eloquence, hardly a surprise in an era that lauded oratorical excellence.[57] For Emerson and others, Webster was the brightest of elocutionary stars, though Emerson became increasingly disenchanted with his onetime hero.

If Webster had any claim to genius, it was as an orator; and accordingly "Address to the Citizens of Concord" attacks him on this very point. After praising Webster's erstwhile "eloquence" and superior "perception and statement" (AW 66), Emerson's comments turn increasingly hostile: "The scraps of morality to be gleaned from his speeches are reflections of the minds of others. He says what he hears said, but often makes signal blunders in their use" (AW 67). One of Emerson's most comfortable postures is that of a literary critic; and here he accuses Webster of plagiarism (and shoddy plagiarism at that) on the first anniversary of "The Constitution and the Union," Webster's (in)famous speech that

---

55 Theodore Parker, "Daniel Webster" (1852), in *Theodore Parker: An Anthology*, ed. Henry Steele Commager (Boston: Beacon Press, 1960), 242.
56 John Greenleaf Whittier, "Ichabod!"
57 For Emerson's general participation in antebellum oratorical conventions, see Warren, *Culture of Eloquence*, 29–52; and Buell, *New England Literary Culture*, 137–65.

swung the Senate in favor of the Fugitive Slave Bill. Such oratory is not what Emerson means when he praises the power of words. Surely Webster has abused his limited store of eloquence. Thus Emerson, the anxiously influenced artist dedicated to original words, says his worst: *Webster is immoral, and I don't like his prose* – two charges that, as we shall see, are intimately linked. Overall, "Address to the Citizens of Concord" marks a shift in Emerson's expression and thought. The speech contains some of his harshest public language and least reflective claims, particularly when discussing policy questions such as African colonization and monetary compensation for slaveholders.[58] Often read on the campaign trail of the antislavery congressman, John Gorham Palfrey, "Address to the Citizens of Concord" shows Emerson at his most political, even as his dialectical mind keeps him from an unequivocal commitment.

In 1853, Wendell Phillips gave Emerson cordial though hardly exuberant praise when refuting an opponent who characterized Emerson as an anti-abolitionist. Phillips responded, "I do not consider [Emerson] as indorsing any of these criticisms on the Abolitionists . . . . Making fair allowance for his peculiar taste, habits, and genius, he has given a generous amount of aid to the antislavery movement." Phillips considers Emerson an ally, though peculiar differences remain, even if such differences largely involve matters of literary style. The alleged criticisms that Phillips disassociates from Emerson were made by the anti-abolitionist "Ion," who objected to abusive antislavery rhetoric. Indicative of the dialogic complexity of the slavery debate, Ion quoted Emerson's "Emancipation in the British West Indies," "Let us withhold every *reproachful*, and, if we can, every *indignant* remark" [Ion's emphasis].[59] It is fitting that in this conflict over the propriety of

---

58 Emerson seems largely unaware of, or at least uninterested in, the extended controversy over colonization, a controversy that became more heated with the passage of the Fugitive Slave Bill. Similarly, it is surprising that Emerson advocates monetary compensation, for the policy conflicted with his usual insistence that slaves be treated under the law of men, not under the law of things. Emerson would later qualify his support of compensation in 1855 (AW 105–6) and renounce it in his "Boston Hymn" (1863):

> Pay ransom to the owner
> And fill the bag to the brim.
> Who is the owner? The slave is owner,
> And ever was. Pay him.

See the aptly named Roger Ransom for the unfeasibility of economic compensation (*Conflict and Compromise: The Political Economy of Slavery, Emancipation, and the American Civil War* [Cambridge: Cambridge University Press, 1989], 70).

59 Wendell Phillips, "Philosophy of the Abolition Movement" (1853), in *Speeches, Lectures, and Letters* (Boston: Walker, Wise, and Co., 1864), 104, 103. For the relation of Phillips and Emerson, see Gougeon, *Virtue's Hero*, 190–91, and Warren, *Culture of Eloquence*, 13–15.

speech both the decorous Ion and fire-tongued Phillips claimed Emerson's support. Even after "Address to the Citizens of Concord" pictured Webster urinating on the Bunker Hill Monument, Emerson retained reservations about contentious, partisan language, worrying in a journal kept in 1853 and 1854 that Phillips's "eloquence" did not save him from being one of the "[m]ere mouthpieces of a party" (JMN 13:281–82).

Such ambivalence is particularly telling in "The Fugitive Slave Law" (1854), a speech that revisits Webster's treachery to ask how – or if – a true eloquence can serve righteous political ends and how – or if – the poet-philosopher can engage in polemic speech. Emerson's second assault on Webster, who died two years before, may be a belated and even mean-spirited production, though much suggests that Emerson profited from an extended reflection on Webster's compromise.[60] Borrowing from a journal entry of 1843, "The Fugitive Slave Law" remembers Webster as "the representative of the American continent" (JMN 8:425–26; AW 76). Like the "eloquent man" of "personal ascendency" from "Lecture on the Times," Webster possessed a "natural ascendancy," a "perfection of . . . elocution," a "voice, accent, intonation, attitude, [and] manner" that made him the orator of his day. Emerson gushes, "Ah! great is the privilege of eloquence." But so, too, is the tragedy of impotent words – "the sterility of thought, the want of generalization in [Webster's] speeches, and the curious fact, that . . . there is not a single general remark, not an observation on life and manners, not a single valuable aphorism that can pass into literature from his writings" (AW 77). Augmenting Emerson's literary criticisms from 1851, "The Fugitive Slave Law" accuses Webster of lacking the largesse of vision that might unite a fractured nation under aphoristic truth. That Emerson believes that such speech is still possible testifies to his faith in words. That he continues to dwell on Webster's weaknesses after the Senator's death shows how troubled Emerson is by the fall of the once-eloquent man. Emerson's negative review of Webster also flies in the face of popular opinion, for Webster's speeches were collected and widely praised after 1852. A glance at most modern literary anthologies vindicates Emerson's dismissal of Webster's art. But why does he fight a posthumous battle over Webster's literary merits? Is not Webster's countenance of chattel bondage a greater crime than his prose?

Not really, because Emerson is convinced that "the moral is the occult fountain of genius" – a reminder that aesthetics are never far from morals

---

60 Gougeon and Joel Myerson suggest that "The Fugitive Slave Law" is not an especially realized piece (AW 214). For a more positive view of the speech, see Gertrude Reif Hughes, *Emerson's Demanding Optimism* (Baton Rouge: Louisiana State University Press, 116–25).

in the antebellum (and neo-platonic) mind, and a point that Emerson makes as early as the "Beauty" chapter of *Nature*.[61] For Emerson, as Eduardo Cadava writes, "[I]t is always a matter of words."[62] Corruptions, including political misdeeds, show themselves in rotten language, even if as Harold Bloom suggests an "aesthetic of *use*" can be difficult to hold.[63] Emerson experiences – or better yet, dramatizes – this problem in "The Fugitive Slave Law" as literary critique only slowly corroborates political disapprobation. Webster's oratory is "clever and fluent," Emerson admits (AW 78). "Nobody doubts that Daniel Webster could make a good speech," he grants. But just when Emerson seems to sunder eloquence and virtue, he insists, "[T]his is not a question of ingenuity, not a question of syllogisms, but of sides . . . . There are always texts and thoughts and arguments; but it is the genius and temper of the man which decides whether he will stand for Right or for Might." True eloquence thus becomes a matter, not of texts and logic, but of character and "sides." As if anticipating the multicultural criticisms that are sometimes brought against him, Emerson insists that literature should be judged at least in part by moral and political standards, an acceptance of a potentially polemical criteria that, as Cavell has written, can ultimately lead to "an evasion, or renunciation, of philosophy."[64] Emerson does worry that his entrance into the politics compromises his aspirations as a poet-philosopher. Yet Emerson also imagines the transformation of genius into a practical power that by the 1850s looks increasingly like abolitionism. Emerson never precisely defines how philosophy as a calling relates to other modes of intellection and social action. He variously defines his work as simultaneously separate from the civil world and necessarily linked to it. This is not necessarily a mystifying paradox. For Emerson, distance also implies the nearness of relativity, distinction brings with it connection, and the fact that a discourse is separate from politics gives that discourse leverage to move it. Or in terms of political speech, eloquence by transcending the fury of faction may be able to encourage solutions.

For Emerson, abolitionist rhetoric was a site for the failure and success of such efforts. Previous chapters have shown how partisan speech worried many Americans who hoped to settle the slavery conflict with rational

---

61 See Thomas Taylor's claim (borrowed from Plotinus) that "the Good is considered as the fountain and principle of the Beautiful" (*Thomas Taylor the Platonist*, 144).
62 Cadava, *Emerson and the Climates of History*, 21.
63 Harold Bloom, "The Freshness of Transformation: Emerson's Dialectics of Influence," in *Emerson: Prophecy, Metamorphosis, and Influence*, 143.
64 Stanley Cavell, "Emerson's Constitutional Amending," 31.

public debate. Like Ion and others, Webster cried in "The Constitution and the Union" that the "vernacular tongue of the country has become greatly vitiated, depraved, and corrupted"; and he later indicted the "din, and roll, and rub-a-dub of Abolition writers and Abolition lecturers."[65] Phillips responded in 1852 by defending what he sarcastically called his "'rub-a-dub agitation.'" And for his part, Emerson tries to avoid the excesses of both sides. For all his catholic diction and loose argumentation, he dislikes buzz, din, rub, and dub, nor does he want to become a mere mouthpiece of a party. However, in both practice and theory, Emerson's speeches on the Fugitive Slave Law show him moving in the direction of more polemic, less temperate words.

A telling example of this shift appears at the end of "The Fugitive Slave Law" when Emerson, with a repetition suggesting the urgency of his interest, turns to yet another orator in defining proper political speech. Again discussing the slavery question in the idiom of literary criticism, Emerson disparages the recent address of a "literary" man, who as a practical and much admired Senator cannot help but remind one of Webster (AW 87). The speaker in question is Robert C. Winthrop, the man who filled Webster's seat in the Senate after Webster became Secretary of State, and who knowingly provoked his fellow Whigs by voting against the Fugitive Slave Bill. It is surprising that Emerson takes as his target this conservative-but-somewhat-conscious Whig. Winthrop's opposition to the Fugitive Slave Bill garnered qualified praise from Theodore Parker, and in 1854 Emerson signed a petition encouraging Winthrop to join him in the Republican Party, suggesting that Emerson's antipathy to Winthrop's 1852 speech has less to do with ideology and more to do with style.[66]

Winthrop's address, "The Obligations and Responsibilities of Educated Men" (1852), is generically akin to "The American Scholar" in that it discusses the "art of oratory" and, apparently innocent of recent achievements, calls for an "American literature."[67] However, certain differences were sure to antagonize Emerson. Overly encumbered by the corpse of memory, Winthrop incessantly pays tribute to "the memory of our Fathers." More importantly, he condemns the "profanity, sedition, [and] slander" of radical

---

65 Webster, "The Constitution and the Union," 358, and "The Compromise Measures," 433.
66 For Winthrop's role in the Compromise of 1850, including interactions with Webster, Parker, and Emerson, see Robert C. Winthrop, Jr., *A Memoir of Robert C. Winthrop* (Boston: Little, Brown, and Co., 1897), 130–78. Winthrop was also a college friend of Emerson's brother, Charles.
67 Robert Winthrop, *An Address Delivered Before the Association of the Alumni of Harvard College, July 22, 1852* (Cambridge: John Bartlett, 1852), 24, 52 (alternately titled, "The Obligations and Responsibilities of Educated Men").

abolitionism. Calling "evil passions, inordinate affections, and unruly wills" "worse than African bondage," Winthrop ridicules the "extravagant conceits" of abolitionist writers and speakers.[68] For him, an appropriate political rhetoric should not shake public opinion, the very goal that Emerson pursues in his unsettling work and in "The Fugitive Slave Law."

Turning his ire against Winthrop's circumspection, Emerson complains that American orators "have forgotten their allegiance to the muse." Usually Emerson uses the muse as a symbol for transcendence. Now, however, he links literary inspiration to "the specific liberty of America in 1854" (AW 87), a liberty that demands from its speakers an eloquence that is nothing if not politically engaged:

I put to every noble and generous spirit in the land; to every poetic; to every heroic; to every religious heart; that not so is our learning, our education, our poetry, our worship to be declared, not by heads reverted to the dying Demosthenes, Luther, or Wallace, or to George Fox, or to George Washington, but to the dangers and dragons that beset the United States at this time. It is not possible to extricate oneself from the questions in which your age is involved
. . . . [Liberty] is the epic poetry, the new religion, the chivalry of all gentlemen. This is the oppressed Lady whom true knights on their oath and honor must rescue and save. (AW 88)

Self-scrutiny is not lacking here. Emerson dismisses Winthrop's obedience to Demosthenes, Washington, and others. Yet with his over-lengthy list renouncing the reliance on sepulchered fathers, Emerson implies that he, too, can be tempted by great historical men, particularly considering that he himself once lectured on Luther and Fox and published *Representative Men* just a few years before. Emerson insists of Winthrop, his audience, and his own scholarly self that the responsible citizen and innovative author must face the pressing questions of the age. But just when one might rightly expect to hear explicitly of chattel bondage in America, Emerson reverts to a fanciful idiom of chivalry, knights, and damsels in distress. In a substantial journal entry from which "The Fugitive Slave Law" draws, a white-hot Emerson excoriated the "romancing" of Winthrop's speech (JMN 13: 71). This critique, however – and Emerson may know it – can also be turned on him. Can the myth-loving Emerson leave behind his own courtly romantic muse? Can he finally bring himself to a more historically grounded eloquence?

Yes, if only momentarily, for Emerson renounces "epic poetry" with a powerful claim, "Now at last we are disenchanted and shall have no more

68 Ibid., 7, 32, 31, 36.

false hopes." In the essay "Nature" (1844), Emerson praises nature's enticing "enchantments," for if its spell is fleeting and even frighteningly alien, it can make "romance and reality meet" (542). Similarly, Emerson maintains in "The Uses of Great Men" (1850) that even considering the disappointments of history "the world is not therefore disenchanted" (631). However, by 1854 and "The Fugitive Slave Law," Emerson is less inclined to insist on the value of enchantment. Stripping the abolitionist movement of his own romantic language, Emerson flatly reports, "I respect the Anti-Slavery Society" – even if such modest praise betrays some distance from the cause. "The Fugitive Slave Law," like "Address to the Citizens of Concord," demolishes Webster's immoral statute and faulty eloquence. More fundamental, however, is that Emerson fights against his own heroic rhetoric – a further instance of his disenchantment with representative men, and a likely reaction from someone whose role model had so thoroughly let him down.

Emerson, of course, does not utterly deny the prospects of individual speech. Disappointed with the "great men of today, the Websters, Everetts, Winthrops," he concludes his journal entry on Winthrop, "[T]he new times need a new man" (JMN 13:82–3). Familiar sentiments to be sure, but what is striking is that Emerson now calls this hero "the complemental man," suggesting that the true reformer cannot be all-sufficient and that the transcendental self is not supreme at the center of the universe. Predicting that "The Anti-Slavery Society will add many members this year," "The Fugitive Slave Law" finishes with the potentially communal conviction, "[W]e have come to an end of our unbelief, have come to a belief that there is a Divine Providence in the world which will not save us but through our own co-operation" (AW 89). Whether Emerson wants to co-operate with fate singly or as a group is unclear. Yet the drift of his thinking and his use of "we" suggests that he admits the need for co-operation not just with destiny but also with a movement that embodied, howsoever raucously, what he took to be moral law.

Emerson wrote of Phillips and Garrison in the mid-1850s, "Very dangerous is this thoroughly social and related life, whether antagonistic or *co*-operative" (JMN 13:281). Yet in a more complemental mood at the end of "The Fugitive Slave Law," Emerson seeks a solution to slavery not in the hero but in the growing ranks of the abolitionist cause. It is a subtle but important change of emphasis for a self-reliant transcendentalist long wary of organized reform. Under severe political pressures brought about by the Fugitive Slave Law, and suspecting that individual reform may not be an adequate answer to slavery, Emerson – if only for an instance – tempers the romantic eloquence that Nancy Ruttenburg sets at the center of antebellum liberalism.[69] Emerson remains far from Marx, Orestes Brownson, and Charles Fourier, and he does not take social engineering as seriously as some of his contemporaries. Yet Emerson sees the limits of heroic reform and transcendental speech, which is to say that he is a cogent critic of an atomistic Emersonian self. Emerson's second thoughts about political activism spring from his realization that truth-claims must be enacted socially and thus are finally validated by the community. Cornel West has offered individualism as a proto-pragmatist strain of Emerson's thinking, but "The Fugitive Slave Law" indicates that the obverse is also true. Just as the pragmatists held (in Peirce's words) that reasoning requires a "social impulse" that "terminates in action," Emerson recognizes the need for the active and complemental philosopher. [70]

THAT TERRIBLE THOREAU

One consequence of Emerson's abiding optimism is a demanding despair. No American writer more than Emerson so strongly believed in the power of words, so frequently lamented their failure, and (as Poirier, like William James, observes) so deeply and painfully "recognized the limits of his own enterprise."[71] Emerson quarrels with the language of politics for a number of reasons. He prefers a more decorous intellectual discourse to the fractious public speech he sometimes associates with lower-class demagogues and greasy immigrant masses. More theoretically, just as "The Fugitive Slave Law" turns away from heroic enchantment, Emerson worries that even polished polemics do not get at reality. The rhetoric taught to Emerson in college was steeped in the Scottish Enlightenment and liked to think that it was grounded in natural law. Emerson, however – and more profoundly, Thoreau – came to feel what many modern readers are not slow to note, that stylized antebellum rhetoric often sounds artificial. Continuing a trend from the revolutionary era, many Americans of the Jacksonian period also distrusted grandiloquence, not only because egalitarian democrats resented aristocratic airs, but also because they saw the artifice of words as divorced from natural laws. As

---

69 Ruttenburg, *Democratic Personality.*
70 West, *The American Evasion of Philosophy*, 40; Charles Peirce, "The Doctrine of Chances" (1878) in *The Essential Peirce*, 150.
71 Richard Poirier, *The Renewal of Literature: Emersonian Reflections* (New York: Random House, 1987), 70. James writes in his "Address at the Centenary of Ralph Waldo Emerson" (1903), "Rarely has a man so known the limits of his genius, or so unfailingly kept within them" (*William James: Writings, 1902–1910*, 1119).

part of this tradition, transcendentalists honored what Buell calls "anti-eloquence," the impulse toward a plainer speech that imagined itself more directly, philologically, and naturally representative of the actual world.[72]

Deconstruction has disabused many thinkers of this realist urge, and certainly Emerson in his skeptical moods recognizes the gap between signs and things. At the same time, "The Fugitive Slave Law" remembers Webster's very real language, "[H]e was so thoroughly simple and wise in his rhetoric, – he saw through his matter, – hugged his fact so close, – went to the principal or essential, and never indulged in a weak flourish" (AW 76). Webster's later impotent words are as far from essential fact as the Compromise of 1850 is distant from moral law. As Emerson generalizes in an oft-quoted line from an antislavery address of 1856, "Language has lost its meaning in the universal cant. *Representative Government* is really misrepresentative" (AW 113). Emerson holds seriously to the notion that language actually matters. So strong is his desire for the correspondence of reality and words, and so pressing is his hope that a natural rhetoric can have practical political effects, when faced with the failure of public speech, including even the power of heroic words, Emerson turns with some desperation to the antieloquent man.

Emerson glorified John Brown, the leader of the failed Harper's Ferry revolt, whom Unionists labeled a criminal and lunatic, but whom Emerson in two brief addresses of 1859 and 1860 depicts as "a representative of the American public" (AW 117). Just as Thoreau praised Brown for using "no idle eloquence, no made, nor maiden speech,"[73] Emerson applauds Brown's "simple artless goodness" (AW 118) and places his small store of letters above "the purest eloquence in the country" (AW 121). Neither Emerson nor Thoreau judges Brown in a strictly literary sense. For them, his eloquence was in deeds. His sentences were like rifles. He synthesized the "Sayer" and "Doer," for as Emerson writes in "The Poet" (1844), "Words and deeds are quite indifferent modes of the divine energy. Words are also actions, and actions are a kind of words" (449–50). That Brown's acts were explicitly violent did not preclude the approval of Emerson and many abolitionists who were generally committed to moral suasion but increasingly frustrated with the slavery debate. As Michael Lopez shows, Emerson possesses an enduring antagonistic streak.

---

72 Buell, *New England Literary Culture*, 155. See also Michael West, *Transcendental Wordplay: America's Romantic Punsters and the Search for the Language of Nature* (Athens: Ohio University Press, 2000). For antebellum rhetoric in general, see Gustafson, *Representative Words*, Cmiel, *Democratic Eloquence*.
73 Thoreau, "A Plea for Captain John Brown," 697.

Hawthorne, too, noted in 1863 that Emerson's combativeness had swelled, for the speaker sometimes described as angelic had become "as merciless as a steel bayonet" with the advent of the War.[74]

For Emerson, Brown's deeds were cathartic and pointed to the kind of avenging justice that "Experience" predicts. Yet Brown also represents a defeat of sorts, an admission that forbearing reform must finally give way to a form of action that is violently manipular. That is, not only did Brown mark the failure of public debate, he did not transcend the fury of faction and profoundly deepened political divisions. Thus Emerson must take interpretive pains to read Brown as an eloquent hero. He paradoxically describes the attack on Harper's Ferry as the speech-act of a powerfully reticent man, and he chooses to ignore the organizational flaws in Brown's doomed campaign. Not utterly comfortable with physical force or entirely despairing of language, Emerson collapses words and deeds to give an over-determined, quasi-literary evaluation of Brown. Along the way, Emerson praises his subject for knowing "the secret signals by which animals communicate," showing that the unschooled westerner eschews the artifices of civilized language and has, like Stowe's Dred and Thomas Gray's Nat Turner, an authority based in the natural signs of the world (AW 122). Brown's words-as-signals are nearer to the real. They correspond with nature. They also prefigure Emerson's eulogy for his friend and occasional antagonist Thoreau, who serves as a more likely and more complex figure of heroic but antieloquent reform.

Just as Emerson called Brown "an idealist" who put ideas "into action," Emerson admiringly but also condescendingly long saw Thoreau as a disciple who practiced Emerson's own transcendentalism, then as now a popular opinion more convenient than precisely accurate (AW 119). In Emerson's eulogy "Thoreau" (1862), he remembers his younger friend as "a speaker and actor of the truth"; and though the eulogy need not be included in a collection of Emerson's antislavery writings, the text suggests the political limits and power of heroic speech, particularly during the trying years of the Civil War.[75] Testifying to their intimacy, Emerson treats Thoreau with the same unstinting honesty with which he often judges himself. This is specifically true in regards to reform, for

---

74 Michael Lopez, *Emerson and Power: Creative Antagonism in the Nineteenth Century* (DeKalb, Ill.: Northern Illinois University Press, 1996), 190–210. Nathaniel Hawthorne to Henry Bright, 8 March 1863, *The Letters, 1857–1864*, ed. Thomas Woodson, et al., vol. 18 of *The Centenary Edition of the Works of Nathaniel Hawthorne* (Columbia: Ohio State University Press, 1987), 544.

75 Ralph Waldo Emerson, *The Complete Works of Ralph Waldo Emerson, Vol. X*, ed. Edward W. Emerson (Boston: Houghton Mifflin, 1883), 457. Hereafter cited in the text as "TH."

Emerson's description of Thoreau's politics is as much self-referential as biographical, "[I]dealist as he was, standing for abolition of slavery, abolition of tariffs, almost for abolition of government, it is needless to say he found himself not only unrepresented in actual politics, but almost equally opposed to every class of reformers. Yet he paid the tribute of his uniform respect to the Anti-Slavery party" (TH 460).

Certainly Emerson and Thoreau influenced each other's views on slavery. To sense the thickness of their dialogue and the difficulty of determining who taught whom, one can set Emerson's Fugitive Slave Law speeches between Thoreau's "Civil Disobedience" and "Slavery in Massachusetts" (1854), a strategy that invites the critic to seek origins in each author's journals and to speculate about possible conversations in the parlor, garden, and woods. Other correspondences are also evident. In "A Plea for Captain John Brown" (1859), Thoreau goads his New England audience, "[Brown] was not our representative in any sense. He was too fair a specimen of a man to represent the like of us."[76] As mentioned, Emerson later calls Brown "a representative of the American public"; and by naming him "a fair specimen of the best stock of New England," he is more forgiving of his neighbors than is the prickly Thoreau (AW 122). The irony is that Emerson's opinion of Brown for the most part follows that of Thoreau. "Thoreau" praises "A Plea for Captain John Brown"; and Emerson may be speaking of himself when he writes, "[Thoreau's] earnest eulogy of the hero was heard by all respectfully, by many with a sympathy that surprised themselves" (TH 460–61).

Typical of their later relationship, Thoreau and Emerson quarrel over politics, not so much because of their differences, but because of the proximity of their views. As with Emerson's 1854 objections to the speech of Robert Winthrop, controversy in "Thoreau" is as much rhetorical as ideological.[77] Emerson initially lauds Thoreau's words as entirely independent and therefore incontrovertible, "No opposition or ridicule had any weight with him. He coldly and fully stated his opinion without affecting to believe that it was the opinion of the company" (TH 458). Emerson finds much humor and pleasure in relating tales of the truculent Thoreau. When a skittish abolitionist committee asked Thoreau to postpone his plea for John Brown, Emerson recalls Thoreau's retort, "I did not send to you for advice but to announce that I am to speak" (TH 460).

---

76 Thoreau, "A Plea for Captain John Brown," 697.
77 Joel Porte also emphasizes rhetorical differences in *Emerson and Thoreau: Transcendentalists in Conflict* (Middletown, Conn.: Wesleyan University Press, 1966), 31–34.

Emerson is attracted by such unapologetic, self-reliant disdain for audience, in part because Thoreau's oppositional-yet-oblivious stance was one that Emerson himself could not indulge as a public lecturer and anti-slavery activist who had political, temperamental, and financial reasons for appealing to his listeners.[78] Gone were the rebellious days of the "Divinity School Address" (1838). In the early 1850s, Thoreau privately complained of Emerson's growing popularity; and he worried in *Walden*, "What is called eloquence in the forum is commonly found to be rhetoric in the study."[79] Thoreau even told Emerson to his face that "whatever was written for a lecture, or whatever succeeded with the audience was bad," a pronouncement designed to offend his mentor, who was at the time seeking and finding thousands of listeners by his side (JMN 13:270).

Emerson relates this accusation in the middle of "Thoreau," and it is at this point that an ungenerous Emerson returns literary insult for insult. "A certain habit of antagonism defaced [Thoreau's] earlier writings" (TH 479), Emerson complains, though this description might as well apply to "The American Scholar" and the "Divinity School Address." Then, deploying Thoreau's favorite tropes and pleasures against the deceased, Emerson charges, "I cannot help counting it a fault in him that he had no ambition. Wanting this, instead of engineering for all America, he was the captain of a huckleberry-party. Pounding beans is good to the end of pounding empires one of these days; but if, at the end of years, it is still only beans!" (TH 480). At the nadir of the North's Civil War effort, Emerson's merciless, knife-like words are not only reserved for the Confederacy. Suddenly an impatient Emerson turns the tables on Thoreau, pegging *him* as the disengaged dilettante and impractical theorist with the same sort of political charges that Emerson endured in his early career and often brought against himself. Voicing the worries of "The Conservative" and repeating the warning of the world from "The Transcendentalist," Emerson complains that pounding beans and writing *Walden* is fine until one ages and dies. Slavery, Shiloh, and the death of a friend can in this way make one a materialist.

That Emerson is so demanding of Thoreau is neither polite nor completely surprising. Emerson's biographical paeans always include qualifications, even when the subject under judgment happens to be Jesus Christ. But what gives "Thoreau" the mean-spirited edge that shocked at

78 Railton's *Authorship and Audience* is particularly good on the resistant rhetoric of both Emerson and Thoreau (23–73).
79 Thoreau, *Walden*, 92–3.

least one of its listeners may have less to do with Thoreau's foibles as Emerson's own insecurities. It is possible to confess and perhaps even celebrate one's own inconsistencies, but who wants to have a friend and former disciple highlight one's hypocrisies? When Emerson's eulogy mentions the "terrible eyes" of "'that terrible Thoreau'" (TH 465, 478), it echoes "The Transcendentalist" in which "terrible friends" and "exacting children" "severely exact" from their timorous elders an unrelenting idealist faith (202). One place where the aging Emerson relented was in the matter of abolitionism. As if in rebuke, Thoreau proved to have more patience than his erstwhile teacher insofar as his resistance to civil institutions was remarkably consistent over time. Emerson respected his friend's integrity but also found it dogmatic and extortionate. Just as "Circles" complains, "[I]f I have a friend, I am tormented by my imperfections" (406), "Thoreau" dwells on its subject's "accusing silences" and "the satire of his presence" (TH 466, 472). Emerson's picture of the astringent Thoreau is in this sense the defensive response of a thinker who has subtly, stubbornly and, to some extent, regretfully strayed from his youthful convictions by capitulating to active reform and increasingly partisan rhetoric.

Thoreau's unbending political beliefs also cause Emerson to reflect on heroic speech, for reform and the language of reform are for Emerson always entangled. Early in the eulogy, Thoreau appears as a powerfully mythic man, "Snakes coiled round his leg, the fishes swam into his hand" (TH 472). Thoreau discovers arrowheads and herbs as if under Nature's direction. And in an anecdote sure to please academics, Thoreau's "irresistible speeches" not only overcome the President of Harvard but, more impressively, manage to override the regulations of the college library (TH 466). Just as "The Conservative" claims, "It will never make any difference to a hero what the laws are" (188), Emerson paraphrases Aristotle in "Thoreau," "One who surpasses his fellow citizens in virtue, is no longer a part of the city. Their law is not for him, since he is a law to himself" (TH 477). Thoreau is this transcendent man in his "virtue," "sincerity," and "probity" (TH 478). These strengths, however, bring a "dangerous frankness" that too often amounts to "scorn," so much so, Emerson complains, that "the severity of [Thoreau's] ideal interfered to deprive him of a healthy sufficiency of human society" (TH 479). Here Emerson of all people bemoans excessive self-reliance, faulting Thoreau's heroic idealism for lacking complementarity. Precisely here (and tellingly so) Emerson unleashes his ire, accusing the berry-picking Thoreau of political escapism or, closer to the consciousness of the time, of military desertion, for in 1862 the North needed captains of something other than huckleberry parties.

This is Emerson at his most vicious, although the mood does not last. After mocking Thoreau's precious berries and beans and displaying his own severest exactions, Emerson reclaims the patient Thoreau – and by extension, Emerson's own earlier self – as both a tragically unfulfilled youth and a hero-in-waiting. Moving to Thoreau's nature writings, Emerson finds in his friend's pure prose not only antieloquent "elegances" that "scoffed at conventional elegance," but also the possibility of political salvation, howsoever tenuous (TH 481). Like Brown, the literary power of Thoreau lies in his representational fidelity, which Emerson exemplifies in the vivid selections he borrows from Thoreau's journals. Eschewing logical argumentation, grandiloquence, and even narrative itself, these passages, founded in inspired perception and onomatopoeic correspondence with nature, have the crisp, original quality so sadly lacking in Webster. Or as James Russell Lowell had to admit in an otherwise cutting review, "[Thoreau] had caught his English at its living source."[80] Emerson quotes, "The chub is a soft fish, and tastes like boiled brown paper salted . . . . I put on some hemlock-boughs, and the rich salt crackling of their leaves was like mustard to the ear" (TH 482). That Emerson ends by comparing Thoreau to a flower-hunting lover is fitting. It recasts the flaky huckleberry captain as a romantic seeker of beauty and truth, returning Emerson to a peaceful idiom of redemptive nature. "Thoreau" concludes with beauty, not politics, but one should not rush past the sentence, "The country knows not yet, or in the least part, how great a son it has lost"; for even as Emerson returns to ideals he also remembers America (TH 484).

The quiet death of Henry Thoreau in the bloodiest year of the Civil War had little immediate impact beyond his circle of friends around Boston. But having admired and resented his friend's heroic antieloquence, Emerson suggests that Thoreau's true words and irresistible speeches make him as great an American son as any soldier dying for the Union and, less surely, abolition. Such resilient faith was not easy to find during a time in which William Tecumseh Sherman lamented, "Argument is exhausted, and words have lost their usual meaning."[81] However, Emerson saw Thoreau's meanings as extraordinary and

---

80 James Russell Lowell, "Thoreau" (1865) in *The Shock of Recognition: The Development of Literature in the United States*, ed. Edmund Wilson (New York: Octagon Books, 1975), 242.

81 W. T. Sherman to H. W. Halleck, 17 September 1863, in William Tecumseh Sherman, *William Tecumseh Sherman: Memoirs of General W. T. Sherman* (1875; New York: Library of America, 1990), 361.

therefore inarguable. For Emerson, his work is a "broken task, which none else can finish." It is painful that he "should depart out of Nature before yet he has been really shown to his peers for what he is" (TH 485). Still, there is succor in a patience that survives even death. Thoreau's country and his peers have not acknowledged his sacrifice "yet" – a prophecy that in optative moods lifts up leaden hearts, and a stubborn insistence that the transcendental hero holds a high place even in wartime.

As much as a eulogy, "Thoreau" is a literary, philosophical, and political autobiography. Though Emerson feels compelled to defend his drift toward partisan politics, he praises a life that represents the potential of intensely autonomous words. Emerson predicted the worldly triumph of transcendental eloquence in "The Times." In "Experience," he pushed the imaginative limits of the hero's forbearing politics. The Fugitive Slave Law forced Emerson to reconsider and in some ways recast his optimism, to confront the failures and misuses of supposedly representative orators. As the Civil War approached, Emerson moved toward co-operation and complementarity. But in "Thoreau" he recalls his own abiding and profoundly ambivalent faith in the capacities of a heroic language he remembers with chagrin and yet cannot forego. In the year of Thoreau's death, Emerson wrote, "War is a realist," though he countered with a commitment to double consciousness, "I speak the speech of an idealist."[82] Still fighting with dualisms, Emerson discovered in the Civil War both the failure and the prospect of synthesis. As with Waldo's death and Webster's treachery, the War simultaneously shook and reinvigorated Emerson's faith in the victory of justice. As with Thoreau's as yet unrecognized work, there remained the dawning realization of genius as practical power. Retaining such a faith was difficult. For Emerson, the still unfinished possibilities of American transcendentalism played out across his long career at the level of words. Perhaps we love our first sins best, and for Emerson eloquence was one of them. His writings aspire to an inspired expression that when properly attended reconciles the conflicting demands of ideal truth, aesthetic beauty, and political power. Heuristically for his readers, and curatively for himself, Emerson works his way toward the One – clamor, skepticism, the Fugitive Slave Law, grief, and war notwithstanding.

He never gets there; and considering Emerson's restless dialectical mind, it should be no surprise that "Thoreau" is not his final word on slavery. "Fortune of the Republic" (1863) says of the War and the

82 Masur, *The Real War Will Never Get in the Books*, 134.

Emancipation Proclamation, "The revolution is the work of no man, but the eternal effervescence of nature. . . . And not a republican, not a statesman, not an idealist, not an abolitionist, can say without effrontery, I did it . . . . It is the old gravitation" (AW 153). Emerson's proscription of human agency in the face of ameliorative natural law turns back to a faith in the argument from design more than it anticipates Darwin.[83] But if the restriction of self-reliance can fit the narratives of Whicher, Gougeon, and Newfield – that is, if the complemental man submits to fate and co-operation for better or for worse – "Thoreau" insists that heroic words are never finally dead, for the eulogy's "yet" implies both second thoughts and impending vindication, both continuing dialectical doubts and enduring prospects.

Emerson's postbellum work may be weak insofar as he rehashes or (more generously) refines many of his former beliefs. But such continuity also suggests the power of his thinking to integrate even the traumatic experiences of the Civil War. Who knows how Emerson would have handled a permanent sundering of the Union, the defeat of the North, or the survival of chattel bondage. Who knows how such events would have shaped his place in American letters. But faced with existing historical contingencies, Emerson's transcendentalism, with some alterations and not a few (perhaps unforgivable) elisions, was able to justify itself to itself, at least in Emerson's mind. His flexible and potentially hegemonic thought may not be good for civil society. Even his dialectical attention to the demands of double consciousness insufficiently notices material forces of subjugation and race. It may be, however, that to emphasize this objection is to underrate Emerson's political work, to extract a purely theoretical position from a project that understood practical power as both a criteria for success and an enabling condition. In other words, Emerson's transcendentalism is not strictly transcendent, for when he preaches an abstracted and self-possessive individualism from a position of privileged idealism, he almost never loses touch with political questions, the most pressing of which proved to be abolitionism, even if Emerson never learned its co-operative lessons by heart.

83 See Kris Fresonke, *West of Emerson: The Design of Manifest Destiny* (Berkeley: University of California Press, 2003).

Epilogue: An unfinished and not unhappy ending

This book ends with a bang, a whisper, and a box. The bang is the telos of the Civil War, which is often taken to mark an epistemic shift: rational deliberation gives way to violence, arguments from design to Darwinism, romanticism to literary realism, foundational metaphysics to pluralistic pragmatism. One reason why the war makes so strong a climax is that thinkers of the time portrayed it as such. Douglass called the War the "inevitable result of a long and persistent course," while James Russell Lowell saw the great conflict as a consummation after which Americans could only write from "the ashes of the burnt-out mind." Most scholars agree with Henry James's assessment from 1879, "[T]he Civil War marks an era in the history of the American mind," in part because it signaled what Louis Menand and George Frederickson call a "failure of ideas."[1]

However, the literature of slavery shows that ideas were failing before Fort Sumter and that as philosophy in the United States faltered antebellum writers dwelled more skeptically on slavery and the prospects of rational order. In this sense, they anticipated the Civil War and its challenge to intellectual legacies, for though they never formulated an explicitly pragmatist or post-metaphysical worldview, they discerned in the debacle of the slavery crisis and its intimations of war the exhaustion of philosophical systems in what seemed their final throes. Wendell Phillips said in 1859, "Insurrection of thought always precedes the insurrection of arms"; and Emerson noted a year before when asserting the political consequences of ideas, "The people's imagination alone is sometimes the cause of a civil war."[2] Though hopes for a peaceful resolution

---

1 Douglass, "The Slaveholders' Rebellion" (1862), in *Douglass: Selected Speeches and Writings*, 498; James Russell Lowell, "Ode Recited at the Harvard Commemoration" (1865). Henry James, *Hawthorne* (1879) quoted in Fredrickson, *The Inner Civil War*, 1. Menand, *The Metaphysical Club*, x.
2 Wendell Phillips, "The Lesson of the Hour" (1859), in *Speeches, Lectures, and Letters* (Boston: 1863), 263; Emerson, "Powers of the Mind," 79.

remained, and though no one predicted the severity of the fighting, some writers before the Civil War recognized their era to be antebellum.

Among them were Poe, Stowe, Douglass, Melville, and Emerson, who witnessed the failure of rational authority just when their country needed it most. Emerson's patient belief in freedom turned increasingly toward polemics, aggression, and fate. Melville's humanism sank toward obscurity, while Douglass's rose in partisan pitch. Stowe's sentimentality retreated from slavery, and Poe passed without reconciling his politics and philosophy. Nor were these the only major literary figures for whom the War was a kind of conclusion. The main texts of Jacobs and Delany were written by 1862, and Whitman had begun what is largely seen as a slow and stubborn decline. Neither Hawthorne nor Thoreau lived to see the end of the War, though both men had already shown indications that their best years of writing were gone. The Civil War was hardly unwritten, but its texts were not generally from the hands or in the forms that shaped antebellum literature, as if antebellum texts relied so much on tense political energies that its impetus perforce declined with the catharsis of the War. Though it risks a teleology that David Potter warned of decades ago, and though it may re-inscribe nationalist narratives of American literary history, the preceding chapters have found in antebellum literature a prologue to the War as authors faced the limits of their era's philosophy prior to the fact of disunion.[3] Such is the bang – the War as terminus, as a kind of slowly approaching apocalypse that serves as an end for multiple strands of intellectual, cultural, and literary history.

And yet for all the satisfaction that denouement affords, whispers about an always unfinished and uninterrupted age of enlightenment make the possibilities of periodization and the task of epilogue hard. Scottish realism, integrated with German idealism, shaped the increasingly professionalized field of philosophy up through the 1880s, while pragmatism went unrecognized as a movement until the turn of the nineteenth century. Darwinism did not immediately supplant existing theology and

---

3 David Potter names the problem "Hindsight, the historian's chief asset and his liability" (*The Impending Crisis: 1848–1861*, ed. Don E. Fehrenbacher [New York: Harper and Row, 1976], 145). Paul Giles has recently argued against the emphasis on the Civil War in American literary history on the grounds that it tends to "shore up the nation-building agendas of the United States" ("Transnationalism and Classic American Literature," *PMLA* 118.1 [Jan. 2003], 74). Such nation building, however, was a crucial fact in antebellum America – one that need not preclude (and, in fact, calls for) transnational perspectives, particularly if one views the North and South as separate polities. In this sense, Bercovitch appears to be right that the Civil War represents a "latent context of the American Renaissance," though I disagree with his emphasis on the slavery conflict as a "growth toward ideological unity" (*Rites of Assent*, 224, 57).

natural law; and though the South Carolinian Mary Boykin Chesnut
wrote in 1861, "My subjective days are over," pledging instead "to be
entirely *objective*" – to work toward a more empirical truth – a few
months later her reading returned to the idealism of Emerson and Fuller.[4]
Philosophy, then, did not utterly change with the coming of the War,
indicating the residual power of antebellum ideas.

Nor did the trauma of the war entirely disrupt literary histories. Post-
bellum abolitionists memorialized their victory using pre-war rhetorical
forms, while some southerners revived old romantic plots to redeem their
recent defeats. Retaining the trope of marriage as Union, sentimental
fiction imagined a nation reunited in intersectional love; and literary
realism can be taken to follow, not reject, antebellum traditions. As
Saidiya Hartman and David Blight have shown, the end of Reconstruction proved how little some racial attitudes changed as a result of the War,
for reunion took place under much of the logic that preceded the national
conflict, indicating the tenacious prejudices and practices of an unequal
America.[5] Whether or not a less-bifurcated nineteenth century emerges in
United States literary history, the antebellum literature of slavery does
not merely foreshadow the bang of disunion. It projects the course of
American literature and ideas beyond the Civil War.

Which is to emphasize that the literature of slavery participates in
continuing narratives. Poe draws from Schelling and Coleridge and in
doing so explores the modern unconscious. Stowe struggles with questions of affect and agency pursued by moral philosophers and moral
psychologists from the pragmatists to today. Douglass's frustration with
rational argumentation can hint at post-metaphysical views, just as his
ambivalence toward unstable identities adumbrates subsequent thinkers
on race. Never entirely abandoning the piety and natural law by which he
was raised, Emerson's transcendentalism yet looks forward to the pragmatists, Nietzsche, and Wittgenstein, while both anticipating and antag-
onizing recent post-liberal thought. The slavery controversy helped to
shape the thinking of these antebellum writers, but Appomattox and the
thirteenth amendment did not conclude the political or philosophical
discussions in which their writings work. Whispers of their unfinished
efforts continue to this day; and of the possible ways to end a book
that insists on the open-endedness of literature, Melville provides an

4 *The Private Mary Chesnut: The Unpublished Civil War Diaries*, ed. C. Vann Woodward, Elisabeth
   Muhlenfeld (New York: Oxford University Press, 1984), 33.
5 Hartman, *Scenes of Subjection*; Blight, *Race and Reunion*.

emblematic text that shows how faith in an enlightened America wavered but did not fade away.

In Melville's short story "The Happy Failure" (1854), a white narrator, his uncle, and the uncle's black servant Yorpy row up the Hudson River to test the uncle's invention contained in an "oblong box."[6] It is a "Hydraulic-Hydrostatic Apparatus" designed to drain off swamps; and when the test fails, the uncle kicks the machine and becomes so dispirited that he nearly dies, until he decides to give up on the project and shouts, "Praise be to God for the failure!" Having started the story fractious and vainglorious, he ends his days "a good old man" whose experience teaches the nephew-narrator how to become a "wise young one." As with much of Melville's short fiction, the story can be an allegory of Melville's career.[7] With *Moby-Dick* and *Pierre*, Melville's highest aspirations ended in despair, and like the uncle who fruitlessly hoped to win "any price for [his invention's] publication," Melville needed to find a way to move beyond his personal and professional bitterness.

The story, however, also points to another type of authorial frustration – the failure of an American enlightenment thinker on the verge of civil war. The boxed apparatus can stand for America flush with manifest destiny, for the uncle predicts it will fetch "a million of dollars" and bring him immortal "glory" by converting wilderness into "fields more fertile than those of the Genessee." With a word that antebellum political theorists still used to describe America, the story's "experiment" turns out to be an imperialistic endeavor associated with land-grabbing, roman emperors, and the uncle's dictatorial ways. But just as slavery simultaneously spurred and inhibited antebellum expansionist desires, the uncle's project is balked by problems of chattel bondage and race. Or as Richard Hildreth wrote in 1854, "[T]he experiment of Democracy . . . is quite overshadowed . . . by the *experiment of Despotism*."[8]

The uncle tests his box on "Quash Island" ("Quashee" being a derogatory term for blacks), while Yorpy bristles under the uncle's tyranny, "De pox has been my cuss for de ten long 'ear." When the experiment fails, perhaps because Yorpy has his foot ground under the box, the uncle flies into a rage and tries to destroy the machine. Here fears of disunion rush to the fore as the narrator remonstrates, "Hold, hold, my dear, dear

6　Herman Melville, "The Happy Failure," in *Herman Melville: Pierre, Israel Potter, The Piazza Tales, The Confidence-Man, Uncollected Prose, Billy Budd, Sailor*, 1188–95.

7　William Dillingham, *Melville's Short Fiction: 1853–1856* (Athens: University of Georgia Press, 1977), 359–60.

8　Hildreth, *Despotism in America*, 8.

uncle! . . . Don't destroy so, in one frantic moment, all your long calm years of devotion to one darling scheme . . . It is not yet wholly ruined, dear uncle; come put it together now . . . [H]ere, here, put these pieces together; or, if that can't be done without more tools, try a *section* of it." Whether the nephew wants to save the Union or a single section is unclear. Whatever the case, the uncle finally gives up on his experiment and, by extension, stops pursuing the dream of an American empire of reason. Just as the carvings on Queequeg's coffin form a "complete theory of the heavens and the earth,"[9] the uncle's coffin-like box suggests a cosmology, a machine-like symbol for what he calls "the present enlightened age." But whereas Queequeg's Polynesian system eventually saves Ishmael's life, the uncle must learn a difficult lesson and leave his intellectual hubris behind. Nearly destroyed by his invention, he gives the box to Yorpy to sell for "tobacco-money," teaching his nephew the reiterated moral, "Praise be to God for the failure!"

Perhaps it is better to forbear and leave impossible projects unfinished, whether the project is a literary opus or an empire of reason that was proving itself to be unworkable and a pox on African Americans. Such might be a didactic ending to a relatively straightforward story, except that the conclusion of "The Happy Failure" has an ironic hook.[10] The uncle's supposed newfound benevolence only extends tobacco-money to Yorpy, who remains a servant trapped within the economy of slavery and whose overwrought enthusiasm for the uncle's slight charity can be taken as a sarcastic complaint, "Dear massa! Dear old massa! Dat be very fust time in de ten long 'ear yoo hab mention kindly old Yorpy. I tank yoo, dear old massa; I tank yoo so kindly." The supposed wisdom and goodness of the uncle and nephew are thus subverted. They may learn to abjure their enlightenment project, but this does not right their country's experiment, for the threat of slavery and disunion did not simply disappear when citizens turned their backs on the problem.

Indeed, Melville himself proved unable to follow his story's ostensible advice. His subsequent fiction and poetry continue to interrogate slavery and philosophy in America as he carefully and unrelentingly examines the limitations of reason and democracy. Cornel West has written, "[O]nce one gives up on the search for foundations and the quest for certainty, human inquiry into truth and knowledge shifts to the social and

---

9 Melville, *Moby-Dick*, 1307.
10 For an unironic reading of the story, see Ray Browne, *Melville's Drive to Humanism* (Lafayette, Indiana: Purdue University Studies, 1971), 237–40. For a "deeper cynicism," see Fisher, *Going Under*, 161.

communal circumstances under which persons can communicate and cooperate in the process of acquiring knowledge."[11] Melville shares a similar sense of the failure of foundational thinking, but the circumstances that he finds in his culture are not conducive to cooperative discussion, nor is Melville entirely comfortable giving up the quest for certainty. Unlike the uncle and nephew of his story, he keeps laboring to advance a project that he knows is unending. There seems to be no other work for an enlightened skeptic to do.

This quandary can be named in a number of idioms critical to antebellum literature. "Praise be to God for the failure!" sounds the rallying cry of the jeremiad, revealing how the hermeneutic of a providential nation incorporates all contrary evidence. Less theologically, the challenge is also one of immanence insofar as racial and economic ideologies subsume all potential resistance. Melville's story, that is, might object to the slaveholding despotism of American empire, but it still cannot think outside its box to advocate a liberating alternative. For Adorno and Horkheimer, such problems are fundamental to enlightenment thought, in part because the dialectic of enlightenment has long maintained its promise, even in the face of critiques that lament its ever-receding completion. Kant complained in 1783 that metaphysics "strings along the human understanding with hopes that never dim but are never fulfilled." Five decades later, Alexis de Tocqueville found an "ideal but always fugitive perfection" in American political life. When Abraham Lincoln invoked at Gettysburg the nation's "unfinished work," he appealed to both the failure and promise of an enlightened civilization – a guarded optimism shared by William James's sense of the "strung-along, unfinished world," and one that Habermas retains in his "unfinished project" of enlightenment.[12] More recent challenges from anti-foundational and multicultural perspectives also suggest that, if only residually, enlightenment endures.[13] Thus when antebellum writers "rage against reason," they take part in a long and ongoing tradition, for it may be that every modern age experiences the failure of

---

11 West, *The American Evasion of Philosophy*, 213.
12 Horkheimer and Adorno, *Dialectic of Enlightenment*; Kant, *Prolegomena to Any Future Metaphysics*, 5. Tocqueville, *Democracy in America*, 1: 420. Lincoln, "Address at Gettysburg" (1863), in *Abraham Lincoln: Speeches and Letters*, ed. Peter J. Parish (London: J. M. Dent, 1993), 266; James, *A Pluralistic Universe*, 688; Habermas, "Modernity: An Unfinished Project."
13 See, for instance, Anthony Cascardi's claim that recent attempts to critique enlightenment "can themselves be seen as the consequences and continuations of a process of self-criticism that originates within the Enlightenment, rather than as cancellations of Enlightenment thought" (*Consequences of Enlightenment* [New York: Cambridge University Press, 1999], 5–6).

its ideas and that some version of enlightenment is always ending without ever reaching its end.[14]

The more history the faltering optimist reads, the more one can be struck not by radical breaks or numbing repetitions but rather by the tragic variation of perfectionist hopes and brutal failures that remain in their particular historical forms singular and compelling enough. In the antebellum era, the slavery crisis embodied the breakdown of rational authority, even as writers on the verge of war continued to seek consensus. Misguided or not, their texts are hopeful insofar as the possibilities of democracy remain discouraging and yet open-ended, failing but not dead. When looking back on "the middle range of the Nineteenth century in the New World," Whitman fondly remembered it as "a strange, unloosen'd, wondrous time." Whitman and his contemporaries were not innocent of the horrors of slavery and war, but they managed to salvage some remnant of faith in an enlightened America. Matthiessen located this "optative mood" with Emerson, Thoreau, and Whitman as opposed to the "tragic" Melville and Hawthorne. More attuned to irony, R. W. B. Lewis found a more general "tragic optimism" in the period, while Myra Jehlen has criticized "the tragic fiction of the doctrinally optimistic American Renaissance." Generations before, William Dean Howells ventured an explanation for such ambivalence, "[W]hat the American public always wants is a tragedy with a happy ending."[15] The writers treated in the foregoing chapters often fulfill this desire when their self-conscious struggles with philosophy cohere around the slavery crisis – in Poe's carefully plotted catastrophes, in Stowe's desperate attempts to fix sentimentality, in Douglass's willfully displayed disappointments, in Emerson's stubborn revisions, and in Melville's subversion of the unfinished project he could not finish or put down. Almost a century and a half after American slavery was abolished at a frightening cost of lives, their efforts to put ideas to practical use seem neither happy nor entirely a failure.

14 Richard Bernstein, "Rage Against Reason," in *The New Constellation: The Ethical-Political Horizons of Modernity/Postmodernity* (Cambridge: The MIT Press, 1992), 31–56. Bernstein adds Nietzsche, Weber, and Foucault to the list of thinkers who resist enlightenment and yet remain within its purview. Stanley Cavell's formulation also speaks to the increasing self-criticism of philosophy, "We are more prepared to understand as philosophy a mode of thought that undertakes to bring philosophy to an end . . . Ending philosophy looks to be a commitment of each of the major modern philosophers" (*The Senses of Walden*, 129–30).

15 Whitman, *Specimen Days*, 690; Matthiessen, *American Renaissance*, 656; Lewis, *The American Adam*, 7; Myra Jehlen, *American Incarnation: The Individual, The Nation, and The Continent* (Cambridge: Harvard University Press, 1986), 18; Howells quoted in Edith Wharton, *A Backwards Glance* (New York: Scribner's, 1933), 147.

Index